Organizational Change and Innovation

For other titles published in this series, go to
www.springer.com/series/8833

Paddy O'Toole

How Organizations Remember

Retaining Knowledge through Organizational Action

Springer

Paddy O'Toole
Faculty of Education
Monash University
Clayton, Victoria, Australia
paddy.otoole@monash.edu

ISBN 978-1-4419-7523-2 e-ISBN 978-1-4419-7524-9
DOI 10.1007/978-1-4419-7524-9
Springer New York Dordrecht Heidelberg London

Library of Congress Control Number: 2010938788

Printed on acid-free paper

Springer is part of Springer Science+Business Media (www.springer.com)

Acknowledgments

Silent gratitude isn't much use to anyone

-- Gladys Brown Stern (The Last Word)

Many thanks to my husband Mark for all of his love and support. His help was invaluable in bringing this work to a happy conclusion. My thanks also go to Associate Professor Halia Silins and Professor Mike Lawson for their support through the study. They are also noteworthy for being the only two people at Flinders University, besides my husband Mark, who really believed that I went to Las Vegas to conduct research.

The research conducted in this study was very labor-intensive, and the international component added significantly to the costs. I would like to express my heartfelt appreciation to the Premier of the Government of South Australia for the extremely generous Premiers Award for Research in Lifelong Learning and Development that funded my living and research costs. I would also like to thank Denis Ralph and the staff from the now-defunct Centre for Lifelong Learning for their encouragement and stimulating company.

I acknowledge the funding received from Flinders University and my colleagues in the School of Education who encouraged me, particularly Jeanette Holt.

Many thanks also to the people in Springer who believed in this book and brought it to fruition: to Nick Philipson, Executive Editor, Business/Economics at Springer, for being so enthusiastic and facilitating the proposal and editing process so well, and Charlotte Cusumano, Editorial Assistant, who was invaluable in clarifying expectations and helping with the production hiccups. Thanks also go to Jerry and Ann Gilley, the editors of the Organizational Change and Innovation series for their support and feedback.

Most importantly, this research would not have been possible without the generosity of the management and staff of the organizations referred to in this work as XME Australia, XME Ireland, and XME USA. I am very grateful for the openness and honesty of the respondents, and for my experience in an exciting organization. Their tolerance is much appreciated.

List of Tables

Chapter 1
Introduction

The manager cursed under his breath. Could anything else go wrong? His industrial designer had left, and important designs were missing. No one seemed to know exactly the details of the agreement with one of the suppliers. And the accounts personnel were on his back over some paperwork they needed. And he had to induct three new workers this month, all starting on separate days. He was tempted to skip it, but knew that he would be most unpopular with the human resources people if he did. He had to oversee the implementation of the new computer system, just when everyone has got to know the old one. Mind you, the old-timers would love a chance to induct the new people into not using the new technology. Now, he finds that the email system is down. Not only can he not send emails, but he can't even access the ones he has filed. How is he supposed to work when he can't retrieve his files?

Introduction

How do organizations remember? Remembering is a problematic issue for organizations. To remember too little is to forget the lessons of the past and to duplicate past effort; to remember too much is to lose flexibility and the ability to innovate (Stein, 1995; Weick, 1979a). In addition, employees may remember what organizational leaders never speak of, or lessons of the past that are useful for the future may be forgotten. Memory or knowledge retention is a significant component of organizational learning and knowledge management, but may also block innovation when old knowledge obstructs the retention of new learning. The hapless manager described in the above vignette is being confronted by a series of problems involving the retention of knowledge, or lack of it, in his organization. Knowledge retention can be a strategic issue, such as a new organizational-wide computer system or a tactical one such as an agreement with a supplier.

When studying knowledge at different levels in organizations, the components of knowledge acquisition, retention, retrieval, and usage are easily confused. The focus of this book is retention. Thus, while acquisition, retrieval, and usage may be incidentally involved, this investigation is limited to how these affect retention. Also, this book refers to "knowledge retention," rather than "memory." "Memory" is a confusing term, meaning both the way memories are retained and the thing

P. O'Toole, *How Organizations Remember: Retaining Knowledge through Organizational Action*, Organizational Change and Innovation 2, DOI 10.1007/978-1-4419-7524-9_1,

retained. The term "knowledge retention" has a more focused meaning, and is generally used through this book. The exceptions occur when citing other authors who use the term "memory."

This book contributes to the understanding of knowledge retention in organizations by closely examining knowledge retention in one organization. Both good practice and not so good practice are examined for the implications with regard to the organization. Knowledge management is a complex task; knowledge permeates every aspect of organizational life and much of the knowledge within organizations may be counter to that espoused by the organization's leaders. My primary aim in this book is not to solve all organizational problems surrounding knowledge management, but rather to help the reader understand the complexity and the issues involved. I hope that academics, students, and practitioners will find value and can draw lessons from one intensive study of a high-performing organization.

Many of the texts on knowledge management deal largely with the strategic aspects of knowledge management. Sometimes an emphasis on the strategic ignores the tactical issues of the day-to-day and the local knowledge that is counter to the dominant culture. Certainly the contribution of the individual to the organization may be ignored, particularly when that contribution is deemed to be low status, local, and context-specific. In this book, the low status, local, and context-specific are included in a "warts-and-all" examination of the knowledge retention structures of an organization that is deemed to be successful and growing.

Knowledge Retention in Organizations Past and Present

Prior to the mid-nineteenth century, the knowledge retention structures of organizations were generally based in the individual and communicated through apprenticeship, although there were some simple organizational processes and paper records of financial transactions with external entities (Yates, 1988). Artisans had to do many things well in order to create a supply of products and it was usual for master craftsmen and craftswomen to train apprentices and journeymen and journeywomen in their crafts (Stinchcombe, 1990; Wiig, 2000). As organizations grew larger, management became separated from production. With new challenges caused by this separation, managers started looking for ways to coordinate and control activities within the firm. The systematic management movement gained momentum, which was the start of attempts by management to remove the dependence on knowledgeable individuals and to embed knowledge within the organization (Yates, 1988). This systematic management entailed far more extensive documentation both for internal and external communication, formalized record keeping, and operation results reporting, and policies and procedures. Knowledge was no longer sited just in the head of the artisan and specialist. People in organizations could refer to other sources in order to learn.

In the 1990s and beyond, the forces of globalization and improvements in information and communications technology have led to knowledge and information being a major source of competitive advantage for organizations (Davenport & Prusak, 1998; Drucker, 1995; Marquandt & Reynolds, 1994). The scientific management approach heralded by F.W. Taylor focused on control over the production process and separated the knowledge from the individual. If knowledge could be embedded in processes and technology, then the knowledge would stay with the organization when the individual went elsewhere. In the 1990s the resource-based theory of the firm that evolved from Penrose's theory of the growth of the firm (1980) was extended to a knowledge-based theory of the firm as knowledge was acknowledged as a primary factor of production (Spender, 1996a, b). The acknowledgment of knowledge management as a critical issue for organizational leaders has led to a genre of literature that concentrates on knowledge as an object to be stored and transferred by explicit means, and separated from the individual (Mentzas, Apostolou & Young, 2001). Yet another genre of literature is concerned with knowledge as a process (Spender, 2000), where knowledge and people are embraced as a unity and it is focused on communication, creativity, and often collective social structures. The knowledge worker is considered to "own the tools of production" and organizations must learn what "the knowledge worker needs, requires and expects" (Drucker, 1995, pp. 246–7). A more sparse genre of literature involves the knowledge that may not be manageable, the knowledge that causes the generation of gossip, stories, and rumors, a type of knowledge that may not contribute to an organization's effectiveness (Gabriel, 1995) and that falls outside of or is counter to managerial concerns (Styhre, 2003).

In management and business circles, the understandings and assumptions related to knowledge deal primarily with how knowledge can improve an organization's competitive performance. This implies that little else happens in corporate organizations other than the production of goods and services, which enable profits to be distributed among stakeholders. Organizations are, however, also structures where people make sense of their surroundings (Weick, 1993, 1995), and the sense that they make may not always be in accord with the values and beliefs of the leaders. Stories, sabotage, rumor, and activities of resistance are manifestations of knowledge that is evidence of an unmanageable side to organizations and which is often ignored by the management pundits (Boje, 1991; Boyce, 1996; Gabriel, 1995, 1997; Gottfied, 1994; Hansen & Kahnweiler, 1993; LaNuez & Jermier, 1994; Martin, Feldman, Hatch & Sitkin, 1983).

Huber pointed out that organizational memory, or knowledge retention, has a critical impact on organizational learning. According to Huber (1996) and Weick (1979b), before learning can be said to take place, the knowledge must be retained and retrievable. Huber (1996) also pointed out that learning is influenced by attention, which in turn is focused by knowledge already retained; that information distribution is affected by decisions made according to criteria and facts retained in knowledge retention structures; and that interpretation of new knowledge is affected by the cognitive maps or schemas that are created via past experience.

The empirical research that is the basis of this book was conducted in an organization known in this work as "XME." There are three sites: XME Australia, the corporate center and XME Ireland and XME USA, the two subsidiaries.

An Organization Called "XME"

The organization called "XME" in this text is a technology company that commenced in 1985 and had operations in Australia, Ireland, and the USA. XME is a pseudonym used to protect the identity of the organization and the people within it. XME had been lauded by the government and won awards for its achievements from peak business councils. The technology invented within the organization gave it a significant competitive edge over its rivals and the products derived from this technology were sold to the retail, military, and industrial sectors on a global basis. XME had experienced dramatic growth in the preceding 3 years, and approximately 70% of the approximately 110 staff had been employed during this period. XME did not have a formal knowledge management system. Instead knowledge management occurred through information and communications technology (ICT) protocols, the quality management system (QMS) and other management-endorsed systems.

During my time in XME there was a change of leadership where a new Chief Executive Officer (CEO) was appointed. I had negotiated my entry into the organization through the former Managing Director, with whom I had acquaintances in common. Fortunately, the new CEO had no objection to the continuation of my research. Thus, during my time in XME, I witnessed the turnover of the senior leaders of the company. The head office, which was in Australia, was visited over a period of 10 months. The Irish office was visited for 3 weeks and the USA office was visited for 1 week. XME Australia is the main site studied, with XME USA and XME Ireland providing useful contrasts.

During this time participant observation and interviews were conducted, documents and objects were scrutinized and the floor plans and physical layouts were recorded (see O'Toole 2003; O'Toole & Were 2008). The data from this field work were analysed using Grounded Theory Method techniques. The text contains quotations from these interviews and field notes, with names altered to protect the anonymity of the respondents. Although people were generous with their time and conversation, I was aware that there was a certain amount of wariness concerning my presence in the first weeks of my arrival in the Australian operation. This was gradually and largely overcome when people observed that I did not cause trouble for them and that I adhered to the normal academic ethical conventions concerning privacy and confidentiality.

Organizational knowledge research has been typically functionalist, with an emphasis on managerial relevance (Burrell, 1997; Porac & Garud, 1999; Styhre, 2003). Organizational research in general has tended to focus on quantitative techniques in spite of Van Maanen (1979/1983b, p. 11) voicing the fear as far back as 1978 that

> there is a growing concern about where quantitative techniques are carrying us. For example, questions have been raised about the extent to which our methods are guiding our theory and concern has been expressed about the degree to which our procedures have become so ritualized that the necessary connection between measure and concept has vanished.

This research, in contrast, was conducted from an interpretive/constructivist perspective that aims to depict many voices in the organization, not just the organization's leaders (Field, 2000) and to promote understanding of the context. Although identifying most strongly with the interpretive/constructivist paradigm, I blended elements from other paradigms where it added richness and rigor to the study (Lincoln, 2000; also see O'Toole 2010). I consider that knowledge is constructed and retained both by the individual and at the group and organizational levels, and that the interaction between the individual, group, and organization affects how the knowledge is retained. An understanding of the nature of knowledge is also an important aspect of how we research organizations. If knowledge is deemed to belong in the top echelons of an organization, there is little point in investigating the shop floor. If the knowledge is deemed to dwell within the organization's information technology infrastructure, there is little value in using interviews and participant observation as research tools.

More information on how the research was conducted can be found in my other publications.

The Structure of This Book

Each chapter is prefaced by a vignette relating to a new recruit's experiences of her new organization, and her efforts to make sense of, access and use different knowledge retention structures. These vignettes help orient the reader to the content and meaning of each chapter in a practical and, I hope, engaging way.

This book is structured to combine theoretical perspectives and empirical research to generate insights that will be of value to organizational leaders in both increasing the understanding of an important component of organizational learning and formulating knowledge strategies. The structure is as follows:

Chapter 2: Knowing About Knowledge explores the nature of knowledge, the different aspects of knowledge, the commodification of knowledge and knowledge as a part of action.

Chapter 3: Developing Knowledge Retention Structures introduces the three operational sites of the XME group and shows how the knowledge retention structures evolved through the history of the organization, the contribution of its people and the interaction with the external environment. This chapter also shows the dominant knowledge retention structures and how they are utilized and maintained within the operational sites.

Chapter 4: Knowledge Retention by Communication illustrates how communication within an organization is essentially a means of knowledge retention. This knowledge may be formal or informal, endorsed by the organization's leaders or counter to the endorsed dominant culture.

Chapter 5: Managing Knowledge Retention develops a model of knowledge retention. This model synthesizes the dimensions of knowledge with an aim of discerning the character of different types of knowledge retention structures to enable their management. Issues are raised and explored that deal with the pitfalls of managing knowledge retention poorly. A discussion of core competency and core rigidities within XME Australia illustrates the pitfalls of managing knowledge in a successful organization.

Chapter 6: How Organizations Remember draws together the literature and the data to bring forth a theory of knowledge retention. This chapter shows how an understanding of knowledge retention can indicate strengths and weaknesses in organizations.

The final chapter, *Chapter 7: Theory and Implications*, shows the theoretical propositions that arose from the study. These theoretical propositions include the implications for managers and leaders who desire to more effectively manage knowledge in their organization.

Knowledge can be viewed usefully both as a dynamic process that permeates the organization and as the residue of experience that human beings construct to survive in a variety of contexts. Knowledge management, in many ways, is a relatively new term for a series of old practices. The setting of these practices and the epistemologies that underpin them in the framework of knowledge management, however, causes us to view practice and activity within organizations from a different perspective. The way that organizations remember will determine the effectiveness of their practice and their continual operation and is affected by the dimensions of the knowledge within the organization. The next chapter explores the complex construct of knowledge.

Chapter 2
Knowing About Knowledge

The new recruit pauses before walking through the door. It looks like a good place to work, but one never really knows. Look at what a psychopath her last manager turned out to be! The manager invites her to sit at the conference table. He smiles at her: "Now, prepare to be inducted!" The induction proceeds well until the manager produces a form for her to sign. The new recruit looks at the form uncertainly. "Just what is this all about?" The manager reassures her that it is just a standard form to protect the company from people selling its secrets to competitors. "Umm, has everyone signed them?" "Nearly everyone," replies the manager going a bit pink around the ears. "Let me take you for a tour." The manager and the new recruit walk down the stairs to the production area. People are standing next to benches, watching intently while they carefully poke solder onto terminals, wind wire on spools and assemble components into the final product. In one part of the area, a group of people are talking animatedly while turning a part over and over in their hands. "Ah-ha, looks like Sanjay has had another brainwave!" exclaims the manager. "Which one is Sanjay?" asks the new recruit.

Introduction

It is difficult to reach an understanding of how knowledge is retained if there is no understanding of whether knowledge is fluid or static, dynamic or stable, or an unchanging feature of an objective reality or a quixotic part of a subjective interpretation. An investigation relating to the communication of knowledge, for example, will be incomplete if there is no understanding of the social and power relations attached to knowledge.

Because this book is centered on knowledge retention, some discussion regarding the meaning and aspects of knowledge, particularly knowledge within organizations, becomes imperative. This task is problematic. According to Alvesson (1993, p. 1000):

> To define knowledge in a non-abstract and non-sweeping way seems very difficult. Knowledge easily becomes everything and nothing.

This chapter thus explores the nature of knowledge, the different aspects of knowledge, the commodification of knowledge, and knowledge as a part of action.

P. O'Toole, *How Organizations Remember: Retaining Knowledge through Organizational Action*, Organizational Change and Innovation 2, DOI 10.1007/978-1-4419-7524-9_2,

It is not intended to be an exhaustive account of epistemological discussions and philosophers through the ages. This chapter answers the following question: How does the nature of knowledge affect how organizations remember?

The Nature of Knowledge: Bedrock or Swamp?

Knowledge is commonly held to be the "body of information possessed by a person or, by extension, by a group of persons or a culture" (Reber, 1995, p. 401). Discussion and debate regarding knowledge have been extended from the arenas of philosophy and education to those of commerce and trade with the advent of the *knowledge economy* and *knowledge management*. At the same time, Western society has seen the postmodern approach promote the recognition of the knowledge held by traditionally silenced groups (Foucault, 1972/1980; Harwood, 2001; Renshaw, 1998).

A discussion of the nature of knowledge, or epistemology, must also take into account an ontological framework, that is, the nature of existence and reality. Classical epistemology has traditionally defined knowledge as justified true belief (Stanford University, 2001). If knowledge is regarded as justified true belief, then retained knowledge is immutable. There is no need for mechanisms to revise or change knowledge, for the sake of acquiring more. James (1987/1995), however, questioned whether we can really know when we have arrived at truth. Although many classical philosophers and scientists were more disposed to regard knowledge as universal and absolute, James was pragmatic about the necessity for acting as if our beliefs are knowledge, and accepting the consequences if we are found to be mistaken. For James (1987/1995, p. 206), truth is the product of an individual desire, with "our social system" backing us up. Hence, beliefs pass into a group's system of knowledge as each member believes in it and cooperates to perpetuate it. Instead of knowledge being absolute and universal, it becomes local and socially agreed.

According to Popper (1959, p. 111), even that bastion of "true knowledge," science, cannot be said to be unassailable:

> The empirical basis of objective science has thus nothing "absolute" about it. Science does not rest upon solid bedrock. The bold structure of its theories rises, as it were above a swamp. It is like a building erected on piles. The piles are driven down from above into the swamp, but not down to any natural or "given" base; and if we stop driving the piles deeper, it is not because we have reached firm ground. We simply stop when we are satisfied that the piles are firm enough to carry the structure, at least for the time being.

Geertz (1983) pointed out that understanding new concepts is often allied to previously known analogies. The analogies chosen, therefore, will influence the new understandings. Common sense, according to Geertz (1983), is a cultural system, rather than a universal recognition of sensible practice. This is consistent with the concept of schemas, discussed later in this chapter. Schemas are knowledge frameworks held by each individual formed by previous experience. As the individual perceives stimuli, and retains a representation of those stimuli, they are filtered and sometimes distorted according to the schemas already held (Anderson, 1995, 2000).

Knowledge then becomes part of a context. A knowledgeable person is someone who knows much about a particular field or context, and the knowledge, when taken outside this context, may be devalued or unregarded (Anderson, Reder, & Simon, 1996). A university professor of mathematics may be ignorant if placed in a work group in a clothing factory. She may know nothing about the industry; the culture of the company or her work team; operating a sewing machine, obtaining fabric; or relating to her superiors or peers. She may be intelligent and learn these things quickly, but when first entering the factory, in a new context, she is not a knowledgeable person. In becoming a knowledgeable person, our university professor will perform actions and undergo experiences. She may read the sewing machine manual; she may ask her peers where things are; and she may learn the proper way to deal with them from the way they interact with her. She will learn things about boss–worker relations as the boss blames her for things that she did not do, and congratulates her for one achievement while ignoring others. She will learn where to thump the machine when it refuses to work and where to place her work so it does not become damaged or dirty. As time goes on, our university professor constructs knowledge in and about her new context as she interacts with others and with her physical environment.

As far as the university professor is concerned, however, constructing knowledge is only part of what she needs to do to be successful in her new environment. It is necessary that she remember what she learns, and that she can recall these lessons when necessary.

Knowledge as an Individual Construction

Classical empiricists, who believed in observation as the keystone to the discovery of knowledge, saw the human mind as a *tabula rasa*, a blank slate, which was unaffected by emotion, belief, or prior experience (Lakatos, 1978; Locke, 1987/1995). The classical empiricists' belief in an objective reality was generally accompanied by an assumption of a dichotomy between body and mind (Ryle, 1949). In contrast, constructivism is essentially an epistemological approach positing that people construct meaning and knowledge as they learn through experience (Dougiamas, 1998) and part of this experience involves bodily sensations and emotions. Although many constructivists may believe in an objective reality, we cannot know that objective truth, and thus we construct reality for ourselves (Smelser & Baltes, 2001). Two people may disagree on how far an external reality may be known and still describe themselves as constructivists (Phillips, 1995; von Glasersfeld, 1984).

Personal or psychological constructivism is commonly associated with Jean Piaget and is centered on the construction of knowledge for the individual. Essentially personal constructivism rejects the notion that knowledge is transmitted unchanged from one person to another, for example, from a teacher to a student. Rather than the knowledge being preserved in an unchanging form, it will be filtered through the lens of the receiver's experience and previous constructions. Instead of the receiver being an empty vessel, she/he is an active builder of knowledge (Papert, 2003).

Our knowledge, born of our experience, is a critical part of our personal identity. According to Pojman (2001, p. 232):

> We know ourselves in the context of a backdrop of memorial beliefs, having to do with family and personal history. We see ourselves as the person who did so and so and whose parents are such and such, and whose beliefs and desires and habits are this and that – all brought to mind through memory.

Hence, as we build our knowledge as individuals, we also build and/or maintain our personal identities within the settings we find ourselves in, and as a result of our interactions. This construction of knowledge occurs both at a conscious and unconscious level (Garrison, 1998; von Glasersfeld, 1984), which contradicts the classical philosophers' emphasis on Reason and its division from the body, the emotions, and the unconscious. According to Garrison (1998, p. 44): "Embodied action rather than abstract Reason lies at the core of pragmatic social constructivism. For the pragmatist, the 'I can do' rather than the 'I think' constitutes the (relatively) stable core of personal identity." Action, rather than static storage, is in fact a key component of knowledge retention in organizations.

Our constructions embrace the influence of cultural symbols and tools in affecting the way we think. Foucault (1977) introduced a more sinister aspect with the construct of dressage, that is, the adoption of symbols and actions by social institutions for the purpose of inducing compliance. Essentially, the constructions of knowledge that incorporate a given set of symbols, behaviors, and artifacts that surround us mean that the learner may construct knowledge that reinforces current social orders (Larochelle & Bednarz, 1998) and may assume roles and stances that are consistent with that social order (Garrison, 1998). Hence, as people construct their own knowledge, they build up images and structures within their own minds that they have gained and interpreted from their own experience, other people, and their environment. As people construct their knowledge within certain settings, their knowledge will reflect those settings, and may often reinforce cultural rules and customs so that they can survive. At the same time, however, people may also influence their surroundings and their culture.

Giddens, in his theory of structuration, outlined how social structures and individuals served to influence each other; individuals may reproduce social structures or they may choose to transform them (Giddens, 1984; Turner, 1986). People may erect buildings and monuments that reinforce cultural messages, which are perceived and interpreted, albeit often implicitly, by others (Assmann, 1995). On the other hand, they may tear the buildings down and build a mall (Brand, 1994). Throughout the interaction of ourselves with others and our environment, our constructions remain our own. According to Larochelle and Bednarz (1998, p. 8):

"Knowledge cannot be transmitted; it cannot be neutral either. Instead, it is constructed, negotiated, propelled by a project, and perpetuated for as long as it enables its creators to organize their reality in a viable fashion." Thus the knowledge that we retain as individuals is at least slightly different in all of us as it is filtered through our previous constructions, and interpreted to make sense to us in terms of our previous experience (Shotter, 1990; Weick, 1995).

In terms of knowledge retention, individual knowledge construction means that even where knowledge is communicated from the same source, the knowledge retained may differ from person to person and from retention structure to retention structure. Even where the knowledge is communicated via an explicit format such as text, knowledge has a tacit element that may be interpreted differently according to the constructions/schemas of the person receiving the communication. A group may hold knowledge in common, where the knowledge of each individual is similar enough to perpetuate a group knowledge. Where this occurs, group knowledge retention structures emerge that may be either tacit or explicit. Tacit and explicit knowledge are different aspects of knowledge that are discussed in the next section.

Different Aspects of Knowledge

This section explores different aspects of knowledge that influence the method and way of retention.

These aspects involve classifying knowledge as:

- Tacit and/or explicit
- Declarative and/or procedural
- Individual and/or collective and
- Data, information and/or knowledge

Although these classifications exist, it can be a fruitless exercise to attempt to isolate a particular bounded area of knowledge into one classification or another. When a discrete task or activity is scrutinized with a view to classifying its knowledge aspects, it is all too easy to assume that the classifications constitute polarities, for example, this one is tacit or that one is explicit. In fact, the aspects of knowledge usually form a duality, where elements of both classifications can be ascertained, which needs to be kept in mind when reading succeeding sections. The term "duality" is defined by Wenger (1999, p. 66) as

> a single conceptual unit that is formed by two inseparable and mutually constituted elements whose inherent tension and complementarity give the concept richness and dynamism.

The value in recognizing different aspects of knowledge is to recognize that different and diverse mechanisms of retention and communication must be implemented if effective communication of the knowledge is to occur.

Tacit Knowledge and Explicit Knowledge

Both individuals and groups retain explicit and tacit (also termed "implicit") knowledge. The common definitions at the individual and group level are slightly different, although the concepts remain similar. At the individual level, the major distinctions between tacit and explicit knowledge are as follow:

- Tacit knowledge is not accompanied by any sense of awareness of remembering, while explicit memory is "accompanied by the subjective experience of remembering" (Banaji, 2001; Kelley & Lindsay, 1996, p. 54).
- Tacit knowledge "may unconsciously influence our perceptions, thoughts, and actions" (Schacter, 1996, p. 9) whereas explicit memory is accompanied by the awareness of the influence of the past. According to Reber, "knowledge acquired from implicit learning procedures is knowledge that, in some 'raw' fashion, is always ahead of the capability of the possessor to explicate it" (Reber, 1993, p. 64).

These forms of knowledge have found their way from the disciplines of psychology and epistemology to organizational disciplines through the work of Michael Polanyi (1962, 1967) and later authors (e.g., Anand, Manz, & Glick, 1998; Cook & Brown, 1999; Gopalakrishnan, 1997; Leonard & Sensiper, 1998; Saint-Onge, 1996; Spender, 1996b; Tsoukas, 1996; von Krogh, Ichijo, & Nonaka, 2000; Wagner & Sternberg, 1986). Spender (2001) saw that writers on tacit knowledge in the field of management could be classified into two groups. One group believes that tacit knowledge should be made explicit and manageable (Nonaka, 1991, 1994), while the other group believes that tacit knowledge is by definition unmanageable or at least difficult to manage and managers must be aware of this (March, 1996; Saint-Onge, 1996, 2000). In fact, this division is probably based on differences of definition. If tacit knowledge is simply seen as not codified, then it is possible that at least some of it can be, and perhaps should be, codified. If, however, the definition of tacit knowledge is that it cannot be codified, then clearly it is a waste of time to try. Explicit knowledge, on the other hand, is knowledge that is codified or easily codifiable. In this book, tacit knowledge is deemed to be that which is not codified.

Polanyi (1962, p. 7) believed that tacit knowing had two parts. The first part related to what Polanyi termed "proximal terms." The proximal terms come to dwell within the body ("indwelling") and are integrated in the "distal term," which is what we are dealing with. An example may be when we drive a car. We are attending to driving the car (the distal term), while our hands steer, our feet attend to brakes and our eyes focus on the road ahead (proximal terms). However, our concentration on the proximal terms is unconscious. If we try to concentrate on nothing but braking, we may lose control of the car. Our focus has changed from the integrated distal to one proximal, which means we lose sight of the whole. Before the focus changes from the distal to the proximal, the proximal is performed via habitual action. It is not consciously evaluated because our driving is practiced and conditions are normal. However, if, for example, a child runs out in front of our car, pressing the brake is at the forefront of our attention.

It is useful to extend this example of driving the car to what happens when we learn to drive. We may study a manual of road rules and, perhaps, car operation. However, the explicit knowledge that we retain may seem of very little use when sitting behind the wheel of a car for the first time. The plethora of controls is confusing, and the multiplicity of actions as we change gear, take our foot off the brake, press the accelerator and look behind us, at the side and at the front, is overwhelming. Generally, we rely on a sympathetic relative or a driving instructor to help us through the process of learning. They have the tacit knowledge, and can activate the proximal to achieve the distal term of driving the car. With their guidance and a lot of practice we can also drive a car. But the manual on road rules and car operation may seem incidental. The verbal directions are generally given while you are practicing because no one can impart the knowledge of how to drive the car by speech. The knowledge is gained by practicing and building experience, that is, tacit knowledge. Some verbal guidance may facilitate the retention of knowledge, but without the retention of the tacit knowledge, the novice driver remains unskilled.

Ryle (1949, p. 30) made the point that "[r]ules of correct reasoning were first extracted by Aristotle, yet men knew how to avoid and detect fallacies before they learned his lessons." Hence, Aristotle could be said to have converted the tacit skill of reasoning into an explicit knowledge, with explicit rules that people could use to improve their reasoning capabilities. Some authors use inability to articulate certain knowledge as a prima facie determination of its tacitness. Polanyi, however, was quite clear that tacit knowledge could be articulated if sufficient focus was placed on the knowledge requiring articulation (Polanyi, 1962; Tsoukas, 1996). However, he did state that this degree of focus would change the knowledge to another state. This state may be advantageous or disadvantageous, but the change would occur.

The act of focusing on a proximal term changes the proximal term to a distal term. Changing tacit knowledge to explicit knowledge may mean that some proximal terms are ignored or unstated. Even if proximal terms are codified, they are codified in a linear way, in some sort of order in the text. The reader thus will become aware of the proximal terms in a different way to which she would have experienced the communication of tacit knowledge.

Tacit knowledge requires far richer means of communication than explicit knowledge, for example, face-to-face contact rather than a set of directions in a manual. Tacit knowledge has sometimes been described as being "difficult, if not impossible, to transfer" (Burton-Jones, 1999, p. 7). However, this is probably unjustified. Tacit knowledge requires different mechanisms to promote communication. The apprenticeship system is generally an example of how a craftsperson can communicate tacit knowledge to another, using demonstration rather than a documentation to impart what needs to be known. Polanyi's belief that tacit knowledge is changed when explicated has some logical basis, particularly when viewed in terms of his proximal and distal terms. When attention is concentrated on one element, that element becomes proximal and the distal is ignored. For the distal to be explicated, it becomes proximal and other distals are ignored. Because speech and text require attention on one element at a time, the integrated skill becomes fragmented and changed. Thus it needs practice or action for the explicated proximals and the ignored distals to become integrated once more. The richness of tacit knowledge is explained by Huber (1996, p. 145) as "the variety of cues that the medium can convey and the rapidity of feedback that the medium can provide." Thus explicit means of knowledge retention do not have the level of sophistication to retain all the elements of tacit knowledge.

The value in recognizing tacit and explicit knowledge as two different aspects of knowledge is related to understanding that they cannot be retained and communicated in the same way. Although some tacit knowledge may be effectively codified, there may also be an ineffable something that is missed as the knowledge is translated into words or images. In a given operation or task, it is suggested that the tacit and explicit knowledge needed will often be inextricably tangled, and their boundaries in fact may not be easily explicated.

According to von Krogh et al. (2000) and Nonaka and Konno (1998), tacit knowledge has traditionally been undervalued in the West, and hence the repeated calls for the "explicitation" of tacit knowledge. Although some authors (e.g., Tsoukas, 1996) have stated that this is not possible in all cases, the mindset of Western society still seems to undervalue the tacit and unexplainable. A recent example is in the area of interpersonal skills where it has been vaguely recognized that it is important for people to act in a mature way in the workplace. However, it took the badging of interpersonal skills and maturity with the label of "emotional intelligence," the publishing of "how-to" books on the subject and the creation of psychological tests before these skills became formally recognized as an important part of the workforce environment. Another example of this is the esteem in which the professions, with their load of codified knowledge and explicit standards are held, compared to the crafts and trades where much of the knowledge retained is tacit. Polanyi's notion of tacit knowledge has been largely ignored, if not directly attacked, by classical philosophers (Reber, 1993, p. 137).

It has been posited that tacit knowledge can constitute a valuable intangible resource (Berman, Down, & Hill, 2002; Boisot, 1998; Kogut & Zander, 1992). Winter (1998) distinguished between tacit knowledge and articulable knowledge, which may or may not be articulated. The fact that knowledge is not articulated may not be only because people have moved on from the organization and the specifications are lost; equally, an individual may choose not to articulate knowledge for their own advantage. Tacit knowledge may be roughly classified as nonarticulable or articulable; however, the boundaries between these two classifications are difficult, if not impossible, to determine.

The implications for organizations with regard to the tacitness or explicitness of knowledge are significant. Blackler (2002) classified organizational studies literature into whether knowledge was retained via the heads of key members (embrained); via the competencies of key members (embodied); via collective understandings (encultured); and/or within the technologies, rules and procedures (embedded). Blackler warned, however, that knowledge should not be separated from the activity of the agents of the firm. Knowledge is not static, individual, and abstract. It is dynamic, often collective and situated. The retention structures of the organization reflect this; to ignore the tacit aspect of knowledge is to distort the nature of the knowledge that is retained within the organization.

Individual and Collective Knowledge

The field of organizational studies has, at various times, focused on knowledge as either or both an individual and collective construct. Individual and collective knowledge resist sharp delineation as the individual interacts with his/her social context (Spender, 1996a), and the organization depends on the agency of the individual for collective knowledge to form. The individual, although part of the social context, has the ability to depart from the organization, and take their retained knowledge with them. This ability can be a significant issue to the organization if the organization is dependent on unique knowledge for its competitive advantage. In arguing that collective learning was more than the sum of individual learning, Leithwood, Leonard and Sharrat (2000) who suggested that

> [collective] mind may take the form of cognitive interdependence focused around memory processes. ... People in close relationships enact a single transaction memory system, complete with differentiated responsibility for remembering different portions of common experience. (p. 245)

According to Leithwood et al. (2000, p. 246): "[C]ollective mind must be an external representation, mind as activity rather than mind as entity." Spender (1998, p. 18) stated that "collective memory requires the support of a social group delimited in space and time." In this study, collective knowledge is manifested by activity and retained in patterns of behavior, and physical artifacts such as documents, the physical layout of the organization and the computer systems.

Sandelands and Stablein (1987) proposed that the organization was a mental entity capable of thought, although they agreed with March and Simon (cited in Sandelands & Stablein, 1987, p. 145) that the organization's thought processes resembled "more earth worm than ape." They pointed out that

> [t]here are ideas of triggering and traces. Just as the firing of a neuron can trigger the firing of adjacent neurons and thus form a trace of activation, so too can behavior trigger other behaviors and thus form a trace of activity. In both cases, the trace so formed can symbolize an idea or even a sequence or train of ideas.

Weick and Roberts (1996, p. 300) conceptualized collective mind as "a pattern of heedful interrelations of actions in a social system." Even Simon (1996, p. 176), who forthrightly declared that "all learning takes place in individual human heads," saw learning as being dependent to a large extent on what is known and believed by other members in the organization. He saw learning, of which knowledge retention is a significant component, as occurring in a web of social interactions and relationships.

Knowledge retention can occur via one human brain, where one person simply remembers what they have learnt, or on a collective level, where collective mechanisms act to retain knowledge so that individuals and groups may access the knowledge as they need in a workplace environment. Huber's (1996) model of organizational learning clearly identifies organizational memory, or knowledge retention, as a significant feature, with the more usual elements of knowledge acquisition and information distribution and interpretation. This model can be used to determine the effectiveness of a learning system in terms of embedding learning in the organization, that is, transforming the learning into a collective resource (O'Toole & Talbot in press).

Other aspects of knowledge that are significant to the knowledge retention structures of the organization are the declarative and procedural aspects.

Declarative and Procedural Knowledge

Knowledge can be classified according to the type of memory system in the individual in which the knowledge resides. The aspects of knowledge involving these memory systems are declarative and procedural. These aspects of memory were established in the field of cognitive psychology, in the first instance by Tulving. These aspects have also been used in a limited way in organizational studies (El Sawy, Gomes, & Gonzalez, 1986; Moorman & Miner, 1998), but have far greater utility than has previously been acknowledged, as shown later in this publication. Organizations are noteworthy for the interaction between people, as individuals and groups, and infrastructure, such as buildings, technological artifacts, and equipment. In organizations, the declarative and procedural aspects of knowledge retention are manifested both in the cognitive structures of the people and also in the physical environment. Thus, the emphasis on cognitive structures in psychology is expanded to include other facets of organizational life. The different aspects of declarative and procedural knowledge retention have different characteristics, which impact on how the knowledge may be used, and its influence on the organization.

Declarative knowledge is comprised of semantic knowledge and episodic knowledge.

The Semantic Knowledge Retention System

The semantic and episodic knowledge retention systems have been represented as holding particular types of declarative knowledge. The semantic knowledge retention system (also called "factual memory" by Pojman (2001)) "contains concepts and factual knowledge" (Schacter, 1996, p. 17), and is believed to be the site of language (Tulving, 1972). Morris (1988, p. 234) likened the semantic knowledge retention system to a "dictionary or encyclopedia, filled with general facts and information," and the knowledge encoded within the semantic memory system may be both abstract and non-domain-specific. Semantic memory is a network of words, concepts, images, and languages. The sources of input are perception and thought. According to Tulving and Donaldson (1972), it is much less susceptible to transformation and loss of knowledge than episodic memory.

Although much of the knowledge within the semantic memory system is explicit, it also has the intriguing characteristic of allowing the individual to retrieve knowledge through reconstruction, without the knowledge being specifically encoded. Hence, by the manipulation of rules, formulae, concepts, symbols, and algorithms, an individual may know that the surname "Lawson" comes before the surname "Silins" alphabetically without specifically being told of that fact (Anderson, 1995; Schacter, 1996; Tulving, 1972, 1985a).

The Episodic Knowledge Retention System

Episodic memory (also termed "event memory" by Pojman (2001)) is where individuals store their "personal past." Schacter (1996, p. 17), a former student of Tulving's, referred to episodic memory as "recollected in the context of a particular time and place with some reference to oneself as a participant in the episode." Tulving (2001, p. 20) evocatively described episodic memory as "making possible mental 'time travel' through subjective time," which gives an image of us reliving past scenes as participants, rather than retrieving and reconstructing a set of facts such as the semantic memory system retains. Episodic memory is thus autobiographical in nature (Tulving & Donaldson, 1972). It relates to events and experiences in the individual's life. It is "probably quite susceptible to transformation and loss of information" (Tulving & Donaldson, 1972, p. 387). This is because the encoding is temporally cued. Episodic memory does not have the capacity for inferential reasoning or generalizations. Shotter (1990) argued that the nature of remembering was subjective and laden with emotion. When accessing episodic memories, the individual also reconstructs associated emotions and perspectives.

It is this sense of oneself as a participant that clearly resides within the episodic memory. Schacter (1996) described a patient who had lost his episodic memory but who had retained his semantic memory. According to Schacter, the patient was significantly disconnected from the major events in his life and thought about them in an impersonal way. Episodic memory at the organizational level, according to El Sawy et al. (1986), contains stories and myths, critical incidents, symbolic artifacts and other information that relates to specific events and episodes. This sense of self is found within the group episodic memory as well, but it is translated from the sense of "I" to the sense of "We," and forms part of the group culture. When newcomers join an organization, they join part of the group episodic knowledge retention structure as they listen, remember, and retell stories of events that occurred before their time, even though this knowledge of past events should form part of their individual semantic memory (O'Toole, 1999). The emotional response of the newcomer, however, belongs to the episodic rather than the semantic memory. Researchers have discussed how the use of stories within organizations can create and maintain a collective sense of self (Boje, 1991; Boyce, 1996; Czarniawska, 1997; Gabriel, 1995, 1998; Hansen & Kahnweiler, 1993; Martin et al., 1983). Some organizations have created "learning histories" to capture the experiences of individuals and make them accessible to the organization (Kransdorff, 1998; Roth & Kleiner, 1998). These learning histories are intended to transform a personal episodic memory into an explicit organizational episodic memory, to be used in decision-making activities and inviting the reader to share the experience of past events.

Schemas

Within the declarative (semantic and episodic) memory systems, memories are organized into schemas, which are mental frameworks that are used to organize related concepts and images and determine the knowledge constructions we make. Schemas are described as "having slots that may be filled with fixed compulsory values, or with variable optional values" (Cohen, 1996, p. 77). Hence a schema for a house would include "walls," "roof" and "floor."

A schema contains knowledge that may, on occasion, distort retrieved memories. By filling in gaps or things not understood from previously encoded knowledge within the schema or script, an individual may inadvertently add or change details of an event or situation, thus altering their perception and the schema representation (Anderson, 1995; Morris, 1988; Sternberg, 1999; Weick, 1979a). For the individual, memory is a reconstruction of the past, rather than a duplicate image. Schön, in particular, described how professionals see problems in terms of their profession, and according to Schön (1987, p. 5) "those who hold conflicting [professional] frames pay attention to different facts and make different sense of the facts that they notice."

At an organizational level, these schemas have been termed organizational schemas, scripts, mental models, and cognitive maps, and represent the merging of individual schemas and scripts. The scripts and schemas of individuals within a group must change before a group schema or script can change (Baets, 1998), and new members to the group generally accept the group schemas at an individual level through a process of socialization (Ashforth & Fried, 1988).

The Procedural Knowledge Retention System

Procedural knowledge refers to the learned associations between stimuli and responses. This is the individual's skill base and is both tacit and domain-specific. Work routines are performed at the individual level with the skills sited in procedural memory. The procedural memory system (also termed "habit" by Pojman (2001)) is the system "which allows us to learn skills and acquire habits" and is often modeled as a production system (Anderson, 1995; Schacter, 1996, p. 17). A production system consists of condition–action rules, for example:

IF the car is moving
AND a person runs in front of the car
THEN push the brake pedal

The procedural memory system is a stimulus–response system. Singley and Anderson (1989) posited that skill acquisition requires both declarative and procedural knowledge acquisition. An important aspect in the declarative/procedural memory system is that the transfer of the memory type is fluid. Procedural-to-procedural memory transfer occurs, for example, when a new organizational member is taught skills by "osmosis," usually by sitting next to an expert and watching (Spender, 1996b).

Declarative-to-procedural transfer can occur as a person first learns the conceptual basis of a skill (the declarative knowledge) and then practices the skill until he/she can perform the skill automatically. Singley and Anderson (1989) gave the example of when a person learns a telephone number "off by heart": if the number is used frequently, the person may then have trouble verbalizing the number, needing to mentally push the buttons to recall it consciously. An interesting point in Singley and Anderson's example is the function of the telephone numberpad. The positioning of the fingers when pressing the buttons is learned procedurally; if the position of the numbers on the keypad changed, or the learner was asked to mentally turn a number dial, it may be more difficult to recall the telephone number. It is shown later in this book how the presence and placement of physical objects act as a cue to facilitate the retrieval of procedural knowledge.

The distinction between declarative and procedural knowledge is somewhat similar to Ryle's classification of "knowing how" and "knowing that" (Reber, 1993; Ryle, 1949). In Ryle's discussion of "knowing how," however, he makes a distinction between habitual performance and what he calls "intelligent performance." Habitual performance is a performance that is automatic, with no "care, vigilance or criticism" (Ryle, 1949, p. 42); intelligent performance has intentionality and the "how" is ascribed to rules that are learnt through practice. Ryle's analysis of intelligent performance seems somewhat simplistic. He gave the example of a mountain climber who "walking over ice-covered rocks in a high wind in the dark does not move his limbs by blind habit" (Ryle, 1949, p. 42). In fact, it is likely that part of the mountain climber's performance would be habitual. For example, the mountain climber may give no thought to the feeling of the backpack on his back because its balance and burden have become habitual. If the balance changes, then the mountain climber will have to shift from habitual or automatic thinking to intentional thinking with regard to the backpack. The parts of the environment that are not standard will be met by intentional performance. The parts that conform to sufficient prior experience will be met by habitual performance. Ryle believed that "know how" was more than just a habit, and I suggest that Ryle, by excluding habit from the knowledge that he called "know how," excluded an important part of knowledge both in individuals and in groups. Ryle's model of *know how* and *know that* has been expanded in more recent times to include "know who" (who knows what and how) and "know why" (knowledge of theories and principles)

(Organization of Economic and Cultural Development (OECD), 1996). Procedural knowledge in individuals refers generally to skill or habit. In this book, as procedural level is explained at a collective level, the definition of procedural aspects expands to include explicit elements, such as written procedures. This is justified in terms of the contribution of each individual to the collective routines and how individuals come to learn their automatic responses that merge with the collective routines.

Another example of knowledge retained from experience is "practical thinking" investigated by Scribner (1986) that encompassed the practical rules of thumb and least-effort solutions that people learn and employ in the workplace to make their lives easier. Scribner (1986, p. 22) suggested that expertise was a matter of "building up a repertoire of solution modes fitted to properties of specific problems and particular circumstances." According to Scribner, the choice of solution favored a "least-effort" criterion, which takes into account the environment and the values of the problem-solver.

The knowledge retained by individuals derived from former experience is significant within organizations. The experience from which our schemas are developed is diverse. Individuals in Western society are born and usually grow up in some form of family situation, undergo primary and secondary school and sometimes undertake further formal studies. Meanwhile, relationships are formed, travel undertaken, hobbies pursued, and conflict endured. Anderson, Reder and Simon (1997) argued that, although the degree of knowledge transferred from one situation to another may be variable, it does occur. Knowledge, however, has a subjective element to it. The schemas that develop in people can mold the knowledge retained in the future. This strengthens the existing schemas and may act to further mold the knowledge retained. According to Kim (1993, p. 39), who labeled schemas as "mental models," a common term in managerial studies, "mental models not only help us make sense of the world we see, they can also restrict our understandings to that which makes sense in the mental model."

Data, Information, and Knowledge

Fahey and Prusak (1998, p. 266) identified an inability to distinguish between data, information, and knowledge as one of the worst of the 11 deadliest sins of *knowledge management*. These distinctions are considered important in that knowledge is considered the asset that may create a competitive advantage for the organization. Burton-Jones (1999, p. 5) defined data as "any signals which can be sent by an originator to a recipient – human or otherwise." Data are essentially facts, such as quantities and values (Davenport & Prusak, 1998). Information becomes data that was "intelligible to the recipient" by being placed into a structure to inform (Davenport & Prusak, 1998, p. 5). Knowledge was defined as "the cumulative stock of information and skills derived from use of information by the recipients" (Burton-Jones, 1999, p. 5). Knowledge is generally considered to be richer in comparison with data and information (Allee, 1997; Davenport & Prusak, 1998). Burton-Jones created a useful diagram, shown below, that depicts the relationships between data, information and knowledge, and value and meaning.

Boisot (2002) makes a nice distinction, one not incompatible with the definitions and explanations above, that only data can flow between people. Data are transformed into knowledge only when integrated with the mental structures of the individual receiving the data, and then two individuals can be said to "share knowledge" (p. 68). This is supported by Burton-Jones (1999, p. 6), who contended that knowledge may only be captured, that is, acquired or created, through the human brain. This resonance, however, can be impeded if the medium used to communicate the knowledge is not sufficiently rich. Jarvis (2009, p. 100) introduces a helpful learning perspective as he explained that "[d] ata and information are the knowledge of those who propound them but they only become other people's knowledge when they have been learned subjectively." To make sense of data, then, depends on an individual's preexisting knowledge, and their capacity to make meaning of the data. As the individual makes meaning, the data merges with the individual's knowledge while adding to that preexisting knowledge.

Organizations tend to keep large banks of data; for many organizations, such as national taxation authorities, data are a key part of their operations. Information, on the other hand, tends to move through organizations. It is organized so that recipients derive meaning from it and in deriving meaning, construct knowledge (Davenport & Prusak, 1998). Although Fig. 2.1 is useful in showing variation in value and meaning, it does not show the relationship between data, information, and knowledge in a functional way. It is feasible that data could be extremely meaningful and valuable, but it requires interaction with, and knowledge of, a human agent to interpret it in such a way that it is useful and meaningful. For example, data coming in a signal from space would be just so much static for the layperson, but could be of immense significance to the astronomer. Although the data need to interact with the knowledge structures of the astronomer, this does not negate the value of the data. A further implication of this model is that data by itself are of little value. To have value, data need to become knowledge. One can thus challenge the value to organizations of retaining data that do not become knowledge.

The data, information, and knowledge typology, however, has an underlying assumption that knowledge is essentially declarative. For example, the typology fails to take into account the role played by objects. The knowledge retained by a blacksmith may be activated by tools and implements in a process of interaction (Keller & Keller, 1996) typical of procedural knowledge (see Polanyi's notion of "indwelling" on page 6). The tools, however, are not data, that is, facts about quantities or values. Thus, although this typology is useful, it does not adequately account for the procedural knowledge inherent in skilled action.

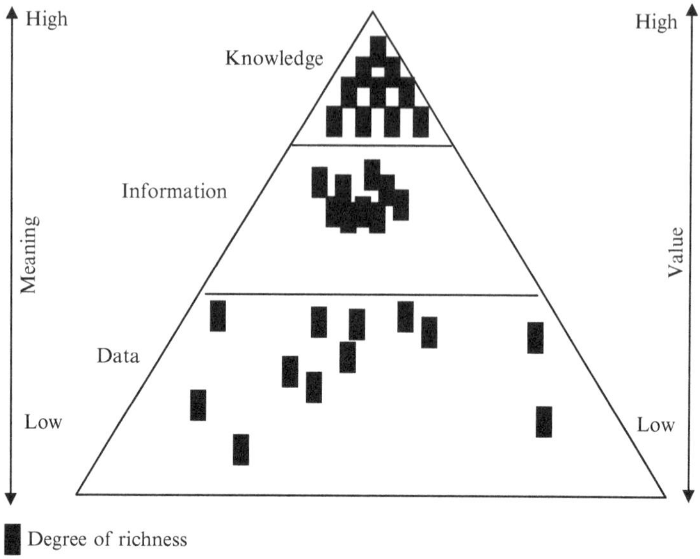

Fig. 2.1 Data, information, and knowledge (Adapted from Burton-Jones, 1999, p. 6)

Unlearning Knowledge

The validity of the notion of unlearning is dependent on whether the unlearning is thought to occur at the individual level or at the organizational level. According to Anderson and Neely (1996), unlearning refers to permanently forgetting experiences in long-term memory due to associative connections among the features of the event being weakened by other experiences. Unlearning has been the subject of experiments in the neurosciences and has been used as part of learning algorithms in artificial neural networks. In this context, unlearning processes, also termed reverse learning (Barrozzo & Penna, 1994; Wimbauer, Klemmer, & van Hemmen, 1994), "locate and remove the unwanted associations between information that obscures the learned inputs" (Robins & McCallum, 1999, p. 1191).

The reception of unlearning as a probable part of human brain function has been mixed (Barrozzo & Penna, 1994; Marks & Tobeña, 1990; Robins & McCallum, 1999; Wimbauer et al., 1994) but unlearning has been widely used as a metaphor to promote the need for changing mental models and belief systems (Hedberg, 1981; Kerfoot, 1999; Solovy, 1999; Starbuck, 1996). Unlearning is said to occur whenever a person has to discard either explicit or tacit knowledge, but this is unproven and the occurrence of unlearning remains unclear. Does unlearning occur whenever a person learns a different way of doing a task, or a different way of thinking? Are there only certain learning events that trigger unlearning, or is unlearning simply part of additional learning, that is, changes in what has been retained in memory systems? Does unlearning occur at all? For example, when a word-processing operator needs to learn new applications that require different key combinations to achieve operations that she/he has achieved in the past, does the operator need to *unlearn* the association of old key combinations with the operations before she/he learns the association of new key combinations with the operation? This seems very unlikely. Our own experience suggests that although at times we have to learn new ways of performing motor skills, some degree of thought will resurrect the memory of how we used to perform the motor skill before we had to change.

Although Hedberg (1981) described unlearning as "a process that discards knowledge" (p. 18), in realistic terms, there is some question as to whether knowledge within the human may actually be discarded, or whether retrieval cues are simply decayed (Anderson, 2000).

It is proposed that a more realistic model for individual learning would embrace the concept of schemas or mental models. According to Argyris (1992/1999) and Argyris and Schön (1978), mental models are most likely to change when they are challenged and reflected upon. This does not mean the knowledge in the mental model is discarded, so much as the commitment to the mental model is lessened. In times of crisis, according to Nystrom and Starbuck (2004, p. 108), "ideologies were powerful than structures as forces guiding organizational responses," and thus considerable evidence may be needed for individuals to critique the ideologies that form their mental models, thus adding to the complexity of the mental models. Interestingly, Hedberg (1981) while discussing the concept of unlearning, notes that people "who make sophisticated responses seem to possess multidimensional stimulus-discrimination networks," which may indicate that people who have complex mental frameworks may be more able to adapt to a variety of situations.

In terms of organizations, the construct of unlearning has more credibility. Argyris' famous construct of double-loop learning, where organizations challenge their underlying assumptions as part of the learning process, incorporated the concept of unlearning. The unlearning component of double-loop learning may have become popular due to the short-term focus of the corporate environment (Kaplan & Norton, 1996), where knowledge may be seen as having a current currency (Davenport & Prusak, 1998). The nature of knowledge means that knowledge must be engaged with the cognitive frameworks of individuals or groups of individuals. In organizations, there are few jobs that encourage the revisiting of "old knowledge" except for current purposes. Knowledge that is not immediately usable may be seen as worthy of being discarded, instead of being seen as an "investment" in experience and adding to the organization's intellectual capital. At the very least, often for legal purposes, this knowledge is put away in archive boxes and forgotten, where it dwindles to the status of stored data and information.

Often implied in the concept of unlearning, however, is the notion that the most recent knowledge is the most "right." In fact, as Levitt and March (1996) pointed out in their excellent paper on organizational learning, individuals and groups may learn "knowledge" that is superstitious in nature and wrong in fact.

Huber (1996) noted that unlearning at the organizational level meant that:

- An organization becomes temporarily inactive because it is without a belief, fact, or script in a particular context where the unlearned knowledge was used.
- Focused search is initiated to fill the gap.
- New learning takes place.

Huber mentions that the most extreme form of unlearning can be the dismissal of employees who cannot change the way they do things. Occasionally, however, the normal attrition of staff and their replacement by new people may cause a form of unlearning. New people learn as a matter of course the systems, technology, and values of their organization. There is usually no value perceived in teaching the old ways of doing things. If, however, a need for "old knowledge" is required, perhaps where a lawsuit arises, or where energy failures or restrictions means that new technology is not viable, the loss of "old knowledge" retained can have consequences for the organization. This indicates a major difference between organizations and people. People may develop differentiated and complex schema, but still have some memory of old learning. Organizations simply unlearn.

The Status of Knowledge

When organizations choose to discard knowledge, that knowledge clearly decreases in value and therefore in status within the organization. The prestige of knowledge and its currency is related to who subscribes to that knowledge. Foucault (1972/1980, p. 81) made a distinction between knowledge and "subjugated knowledges." Foucault pointed out that there is essentially a pecking order in different areas of knowledge. There are fields of knowledge that ignore or work in opposition to institutional fields of knowledge. These fields of knowledge are local, particular and may not be unanimous (Foucault, 1972/1980). Examples in Western societies of the exposure of previously unregarded fields of knowledge are those relating to women and indigenous people (Crowley & Himmelweit, 1992). In organizations, low status fields of knowledge may be held by workers who are lower down in the hierarchy and whose field of expertise is not highly regarded by the leaders of the organization. Examples of this were shown in the work of Orr (1990), where the photocopy technicians had to meet their own learning needs through a community of practice because the organization did not invest in adequate training. Because the knowledge held by these groups was considered manual/clerical, and not "professional," there were few resources allocated to explicate the knowledge in the form of manuals, rules, and procedures. Thus the low status of the knowledge directly affected the structures in which the knowledge was retained.

Knowledge as a Commodity

Drucker (1995) saw knowledge as the primary economic factor for the global economy. This has come to pass with the knowledge economy and knowledge management becoming part of the common economic and business terminology. Knowledge is seen to be something that can be bought and sold and as an asset that produces a commercial value for the firm or the nation (Gherardi, 2006). While postmodernism promotes the recognition and valuing of formerly subjugated and local knowledges, the emphasis in this push for the commodification of knowledge values the knowledge which can be seen to elicit direct profit or add monetary value to the organization or the economy (Matthews & Candy, 1999). Knowledge has become considered to be a significant input to the wealth creation, to the extent that the OECD periodically publishes a "scoreboard" that sets out the performance of various OECD countries in terms of various knowledge indicators (2002).

According to Burton-Jones (1999, p. 3): "[F]uture wealth and power will be derived mainly from intangible intellectual resources: knowledge capital." Knowledge as a commodity, which comes within the auspices of knowledge management, does not seem to include the indirect, informal knowledge that either detracts from, or does not contribute to, the achievement of the organizational goals of the company. Knowledge is a functional construct; one that is transmitted, received, and assimilated, rather than one that is constructed in concert with the previous experience of the "receiver." An issue that arises is just how successfully knowledge can be commodified. As Stafford (2001, p. 229) pointed out, "commercialization thrives on standardization," which is difficult to relate to a construct as complex as knowledge. March (1996) pointed out that, although increased knowledge may decrease variability in performance, it may not actually guarantee competitive advantage. Thus a knowledgeable organization may improve its position from the last in a competitive field, "without changing the likelihood of finishing first" (March, 1996, p. 118–9).

At the organizational level, the knowledge of the organization has varying value. Some knowledge may relate to the strategic advantages of the firm, such as formulae, leading-edge technology or specialist skills of key employees; some knowledge may relate to standard operations within the firm that may be duplicated in other organizations, such as how to operate commonly used software. Other knowledge, such as the employees' knowledge of a chief executive officer's (CEO) incompetence, may have an adverse effect on the firm, assuming that it becomes known in the marketplace. According to Burton-Jones (1999), only tacit knowledge, either alone or in concert with explicit knowledge, can give an organization a sustainable competitive advantage, because explicit knowledge is too easily communicated. If knowledge is considered an economic asset, then it becomes desirable to optimize the knowledge that contributes to the achievement of organizational goals and minimize the effects of knowledge that is detrimental to the goals of the organization. Hence knowledge management becomes necessary.

Knowledge Management

Knowledge management has been defined by Wiig (2000, p. 6) as

> the systematic and explicit management of knowledge-related activities, practices, programs, and policies within the enterprise. Consequently, the enterprise's viability depends directly on:
>
> - The competitive quality of its knowledge assets and
> - The successful application of these assets in all its business activities (i.e., realization of the knowledge assets' value)
>
> ...The goal of knowledge management is to build and exploit intellectual capital effectively and gainfully.

In much of the knowledge management literature, there are essentially two approaches (Mentzas, Apostolou, & Young, 2001). One of these approaches involves semantic knowledge retention in the form of databases, and occasionally an episodic knowledge retention in the form of documented histories and stories of the past so that current members may learn from them (Kransdorff, 1998); this is also termed the "product-centered approach" (Mentzas et al., 2001). The other approach, termed the "process-centered approach" (Mentzas et al., 2001), emphasizes knowledge management as a social communication process. Snowden (2000a, b) emphasized the importance of stories and other cultural devices, which have the element of the personal past, the "I" or "We" that assumes a feeling of participation and experience in the remembered event. Knowledge management has absorbed many of the principles of the Learning Organization, a notion popularized by Senge (1992), which focused on flatter structures, collaborative learning, and viewing the organization from a systems perspective.

The practice of knowledge management holds some underlying assumptions. The knowledge referred to must contribute to the organization's profitability, or at least to its effectiveness of achieving organizational goals. Knowledge that detracts from the achievement of the organization's goals is generally not included in the knowledge that is to be managed. One notable exception to this is the work by Snowden (2000a, b) who has attempted to manipulate organizational stories so that they promote organizational goals, instead of organizational calamities. Finally, knowledge must, in some form, be reproducible so that organizations can reap the benefits on an ongoing basis (Gherardi, 2006).

The knowledge management movement has become a normal part of corporate organizations as evidenced by the creation of chief learning officers from the ranks of human resource areas, as well as the more common chief knowledge officers, who have evolved from the information technology departments (Bonner, 2000).

The development of information and communications technology (ICT) is part of the reason for the development of knowledge management. ICT gave managers the tools with which much of the explicit knowledge could be stored, transmitted, and retrieved across the globe. The most common ICT tools used by knowledge managers, according to Hellström and Raman (2001), are:

- Document or management databases used in the performance of administrative tasks
- Cooperative groupware, enabling the communication of knowledge and
- Human resource databases and portals (Hellström & Raman, 2001)

Much of the earlier work in knowledge management attempted to codify tacit knowledge to ensure that it stayed in the company when individuals left the organization (Hellström & Raman, 2001). This led to the development of IT systems that purported to act as knowledge retention structures but failed to effectively capture the knowledge and experience of the contributing experts. The complex ways in which the procedural and declarative knowledge of experts were entangled could not be explicated, and it was perceived that there was often a schism between the experts' theoretical knowledge and their practical experience. In response to this early failure, the knowledge management field has embraced various sociocultural devices, such as communities of practice (Vann & Bowker, 2001). A community of practice is a social construct that occurs when people of similar occupations and interests form a group of mutual interest, where people tend to share knowledge, help each other with difficult problems and support each other in areas of common enterprise (Wenger, 1999, 2000). Where Wenger initially described groups that had evolved informally, organizations now attempt to manufacture communities of practice to garner the benefits to the organization (Vann & Bowker, 2001; Yi, 2002). Informal communities of practice may arise simply because the knowledge required for a particular occupational group is undervalued and not considered worth fostering by the management of a particular organization (Collinson, 1994; Gottfied, 1994; Orr, 1990; Wenger, 1999). The community arises as the group of workers attempts to overcome the deficiencies of management support by creating their own support mechanisms.

The calls by knowledge management consultants and others to promote communities of practice are perhaps unnecessary and simply confirm their previous existence (Vann & Bowker, 2001). They may also be evidence of the power of making something explicit. Communities of practice are not uncommon in organizations, since they are informal structures of knowledge which make up the deficiencies of the formal structure and processes of the organization. It needed, however, someone to write a book about it (see Wenger, 1999) and to give this informal structure of knowledge a label before communities of practice were recognized as assets to be nurtured.

The challenge for organizations that attempt knowledge management is to simply find out the knowledge resident within the organization. Core competencies are given a special place in the knowledge management arena. They are widely credited as being a key to an organization's effectiveness (Prahalad & Hamel, 1990; von Krogh, Lyles, Mahnke, & Rogulic, 1999). The value in the notion of core competencies is in encouraging organizations to ascertain what they know and do well, which adds to shareholder value (von Krogh et al., 1999). The process of ascertaining this knowledge, however, may be difficult in the light of the amount of knowledge within organizations. Dhar (2001) argued that organizations did not understand or utilize the extent of the knowledge held within their own databases. It seems reasonable to suggest that if organizational leaders do not know the extent of their explicit knowledge resources, then it is extremely unlikely that they will know the extent of their tacit knowledge resources, which are held in the minds of the individuals who work there. Although knowledge creation may occur either within or outside the organization (Garud, Jain, & Kumaraswamy, 1999), the typical knowledge management ethos concentrates on how that knowledge that can be leveraged may be retained and utilized for the maximum profit of the firm.

The Commodification of Knowledge

Many authors (e.g., Burton-Jones, 1999; Grant, 2000) have identified a new form of postindustrial economy that has been labeled the knowledge economy. The knowledge economy is characterized by knowledge becoming the primary factor of production. The knowledge economy is also characterized by rapid change, being networked via various ICT media, and is concentrated on intangibles, that is, a predominance of service over goods (Grant, 2000). Unlike other organizational assets, knowledge, instead of diminishing, grows with use (Adler, 2002).

The emphasis on knowledge in the knowledge economy means that knowledge is a commodity for the individual as well as the organization. Cook and Seely Brown (1999) pointed out that knowledge held within organizations is commonly seen as "possessed" by the organization or the individual who holds it. This perspective of knowledge is consistent with the common interchangeability of knowledge with memory (Reber, 1995). The individual can be viewed as the agent of knowledge. It is the individual who undergoes training and education, scans the Internet, talks to peers, has ideas and tries out new ways of working. For organizational leaders, the threat of the most knowledgeable employees leaving the company and perhaps joining competing companies may be a serious threat to the business. The people in a knowledge-based industry are considered to be a valuable resource, and hence recruitment and incentive schemes become a significant mechanism for retaining an important part of the knowledge resource (Burgess, 2001; Burton-Jones, 1999).

Issues of ownership of knowledge generated during the individual's tenure with an organization can also be problematic. Knowledge created during company time, with company resources on company property is usually deemed to be owned by the company, who can arrange patents. The situation, however, becomes more complex where the individuals are perhaps educated at the firm's expense and where they create knowledge in their leisure time, but using knowledge that has been generated under the firm's patent. Where an individual becomes knowledgeable about a particular process or domain within the organization, there is often considerable pressure to share that knowledge with others, or to embed the knowledge in the firm's IT resources. Employees who refuse to release their knowledge to the rest of the organization are deplored and labeled "silos" (Senge et al., 1999).

For the knowledge manager, the challenge is to somehow transfer the knowledge of the individual to the organization (Hellestöm and Raman, 2001). This, however, is not a new challenge. According to Wiig (2000, p. 4) "the craft guilds and apprentice–journeyman–master systems of the thirteenth century were based on systematic and pragmatic [knowledge management] considerations." This refers to the sharing of valuable knowledge by the craftsmasters with the younger people in their business within the structure of the apprenticeship system. The establishment of Fordist work systems in the 1890s was a significant development in separating individual knowledge from the work process. According to Hellström and Raman (2001, p. 141): "Fordism originated in the Chicago meat industry in the 1890s, and its centre was the conveyor belt that brought the meat to the worker at a speed chosen by management." Later, the principles were adopted and expanded by Henry Ford in his automobile factories. Fordism has evolved in and has been adopted by various industries, and is typified by the following principles:

- Technology and labor are integrated so that production speed and managerial control is optimized.
- Individual differences between workers are minimized so that workers may be changed and replaced with little or no effort.
- Technology replaces workers where feasible.

Fordism is often associated with Taylorism, which "effectively treats the workers as machines (Braverman, 1974) by 'extracting' and 'embedding' their skills in technical and abstract systems" (Hellström & Raman, 2001, p. 142). Although workers with high levels of knowledge are valued in a knowledge society, it would be fruitless to argue that knowledge management activities do not try to embed as much knowledge as possible in organizational mechanisms in order to diminish the amount of knowledge that can leave the organization when the individual departs. The differences to the Fordism principles lie in the need to recognize the individuals as the original owners of the knowledge and compensate them in terms of opportunity, reward and recognition.

Knowledge is used in the performance of organizational tasks. The next section investigates the nature of knowledge and the role it plays in action.

Knowledge as Part of Action and Knowing

Spender (1996a, p. 47) pointed out that discussions of organizational knowledge

> remain divided over whether we mean individual knowledge shared by all the organization's members, focusing us on the management of the "sticky" knowledge that must be moved around the firm (von Hippel, 1994) and on the prevention of leakage of information to others, or on the generation of some kind of objectified knowledge that, embedded in the organization's rules and routines, acts as a Hobbesian constraint over its individual members.

Both descriptions are relevant as knowledge is an umbrella term for a construct that has many forms and aspects. Walsh and Ungson (1991, p. 58) posited that an organization's "retention facility can be structured in terms of five retention bins." The imagery afforded by the notion of retention bins is probably contrary to later commentary by the authors. Walsh and Ungson (1991, p. 59) mention elsewhere in their work that "memories are distributional and transient in character." However, the bins metaphor suggests stable, stationary, and central modes of retention. Walsh and Ungson's definition of knowledge retained is limited to the knowledge that is useful for the purposes of decision-making in the organization. The bins, however, provide a useful starting point for conceptualizing knowledge retention structures.

The combination and interaction of an organization's knowledge retention structures will affect the generation and emergence of future knowledge retention structures. As individuals continue to use one knowledge retention structure and cease using another, different patterns of dominance in knowledge retention structures will emerge. The organization's physical environment, although explicit and tangible, will often contain symbolic and tacit knowledge that may be drawn upon by organizational members (Domingues, 1997; Doxtater, 1990; O'Toole, 2001; Proshansky, Fabian, & Kaminoff, 1995). Culture, process and structure are organizational repositories of tacit knowledge, although many organizations attempt to codify this knowledge in the form of written procedures, manuals, and rule books (Fahey & Prusak, 1998).

In many of the texts that examine knowledge, knowledge is seen as an end in itself, instead of a construct that is part of some form of purposeful action. Knowledge held by an individual, however, interacts in the context in which the individual is situated. Part of this context includes other individuals with whom the individual interacts. Thus the individual will draw knowledge from the context, which is combined with his/her own previous experience. The characteristics of the context will affect the action that comes from the individual's knowledge. For example, the computer system malfunctioning will affect the actions of the individual who has to complete a task urgently; that is, they will not try to use the computer system. As the action takes place, the practice incorporates an interplay of tacit and explicit knowledge and an interaction with the context. This serves to add to or change the individual's knowledge in a dynamic and situated way.

Argyris (1993, pp. 1–3) defined actionable knowledge as "the knowledge that people use to create … [their] world. … How do you know when you know something? When you can produce what it is that you claim to know." This theme is further developed by Cook and Seely Brown (1999, p. 383), who promoted an epistemology of practice that incorporates knowing as a part of action. Cook and Seely Brown (1999) distinguished between knowing and knowledge by defining knowledge as *what is possessed in the head* (1999, p. 382) in what is described by them as *the epistemology of possession* (1999, p. 382), where knowledge is an asset or tool that is owned and can be called upon by the individual. Knowing is *part of* action (1999, p. 383), conceptualised as an *epistemology of practice* (1999, p. 383). In other words, knowing is part of doing, of acting, rather than bringing knowledge possessed to bear as a tool in a given situation. Cook and Seely Brown posit that knowing is about interaction with the physical and social world.

In their words: "One cannot make reliable objects through the haphazard use of clay and steel ... objects give way when design pushes them beyond the constraints of their materials. ... Similarly, in the social world, one must honor the strengths, limitations, and character of individuals and groups to engender coordination and directed action or practice" (Cook & Seely Brown, 1999, p. 389). A point about Cook and Seely Brown's thesis is that the individual/group seems very much in control of the knowing. Knowing and knowledge are concepts that will have positive effects for the organization and the individual because the individual is in charge of the action. But, as Cook and Seely Brown state, knowing is about interaction with the social and physical world, and interaction implies that influence flows both ways. Gherardi (2006) extends the processes of knowing into a "texture of practices" that weaves individual, intraorganizational and interorganizational communities, the organization itself and elements into a complex infrastructure mediated by the material world, social relations, and past experience. Later in this book, the impact of the social and the physical world and past experience upon the knowing of the individual are also discussed.

Scribner, guided by the notion of "activity theory" introduced by the Soviet psychologist Lev S. Vygotsky, rejected the notion of separating mind from action and proposed that the primary unit of analysis in investigating the relationship between knowing and doing must be culturally organized human activity (1997a). Action causes ongoing knowledge retention: knowledge is not static because it results from the interaction of individuals and their environment. Although the knowledge itself may not vary in content, action by the individual means that the knowledge is confirmed in its viability or amended to become consistent with the environment. Individual action therefore results in continuous knowledge retention. Knowledge is simply a tool to facilitate knowing, to enable a useful solution to productive inquiry.

Conclusion: How Does the Nature of Knowledge Affect Knowledge Retention?

A fundamental characteristic of knowledge is its construction in the cognitive frameworks of the individual. Although knowledge can be retained by means such as documents, objects, cultural artifacts, and rituals, the individual is the active agent with regard to the process of knowledge acquisition, retention, and retrieval. Individuals, however, can form groups, interact with the environment, and create and retain knowledge that transcends the knowledge of one individual. Knowledge has different aspects that generally work as dualities; that is, knowledge can be both tacit and explicit, and both individual and collective. Where a knowledge retention structure retains an inappropriate form of knowledge, part of the knowledge may be lost.

The construction of knowledge is also germane to the issue of knowledge retention. The retention structures need to be able to be flexible so that they can deal with continual construction. This flexibility takes a variety of forms. In individuals, cognitive structures such as schemas simply become more complex. Documents may be altered or replaced.

If knowledge is constructed in the frameworks of individuals, then it is logical that knowledge is found where individuals are found. This leads to the conclusion that knowledge is dispersed through organizations, and the knowledge retention structures are also dispersed, so that knowledge can be accessible on a local level. For example, where an organization creates a fully automated factory without individuals, this can be viewed as a collection of artifacts, or residue of knowledge: the knowledge within the automation cannot be reviewed and updated without the intervention of individuals. Similarly, as knowledge relies on individuals, it follows that knowledge is as variable as individuals, which means that knowledge that may not be condoned by the organization's leaders can be found in organizations. If not condoned, it is unlikely that the organization's leaders would countenance any form of investment to retain the knowledge and the knowledge retention structures are likely to be informal, local and tacit. Knowledge that is condoned and valued, particularly if it is part of the organization's core competence, is likely to attract interest and investment by the organization's leaders. Thus the retention structures reflect this interest and investment.

As Alvesson (1993, p. 1000) stated, knowledge is a very difficult thing to define in a meaningful way. The understanding of knowledge that comes from this discussion is the knowledge that is constructed from the experience of the individual. As individuals interact with their environment, their experience and thus their knowledge grows and leaves an impact on the environment and therefore on the organization. As their interaction impacts on the organization, others are affected as their own knowledge grows in interaction with the organization, and the knowledge available to the organization increases. Hence knowledge is a dynamic, constructed entity that is retained both within individuals and within their environment on an individual and collective basis.

Chapter 3
Developing Knowledge Retention Structures

The new recruit knocks on the door as instructed. It opens to a face she has seen in the tearoom. The new recruit asks the whereabouts of Thommo's desk. "Walk straight down this aisle and then turn left. Don't take a shortcut through that work area. Doug is working on something there that's a bit sensitive." "Yeah, like the Hiroshima bomb was sensitive!" interjects a passerby. The new recruit edges past a contraption made of balsa wood that takes up most of the aisle space. A leg swings out from under the contraption missing her narrowly. "Sorry!" The body belonging to the leg crawls out. The new recruit picks up a battery that had rolled away from two women sitting on the floor and returns it. They smile and thank her and go on counting. Snatches of conversations about the Osmonds, how water arrived on Earth, the death of Princess Di and the production date of the new release fill the air. A man strides by alternatively clutching his head and swinging his arms. She has fallen down the rabbit hole and arrived in Research and Development (R&D).

Introduction

The diverse ways that organizations remember depends on the knowledge retention structures that develop. Knowledge retention structures evolve through a variety of processes. This and the following chapters describe and discuss processes related to knowledge retention structures through the depiction of three sites in one company. XME is a firm inventing and selling technological products for the consumer, industrial, and military sectors. The growth of this Australian company has been extremely strong, particularly after entry into the North American markets. The corporate/research and development (R&D) center of the firm is designated as XME Australia. The main production facilities are located at XME Ireland, which also serves the UK, European, and African markets, and XME USA services the North and South American markets. The focus in this chapter is mainly on the knowledge retention structures that involve knowledge that is endorsed or accepted by the organizational leaders, at both a collective and individual level. Data and information is transformed into knowledge when it is integrated into the cognitive structures of an individual. This means that knowledge retention structures are created when actively used by people. Thus, a document becomes a knowledge retention structure when an individual reads it, and the information contained therein

P. O'Toole, *How Organizations Remember: Retaining Knowledge through Organizational Action*, Organizational Change and Innovation 2, DOI 10.1007/978-1-4419-7524-9_3,

interacts with the cognitive structures of that individual. A file that is immured in the archives, on the other hand, becomes a repository of information and data. Knowledge retention structures within organizations are thus manifested in a huge variety of forms. Particular examples of knowledge retention structures may be short-lived, such as a worker's "to-do" list that is discarded at the end of the day or extremely durable, such as the buildings from which people elicit messages related to status, hierarchy, and the business of the organization. The worker's to-do list, although in itself short-lived, may be a part of a long-standing organizational routine if the members of the organization habitually use the same type of to-do list every day and use other people's in their absence to check work to be done. Knowledge retention structures may have both explicit and tacit elements, for example, an internal telephone directory shows the telephone extensions of people within the organization, but may also include information relating to titles, hierarchies, and authority structures. It must also be acknowledged that people themselves are knowledge retention structures. Whether as individuals or as members of a group, people retain knowledge on an ongoing basis as they take action and undergo experiences.

The combination and interaction of an organization's knowledge retention structures will affect the generation and emergence of future knowledge retention structures. As individuals continue to use one type of knowledge retention structure and cease using another, different patterns of dominance in knowledge retention structures will emerge. The next section sets out the development and patterns of dominance in the XME group.

XME Australia: the Development Site

XME commenced in 1985, essentially to commercialize an invention of the technical consultant, who was also a member of the board of directors. The release of advanced technology products saw a large growth in sales, which in turn caused rapid growth within the company. During the time of the study, XME was a privately owned company, and there were significant changes in the leadership of XME Australia, both with regard to the Chairman of the Board and in regard to the Managing Director. A new Chief Executive Officer (CEO) and Chairman were appointed, which heralded changes in various aspects of the operation toward the end of the study.

It has been argued that the life cycle of an organization directly impacts on the degree of formalization and structure. According to Cameron and Whetton (1981, p. 527):

> Organizations begin in a stage, labelled "creativity and entrepreneurship," in which marshalling resources, creating an ideology, and forming an ecological niche are emphasised. The second stage, the "collectivity state," includes high commitment and cohesion among members, face-to-face communication and informal structures, long hours of dedicated service to the organization, and an emerging sense of collectivity and mission. The organizational

emphasis is on internal processes and practices, rather than on external contingencies. In the third stage, "formalization and control," where procedures and policies become institutionalized, goals are formalized, conservatism predominates, and flexibility is reduced. The emphasis is on efficiency of production.

XME Australia had entered the "formalization and control" stage, encouraged by their accreditation under ISO9000. The organization chart of the XME group gave various indications about aspects of the company. The first chart seen of the company was notable for the specification of names and titles of managers and the lack of specification with regard to anyone below the title of manager, reflecting the egalitarian nature of the company, which employed approximately 55 people.

XME Australia was structured into departments according to a combination of functions and markets. These departments were:

Accounts/Administration, which was responsible for monitoring and reporting on revenue, expenses, and the financial position of the firm, personnel issues, and information and communications technology (ICT). The manager of this area also chaired the Occupational Health and Safety committee and acted as secretary to the board of directors.

Research and Development (R&D), which was responsible for creating the circuit boards, wiring, housings, and other components of the products.

Operations, which was responsible for streamlining the processes and specifications of the products generated in R&D. Operations was also responsible for assembling the products, warehousing, and physically shipping the products and ensuring that components were planned for and purchased, and that electronic and other problems were dealt with as part of the production process. In XME Australia, there were designated areas for production control and production.

Business Divisions, which were responsible for generating the business, that is, market development, sales, and account management. The Business Divisions comprised Consumer Products, Military, and Industrial. Industrial was a new market for the organization, and the Divisional Manager had been moving between consumer products and Industrial during my time at the site.

XME Australia was structured as shown in Fig. 3.1. Each manager had a varying number of people reporting to him/her. The Divisional Managers reported directly to the CEO, but have been grouped together in the chart below in the interests of room and visual presentation.

The inclusion of XME Ireland and XME USA on the organizational charts depended on whether the chart represented the XME group or XME Australia. Although status was generally not represented on the charts, two groups tended to appear at the bottom. These groups were the casual staff and staff that were removed geographically from XME Australia.

In the XME group charts, XME Ireland and XME USA were represented reporting to the Consumer Products Business Manager in addition to the Australian Marketing & Retail Sales Manager, as follows (Fig. 3.2).

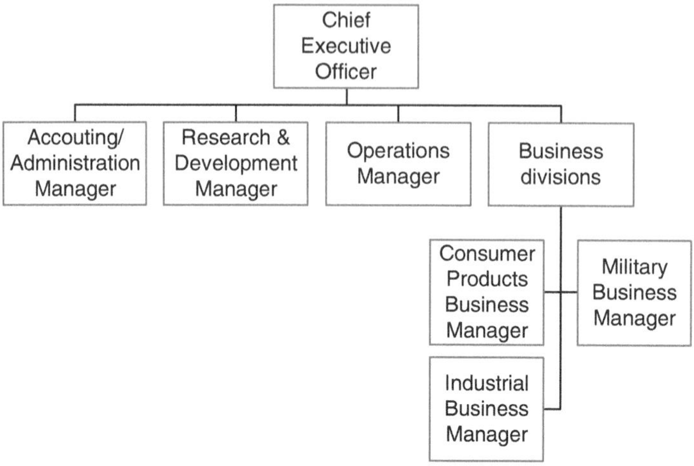

Fig. 3.1 A representation of XME Australia organization chart

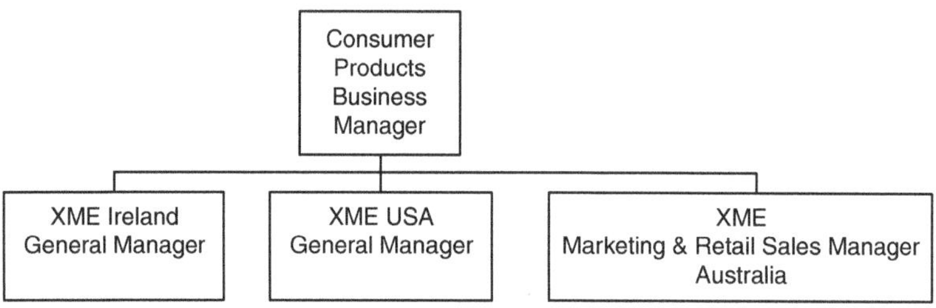

Fig. 3.2 Reporting structures in XME consumer products

Although not represented either by the XME group or the XME Australia charts, there seemed to be significant structural relationships between XME Australia managers and their counterparts in XME Ireland and XME USA. The accountants in Ireland and the USA would work together to reconcile their accounts before sending them to the accountant in Australia. When satisfactory, the accounts were passed to the Accounting/Administration Manager. It also appeared that the Operations Manager in XME Australia had some degree of power over the Operations Manager in Ireland, at least in the form of veto.

A significant difference between XME Australia and the other XME sites was the presence of the R&D department. The focus of the company was on the technologically sophisticated products that it sold; its increasing dominance in the market was due to the technical superiority of XME products over those of their competitors.

The Development of the Organizational Knowledge Retention Structures

The capacity and effectiveness of the knowledge structures at both the individual and the collective level are important from the perspective of how the individual and the group make sense of the organization as part of their world. Although the cognitive structures in a person's head give a useful starting point for understanding knowledge retention, it is also necessary to see how social interaction and social artifacts affect the individual's capacity to remember and make sense of their world (Anderson, Reder, & Simon, 1996; Greeno, 1997). Weick (1979a) pointed out that within the organization exist the social constructions of the members of the organization, but that these constructions exist independently of the members, even though the members may "embellish and elaborate" them, or even change them. These constructions represent the convergence of the constructed knowledge of members both past and present. The knowledge may not represent reality as outsiders may see it, but will represent reality for the members unless something happens to contradict the reality. However, the construction must be available for retrieval if it is to be used in sensemaking activities. The sensemaking activities of organizational members contribute to the organizational culture, as the members make sense of their environment and events in a particular way (Choo, 2002; Weick, 1979b, 1993, 1995). Previous memories act as a reference when new stimuli occur, and enable the members to fit the new stimuli within the existing cultural framework. In XME Australia the stimuli that greatly influenced the development and use of knowledge retention structures at an organizational level were:

- The historical emphasis on R&D
- A more subtle emphasis on accounting
- The rapid growth of the company
- Various external legal and other requirements and
- The demands and decisions of the organization's leaders.

The Historical Emphasis on R&D: "I was REALLY hit by the strong R&D focus"

The emphasis on R&D could be discerned both directly and indirectly. The company had grown from mainly an R&D company to one that included production and engineering facilities. R&D was distinguished by a stew of people, conversations, materials, and equipment. People would walk off with other people's tools and equipment and forget to return them; and they would intersperse questions of the physics of the universe with the details of a popular television show, while crawling on the floor investigating the dimensions of a prototype. This extract from my field notes illustrates the variety of interactions in one place in R&D within a few minutes:

> Terry tells George how he tidied the area. Simone comes over for Hubert's hammer which Terry borrowed "Don't want an angry Hubert up my arse."
> Hubert asks Robert "Do we want a screen in there?"
> Colin starts testing software on a circuit board.
> George gets more wire. Terry mutters that "I had some black ones, but someone pinched them."
>
> Field notes

There was an egalitarian camaraderie, which was a distinguishable trait of the XME Australia culture. A small but interesting observation was that the widely used list of internal telephone extensions was sorted in order of people's first names, a manifestation of this egalitarian culture. This egalitarianism is illustrated in the following interview extract by a person outside of R&D describing the R&D people:

> You know, they must be very, very smart people and also they manage their time, they must manage that very efficiently with having families as well, and yet they've got all these degrees and things and yet they still treat me and talk to me on the same level – and I'm not putting myself down in saying that, it's just that I'm in awe of them. But they do, they think that my job is just as important as theirs, which is good, though.
>
> Interview

Part of the XME Australia culture that could be attributed to the R&D roots of the organization was the amount of autonomy or space given to each person in which they could organize their tasks and their role. Individuals could take it upon themselves either to innovate within their own space or to negotiate with others who would be affected by the change. This aspect of the culture was responsible for the fairly constant changes and improvements witnessed during the period of data collection. A variety of authors (Pedler, Burgoyne, & Boydell 1991/1997; Spender, 1996b; Shields & Newton, 1994; Senge, 1992; Senge, Kleiner, Roberts, Ross, Roth, & Smith 1999; Leithwood, Leonard & Sharrat, 2000) noted the positive effects of autonomy in organizations with regard to organizational learning and the improvements that result from such learning. In XME Australia, the degree of learning experienced was considered a benefit of working with that organization:

> I think generally people's willingness to learn, I think that's where the culture of being a technology company really, really works, because people want to learn, they want to change, they want to really improve, you know.
>
> Interview

> Although I am in the same position for the last [number] of years and don't feel, not even WANT to move to another position, it's not about changing position, it's about you are not stationary in learning, you are not stationary in getting new experience. There is ALWAYS something happening where it actually helps you to grow and get better and better.
>
> Interview

This emphasis on learning implies new knowledge being retained, which is consistent with an R&D focus on invention and innovation. But although this R&D focus had benefits, there were some drawbacks. A historical shortcoming of the company was the lack of management and retention of important records. The exception to this was seen in the focus on accounting, which is discussed in the next section. It was obvious, however, that, in terms of product drawings, specifications, and inventory management the innovative but somewhat informal work practices of the R&D culture could not be maintained in a company that was rapidly increasing production, as shown in this quote:

> but I was a bit shocked. I thought we were a little backward in the way we managed inventory and warehousing. What hit me mostly was the fact that the warehouse didn't use the MRP system and we sort of worked around it, like that staggered me, and yeah, following on from that, production scheduling, even purchasing, it's like I was REALLY hit by the strong R&D focus and the logistic side of it [was] a bit of a side issue.
>
> Interview

R&D people tended to retain information in individual knowledge retention structures such as their personal logbooks and field notes, and on their own computer hard drives and diskettes rather than the central server. There was anecdotal evidence that pointed to R&D staff causing problems in the management of inventory and even in the retention of equipment. The IT consultant complained bitterly that R&D people had taken apart computers from other areas to salvage network cards which were needed to finish testing products. In another case, physical space had been changed in the repair room to prevent the R&D people helping themselves to components:

> Gary comes in a with a service form. I notice that there is an entrance to Warehouse from Service behind shelving. Apparently the shelving was erected to stop people from helping themselves to parts.
>
> Field notes

There were some signs of change, however. The industrial designers located in the R&D section kept orderly drawings and records, and the imposition of order by a technician with regard to components storage encouraged more order in relation to many people's personal management of components.

There were complaints, however, that at times needed information could not be found.

An Accounting Focus: "We tend to be disciplined because we need to be"

The occupational culture of accounting also had an influence on the XME knowledge retention structures. The contribution of accounting to XME Australia, and the rest of the XME group for that matter, could be attributable firstly to the fact that the former Managing Director and the Accounting/Administration Manager were both accountants. These two staff members between them had more than 33 years' experience in the organization, which gave them, in addition to their status within the authority structures, a credibility in terms of their knowledge of the past. This credibility was marked in a fast-growing organization where only one other staff member had over 10 years' service. In addition to the normal requirements of the taxation and company authorities, XME received grants relating to the encouragement of export activities. The requirements of the regulating bodies involved meant that XME had to have strong record-keeping practices in regard to transactions, and so forth, as shown in this interview with a staff member from the Accounting area.

> I'm probably biased there, but I think we tend to be disciplined because we need to be in this area. There are already so many rules that we have to work by, that are external rules that we have no control over that we are just used to following that sort of thing. Yeah, I think we are naturally, have to be a lot more disciplined.
>
> Interview

The Accounts/Administration area had a preoccupation with order. An inability to balance accounts caused a degree of anguish among the staff, while the event of balancing caused celebration. Procedures were easy to find and follow on the computer server, papers were filed, and stray transactions tracked down. Factual accounts of previous events were easily recalled by accessing the department's meeting minutes.

Although the accounting focus did not seem very overt, it could be detected in the use of the software application DO_IT. DO_IT was an integrated computer package that dealt with accounts, inventory, product structures, pricings, and many other aspects of business. The software was marketed in modules, with customers like XME choosing which modules they wished to purchase, and whether they wished the package to be customized. Various people from different operations and areas in XME told me that XME used DO_IT because it was strong in accounting, and the former Managing Director had been an accountant. It was noticeable that many people in the organization were not impressed by DO_IT's capabilities, and its lack of functionality in various ways meant that people created spreadsheets and other documents to compensate for the software's shortcomings. Thus the demands of the work meant that people created new knowledge retention structures to deal with the deficiencies of an organizational knowledge retention structure that was imposed upon them by the organization's leaders.

Having an integrated application, however, meant that people across the company had a terminology in common. Where problems were discovered, meetings among the user departments were convened to ensure that actions taken did not act adversely on other parts of the system. Although this may have taken more time, it did encourage communication between departments, and encouraged a common language across organizational subcultures, a necessary factor in effective communication according to Wenger (2000) and Cyert and Goodman (1997). Having an integrated system has meant also that the Accounts area fulfilled a function that combined the roles of backup and monitor. It was often mentioned that if something were missed at some stage, then it would be picked up by Accounts. On some occasions, this led to Accounts staff also acting as trainers to ensure that the system was used in such a way as to generate the correct accounting information.

Rapid Growth of the Company: "It's a growing company..."

XME had clearly grown dramatically, which was reflected in the expansion of premises, and the planned building that was to be erected after the data collection had been conducted. As the physical space expanded, so did the distance between people and departments, which has caused some problems with communication and these are further explained in the next chapter.

The organization grew to keep up with the increased demand for its products, which meant that production had to become more efficient and standardized. This influenced the entry of more people to work in or with the production area. They in turn influenced the company with their previous experience and expertise in production process and engineering, and introduced a discipline with regard to explicit knowledge retention structures. March (1996) saw the entry of new people into an organization as opportunities for organizational learning. The number of people entering XME Australia, many of them with similar experience and values, meant a change in the way organizational operations were conducted. There was a perception among many of the new staff that being with a growing company meant a degree of security, as shown by this remark:

> It's a growing company so you feel quite secure. From time to time there is some time, short time, when you aren't really SURE you are standing FIRMLY on the ground but still, you can look into the future seeing yourself in this place and still learning; and I think quite important you are not stagnant, you are not standing in one spot not moving anywhere.
>
> Interview

The growth of the company, of course, also encouraged the board of directors to create and incorporate XME USA and XME Ireland to fulfill production and sales functions in their designated areas. This in turn necessitated the connection of the organizations through ICT and other means. The growth of the organization also saw XME having to comply with an increasing raft of legal and other requirements, which is explained in the next section.

Various Legal and Other Requirements: "For instance, when the GST came in, all businesses had to learn new ways of doing things..."

As the organization grew, became international, applied for government grants, and was subject to legislation, the need for explicit proofs of transactions and activities became more necessary.

Income tax, goods and services tax (GST) and workers' compensation requirements demand proof of personnel and commercial transactions. ISO9000 requirements demand documentation of procedures, organization structure, and customer feedback mechanisms. The accreditation of the company under ISO9000 also had encouraged more structure in the company. The adoption of ISO9000 meant that a raft of procedures was written and stored on the computer server. A consultant was employed to write human resources policies, which furthered engendered human resource bulletins to inform the staff of news in this area.

As more non-R&D people were employed, the culture changed. The non-R&D people enjoyed the culture of their new company, but themselves usually encouraged more discipline and documentation. This documentation was needed by suppliers to produce components according to specification. The documentation and discipline was also required under ISO9001, an international quality standard that demanded that XME Australia implement a Quality Management System (QMS). The Quality Manager of XME Australia was an engineer in the Operations area, although the Quality committee was drawn from all parts of the organization. It is noteworthy that some R&D people firmly believed that the QMS had no application to their work.

The increase in discipline and documentation was especially necessary to facilitate the transfer of production from XME Australia to XME Ireland. Comparing XME Australia to Cameron and Whetton's (1981, p. 527) model of the life stages of an organization, the stage of "creativity and entrepreneurship" and the stage of the "collectivity state" had passed. XME Australia was in the process of implementing "formalization and control" in order to coordinate activity between the different sites and to comply with external regulatory authorities. Thus there was an increase in the explicit documentation of semantic knowledge that dealt with the facts of activities of the organization. This type of explicit knowledge structure was often based on predetermined formats provided by the external entities or in a format that was generally used within the industry; in other words, the explicit knowledge retention structures were based on a professional group's agreement of meaning and significance in terms of the knowledge collected and recorded.

Also, the investment in the company by external parties heralded due diligence investigations, which commented on the managerial and other practices of the company. These due diligence investigations determined whether an organization was a good risk for investment, and hence it was incumbent on the organization to fulfill expectations of potential external lenders or investors.

The Dominant Knowledge Retention Structures

As the people of XME Australia coped with the changes to their organization, knowledge retention structures were implemented, used and/or discarded according to the needs and the demands of the work and the organizational leaders. The computer system DO_IT has been mentioned as a manifestation of the accounting dominance through the organizational leaders. Despite many people being dissatisfied with the software's performance, DO_IT became a dominant knowledge retention structure because the majority of people had no choice but to use it, and to use it the best way they could. The use of DO_IT meant a heavy reliance on spreadsheets in some departments because of DO_IT's poor reporting functionality. DO_IT was part of the ICT network upon which XME relied to facilitate communications within XME Australia, within the XME group and with external entities. The ICT network was also used to store and manipulate data and information.

The ICT Network

XME Australia had a computer system based on networked servers. Microsoft Windows was used as the generic office software throughout the XME group. Organizational members could choose to save files on the server, in their own computer's hard drive or on a diskette or CD. The server was regularly backed up on DAT tapes according to a documented procedure, but the tapes were stored on the premises. The vulnerability of computer files seemed to vary from department to department. In some departments, each member seemed to save files on the server directories, rarely using their own hard drive or diskettes. In the R&D area, however, there were people who commonly used these more vulnerable means of saving files.

There seemed to be almost universal Internet access across XME Australia. Staff were seen doing company banking, market research, searching for components, using calculations software found on the Internet, researching legislative and even working out the distances involved in business trips. It was clearly regarded as an important research tool within the company. In particular, people in R&D used the Internet as a means of obtaining software for particular uses.

Despite the heavy use of the ICT network, corporeal records were still an important part of the knowledge retention structures of XME Australia. In contrast to the underlying assumption of the "paperless" office espoused in the 1990s, in XME Australia – and the XME group for that matter – the electronic documents on the ICT network and the corporeal paper documents complemented each other.

Paper Records and Documents

XME Australia often used paper documents and records in addition to computer files. The corporeal nature of paper means that it retains visual cues; for example, people can see how high their in-tray is stacked. Paper was preferred when the information needed to be stable and immediate, and to be visually compared with other documents. The computer system was better when information needed to be more fluid; for example, when several months of transactions needed to be scanned.

The records significant in this study were printouts of computer records and personal notes and logbooks.

Printouts of Electronic Records

There was some evidence of people choosing to maintain dual record systems of both electronic and paper. Despite the extra work involved, the people concerned stated that it was quicker and easier to check the paper record than to conduct a DO_IT enquiry. The practice of dual record keeping, although not specifically encouraged by the organization, was copied from one individual to another, as the people saw the ease with which individuals could quickly check records in response to, for example, telephone queries. The format of the paper record keeping was generally copied or adapted, as well as the practice, as individuals built on the experience of others. Generally, although these records were kept by individuals, they could be referred to by other individuals who needed to quickly check the arrival, for example, of specific components, where the record keeper was absent. Thus the common format made this individual-level knowledge retention structure accessible to others who needed it.

Personal Notes and Logbooks

In contrast, the notebooks often seen in XME Australia were generally created and used by one individual. They were used to record the salient facts of meetings for the individual; they retained product test results; and they retained new things that the individual needed to learn. These notebooks were often simple exercise books, where items were written down of necessity in chronological order. Because these notes were only used by the writer, however, the presentation and order were not important. Individuals knew approximately when they had written an item; individuals had an idea of how the item was presented. There were no instances witnessed when an individual had trouble retrieving information from his/her notebook.

The disadvantage to these personal notebooks and logbooks was, of course, the lack of accessibility by the organization. Because the notebooks were corporeal, if they were in somebody's backpack they could not be read by anyone else. In addition, and the norms of privacy meant that people were reluctant to open other people's notebook in the case of absence. Lack of accessibility was thus both logistical and cultural in nature.

Routines, Processes and Procedures

The formalization of the work meant that the processes of the organization were becoming formalized and standardized as well. Many of the explicit records kept as part of the processes were obviously directly attributable to the implementation of the QMS system. XME Australia, though, was at a stage where processes and procedures could change relatively quickly and easily. In all operations, processes were negotiated among those staff involved to a lesser or greater degree, with the initial idea relating to the process fairly often coming from the nonmanagement ranks. A process was often implemented when individual action had failed to achieve a desired result. An example in XME Australia was the reluctance of people to initiate discussions on salary and performance issues with their managers. The management of XME thus created a new performance appraisal system to overcome this problem. This was an example of a process achieving what individuals felt unable to accomplish by themselves.

The routines, processes, and procedures were heavily influenced by the subcultures of the originating department. For example, an issue for R&D, like other parts of the company, was making sure they had the components they needed to perform their tasks. Unlike component purchases in other parts of the company, R&D frequently required only very small quantities of components in very short time frames. This was a complicating factor in the purchasing process and meant that components were often relatively far more expensive. R&D people would often range around the warehouse and repair area looking for parts, rather than purchase them. Although this was the cause of some frustration with other staff members, there was a tolerance afforded R&D staff that perhaps would not have been extended to similar behavior on the part of Operations or warehouse staff.

The documentation that took place in R&D was often the personal and the current. Logbooks were a significant method of recording test results and observations. Many R&D people saved files in their personal directories rather than on the server directories. Besides producing the products, R&D also had to develop the product's test procedures. In development, however, although the record of testing was kept, it was noticeable that the nature of the tests changed during the development of the product, although the specifics of testing carried out did not seem to be recorded. Hence, although a record would be made that a unit had been tested, what the tests had actually been could only be guessed at.

There seemed to be some degree of order in the work of the industrial designers within R&D. These industrial designers were responsible for designing the housings of the products; they recorded drawings on the server and filed the hard copies accordingly. The drawings completed by R&D and given to Operations, however, were the culmination rather than the record of effort. They did not record the history of the development of the product, which caused concerns that changes made by Operations to the product in development could lead to problems. Within R&D, the prevailing opinion was that, rather than R&D recording the development more comprehensively, Operations should refrain from changing the product without involving R&D.

In contrast to R&D, Operations had to find component sources that were reasonably priced, reliable, and could deal with the volumes needed. In addition, housings and component assembly had to be adapted and fine-tuned to enable mass production. Processes and procedures had to be created for use by production workers. Thus, besides the engineering knowledge required to adapt the product, drawings and procedures must be created. Putting a product into production thus required drawings, specifications, procedures, engineering action reports (EAR), and product structures that had to be created and loaded onto DO_IT.

All the explicit drawings, specifications, and procedures had to have controlled version numbers, file numbers, and so on. When the drawings and EARs were completed, they were uploaded into a special directory of the XME Australia server, for access by people in all three XME operations. All documentation in this directory was the most recent pertaining to products in production.

Operations retained a far higher level of documentation compared with that of R&D. Emails were saved and registers were kept relating to parts evaluations, tool trial reports, price lists and so on. Obsolete drawings are also kept. On the Operations directory a "postmortem" for the New Year's resolutions 2001 reviewed the year to see strengths and weaknesses of the Operation team's performance. This was one of the few instances of collective explicit episodic knowledge discovered in the organization.

The weaknesses in the past, however, impinged on activities of the present. On one occasion, it was discovered that information relating to a product had not been transferred to other documentation, and a product had subsequently been made with a wrong component since March 2001. There was a significant issue involving a product where ongoing defects had not been resolved.

Several people in XME Australia were of the opinion that XME did not seem to learn from the mistakes of the past. These mistakes revolved around not having enough time to fully test and check new products before releasing them to the market, and not having the time or inclination in the past to formulate proper product specifications and drawings. I was shown an electronic component where a switch had gradually "floated" across the box because the supplier was never given drawings. Thus, as time went on, the position of the switch on the component moved, and kept moving. This situation was changing.

> Interviewee: Yeah, it was always a struggle to sort of ... use the engineering stuff as an example – to find a drawing from 1997, you wouldn't bother to go look for it because there was only a five percent chance of it actually existing and if it did exist there would be a minimal chance it was actually correct. So ah, something we've tightened up on, a LOT.
>
> Interview

During the process of development, streamlining and production, the relevant business manager was keeping an eye on the progress. Project timelines were created for each product; however, there were complaints from both the R&D and Operations people that there was no margin for setbacks and problems. They believed that management did not realize, as the products became more sophisticated, that more things could go wrong.

Processes were also implemented following the adoption of the QMS. For example, when components arrived from suppliers, they had to be tested and the testing results, if faulty, were recorded via a non-conformance report (NCR), which is a common report in ISO9000 systems. The NCR forms were entered onto a database to keep records of faulty components from suppliers. The supplier was sent a copy of the ensuing report to assist their improvement. The stock was then moved to the appropriate numbered location in the warehouse until requisitioned. Stock takes occurred twice yearly. Some cycle counting was done, but it was mentioned that probably more would be of benefit, although time pressures were a problem. Reports from DO_IT assisted in keeping data current. At this stage, innovation occurred in the areas of storage, movement and accounting for the product. Knowledge was retained via electronic documents, external documentation from suppliers and clients and in the physical embodiment of the products themselves, in terms of the height of a stack on a palette. In addition, however, the individuals had various mental histories of suppliers and customers to draw on and rules of thumb about priorities of supply and utilizing supply loads to save money. Thus the knowledge of the individuals acted in concert with the knowledge retained in the processes, routines, and procedures to accomplish the business of the organization.

The Individual as a Knowledge Retention Structure

The individual may be thought of as a knowledge retention structure, albeit often an unregarded one. In XME Australia the actions of individuals caused changes to the work environment and how the work was done. These actions were usually the result of the experience and training of the individual. Thus the individual can be thought of as a knowledge retention structure that influenced the use of other knowledge retention structures, without regard to the status of the individual in the organization. In XME Australia, several themes relating to the individual's capacity to retain knowledge were discerned, namely, how the individual interacted with their work environment, how the individual created their own local ways of working and the contribution of their previous experience.

The Situating of the Work Environment

Gibson's (1979) theory of physical affordance sheds light on how the physical environment can shape human behavior, and how human behavior can change the physical environment. An affordance is what is offered to someone, and what it provides or furnishes, either for good or for ill. A chair affords seating or a storage area, for example. As Gibson pointed out, human beings alter the environment and thus change the affordances offered. Gibson posits that "what we see when we look at objects are their affordance" (Gibson, 1979, p. 134). "Affordances are primarily facts about action and interaction, not perception" (Gaver, 1996, p. 114). Physical layout and artifacts can evolve or change according to what is, and what needs to be, afforded (Gibson, 1979). If an in-tray is out of reach, it will be moved to where it affords the placing of the documents in an easier way. People will often order their work environment to suit their own ways of working, and this ordering will have an effect on how the work is done. The incident below describes the discomfort of someone who has just moved to a new working position.

> I noticed Cheryl sitting in June's old position. She mentioned that she felt like she was "in a cave." Her shoulders hunch. She had to move the computer "because it just wasn't me."
>
> Cheryl describes how she took all of June's files that didn't relate to her and put them in the same order on her old desk. She put her files in the new space in no particular order.

> She has to find a way of placing the files to suit her. "Let's find a different way of working in a different workspace, isn't it silly?"
>
> Field notes

The ordering of the workspace is significant to the person working there. As time goes on, their interaction with the workspace and the objects will become habitual. The interview extract below shows the perceptions of an XME employee on the effect of the workplace on her knowledge of the job:

> Researcher: Yeah. Now when you remember back to you work in the [previous employer], do you actually remember the specifics of what you did?
>
> Interviewee: [Long pause] Yes I do. The modifications which I was responsible for, if they asked me to do it today, I would have to go to the documentation and just check, but um, yes, most of it I seem to remember.
>
> Researcher: Oh, you could actually, with a little bit of reference?
>
> Interviewee: Yes. I believe I would sit in the front of the equipment I was doing back then and do most of it.
>
> Researcher: Now that's a very interesting point, yes. If we took you back or gave you a facsimile of that work environment, you could do it. If though, for some reason … you had to do it at XME, so we had to put you in another work environment with slightly different things?
>
> Interviewee: That would be more difficult.
>
> Researcher: Would it?
>
> Interviewee: I never thought about it but, yes, with the environment here you KNOW where the parts are, where to get them from, you know where your documentation is and you feel more comfortable with this particular work because you are in these particular circumstances and the room. I never thought about it but …
>
> Researcher: Yeah, I was just thinking about it, and yeah, the hand goes out to grasp something.
>
> Interviewee: And that's what actually helps you to remember as well, I believe, because you look at the tool you are using and oh, that's what's next. It's the little things which actually trigger memory.
>
> Interview

This relationship between the way people order their physical environment and the way people do their work illustrates how counterproductive it may be to structure the workplace so that individuals lack this small but significant ability. There is a significant amount of literature that propounds that learning is situated (e.g., Greeno, 1997), but very little of the ability of the individual to create their own immediate situation. The automatic cues in the immediate work environment effectively streamline the work through the procedural knowledge retention system, and enable the individual to transfer that automatic action to other places. The procedural knowledge of the individual is dependent on their previous experience, where practice becomes habitual. The next section explores the contribution of previous experience.

The Contribution of Previous Experience

The contribution that the people of XME made to the company was partially due to the skills and knowledge that they brought with them. In many cases, however, they brought more than the ability to simply complete the tasks. Their previous experiences may contribute to the culture of the organization, be used as a teaching resource or add to the habits of the current organization:

> Cheryl likes to pass on information to others because she worked in a place where it was encouraged. Interestingly, it was the same place that taught her to take notes.
>
> Field notes

> Yves tidies up his work space. "One thing I learned from [previous employer], clean up and start afresh."
>
> Field notes

Previous work experiences also engendered expectations on the part of the employee. Employees contrasted (unfavorably) DO_IT with previous systems with which they had worked. Others mentioned that they had learned to appreciate having good tools.

Some of the people had the same previous employers. This had one effect where a small group of staff with previous experience at the same company introduced and lobbied for the use of the engineering action report form, the form that later became a key record of product information for the XME group. This action also illustrates a "bottom-up" influence on organizational knowledge retention structures.

The previous experience of employees not only added to the semantic knowledge base of the organization; it also gave a range of practices that had the potential to benefit XME Australia. Previous experience could lead members to be dissatisfied with the current practices in XME Australia; however, a counterargument would be that dissatisfaction is a prime factor in innovation (Starbuck, 1996) and excellent performance (Senge, 1992). Certainly, in the case of the engineering action report, dissatisfaction had a positive result.

Part of the knowledge retained by the individual was the rules of thumb, the often undocumented expertise that was known and often expressed only by a sentence or two that made the job easier in some way.

Heuristic Ways of Working

Scribner (1986) investigated the way individuals build up a repertoire of least-effort solutions in their work practices. Rules of thumb and practical shortcuts played a significant part in the way people worked in XME Australia. These practices had a variety of formats. In different areas, DO_IT was manipulated to achieve desired outcomes (i.e., the system was manipulated, not the transaction figures). When balancing or solving problems for past transactions, "odd" figures and dates would be recognized as clues to the underlying problem. Where a task had to be performed a number of times, the individual performing the task would often gradually develop a way of performing the task to make it simpler:

> As Zane counts the number of threads around the ring, he mentions that he has developed his own counting system over the years.
>
> Field notes

Although these shortcuts or rules of thumb can be quite simple things, they can save a lot of time for the individual, and ultimately of course the organization. These rules of thumb were not confined to analytically based work.

> She knows the sound and the rhythm of an off-balance spool.
>
> Field notes

> Olive starts. 20 mm wire which she can do by sight and judgement. Olive's experience allows her to nip a few at a time. She would have a new person measure and nip 1 at a time.
>
> Field notes

To generate these shortcuts and rules of thumb, the individual needed to understand the end result and/or the priorities related to their work. This knowledge not only made them effective in completing the task, but enabled them to judge when to bend the organizational rules, for example, the procedures laid down in the QMS manual. There were examples seen in various departments in two of the sites where individuals decided to deliberately deviate from a set procedure to accomplish a task in a particular way or short time frame. Occasionally, however, a personal rule or value would not reflect an easier way of working. It would simply reflect the way the individual believed that things should work, as the following quotation shows:

> "Cash at bank shouldn't have a journal. It should be just in and out money."
>
> Field notes

This accounting clerk was making the point that the "cash at bank" account in the company accounts should reflect the actual cash position of the company. Unlike other accounts, this account is not subject to end-of-month adjustments to reflect an accrued value. Any adjustment in this account must necessarily be the result of an error and be worthy of investigation.

These beliefs about how things should work reveal personal values that are tied to their occupations, and are products of both training and experience. Thus Scribner's least-effort solutions (Scribner 1997a, 1997b) are constrained within the standards and value systems of the individual.

The Influences on XME Australia's Knowledge Retention Structures

The knowledge retention structures of XME Australia have developed in large measure because of the organization's history, culture, and environment. The history and culture of the organization can be seen as the accommodation of two groups, the R&D people and the accountants. The R&D people were more numerous and, in many ways, were the reason the organization existed. Their legacy was the egalitarian, *laissez-faire* approach to work and life that enabled each individual to have a certain amount of autonomy to order their work practice as they saw fit, provided it did not negatively impact on others or on the organization. This autonomy could be seen throughout XME Australia. Unfortunately, the R&D approach did have some negative impact on the organization. The *laissez-faire*, individualistic approach was manifested by a lack of needed knowledge retention at the organizational level, which had an impact on product development.

The accountants were far fewer in number but held greater authority in the organization. They did not affect the attitude of the R&D people, but imposed a computer system on the organization that became the most dominant explicit knowledge retention structure. The DO_IT system, although criticized by many of the staff, had to be used and thus the staff adapted and used other systems to complement DO_IT. In many respects, the Accounting staff became the monitors and trainers of the organization, and DO_IT provided a common language and a common way of doing things.

The growth of the company had caused the entry of another class of professionals – the engineers. The engineers in Operations introduced order and method to enable the mass production of the products. Where the Accounting staff could influence only the aspects of the organization relating to the finances of the business, the Operations staff were charged with the conversion of invention to viable production, which necessitated much more discipline and explicit knowledge retention. Operations was largely in charge of the QMS, the other major system imposed by the organization's leaders in response to pressures from the external environment. The engineers, on the other hand, were able through persuasion to introduce a key explicit knowledge retention structure, the engineering action report.

The environmental factors, which are easy to disregard because they are so prevalent, relate largely to the Western business arena that incorporates government and other regulatory authorities, suppliers, customers, and other stakeholders. Over the years, accounting and other professional standards have required the development of a common language and a common business practice. As people join this environment, they are trained in this common language and common way of doing things, and hence actions are recorded in a common, required format. Thus, XME Australia had a system of knowledge retention structures that were based on the normal business practices of their time and place.

When investigating organizations, it is easy to ignore the role of the individual, particularly the individual who is low in status. In XME Australia, the individuals played a key role as knowledge retention structures, and the prior knowledge and experience of the individual interacted with the other influences to determine how knowledge was used and retained. As individuals acted, successful knowledge retention structures were noticed and adopted by other individuals in a "contagion of usefulness," which meant that individual structures gradually became more collective.

A landmark decision in the fortunes of XME was the decisions to establish operations off-shore, in Ireland and in the USA. Although these decisions had some effect on the skills required in XME Australia to cope with the consolidation of accounts, there was less effect discernible on the knowledge retention structures in Australia when compared with those that had developed in Ireland and the USA.

XME Ireland: the Production Site

XME Ireland was located on an industrial estate near a small town in Ireland. The XME board of directors had agreed that Ireland was an appropriate location for a European operation for a number of reasons, including a young, educated population and significant tax concessions awarded by both the local and national government. Another motivating factor was the establishment of manufacturing sites of major electronics firms within Ireland, which meant that components could be obtained at much cheaper prices than in Australia.

XME Ireland had been incorporated in the late 1990s, and a senior staff member from XME Australia, who later became the Managing Director of XME Ireland, recruited a number of staff, and business commenced. There was a long-standing joke that XME Ireland started life as a cardboard box brought from Australia. At first the organization consisted of two small premises, which were for administration and accounting, and warehousing respectively. The operation then moved to its current premises, and later extended the building to include production facilities.

XME Ireland had been created to become the production center for the XME group. During the time of the study, more products were being transferred to Ireland for assembly, with fewer products being produced in Australia in a bid to make Ireland the production center for the XME group in fact. When I entered the organization, it had approximately 40 staff with an impressive production facility, together with the supporting functions of administration, ICT, accounting and customer service/repairs. XME Ireland was also responsible for sales to Europe (including the former Eastern Bloc), Africa, and Canada. The Managing Director was resident in Australia and periodically visited XME Ireland.

XME Ireland essentially had three areas:

Operations was responsible for assembling the products, warehousing and physically shipping the products and ensuring that components were planned for and purchased, and that electronic and other problems were dealt with as part of the production process.

Administration was responsible for personnel issues, ICT, customer service/repairs, and shipping sign-off and documentation.

Accounts was responsible for monitoring and reporting on revenue, expenses, and the financial position of the firm.

The General Manager's main focus was marketing and sales, but these activities, although generating revenue for the company, did not seem to impact on the

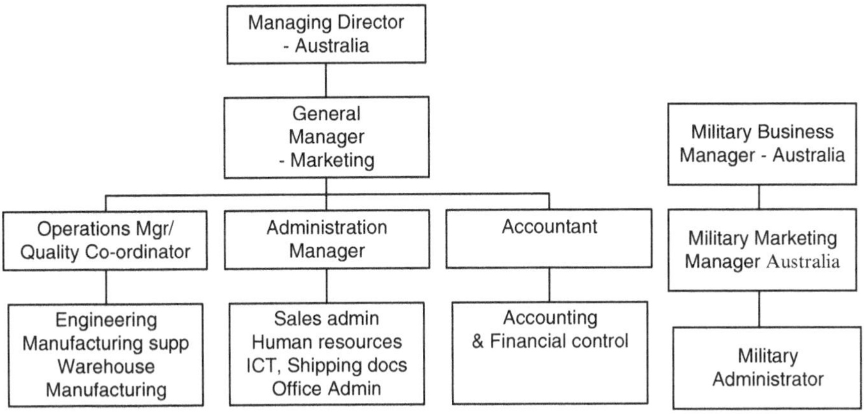

Fig. 3.3 Representation of XME Ireland organizational chart

organization as a whole in an operational sense. XME Ireland housed also two members of the military division of the firm. The military division sold noncombative products to military and humanitarian organizations, and Europe was an extremely lucrative market for the company. The two members from the military division in XME Ireland were a Marketing Manager and an Administrator. The Marketing Manager reported to the Military Business Manager in Australia. The military division was essentially a client of XME Ireland. XME Ireland was responsible for shipping already assembled military products from Australia and filling orders for the military division.

See Fig. 3.3 for an adapted version of the XME Ireland organization chart.

The Development of Knowledge Retention Structures

XME Ireland had a much shorter history than XME Australia, with a planned development. Like XME Australia, the external environment had a large influence on knowledge retention structures. In addition, European events, such as the European Union and the introduction of the Euro as a European currency certainly had an impact that was not felt by the members of XME Australia to anywhere near the same extent. There were two other major differences between XME Australia and XME Ireland. Firstly, XME Ireland always had felt the influence of XME Australia, which was the corporate center, the home of XME Ireland's Managing Director and other powerful figures, and the originating point for the products. XME Australia, on the other hand, did not have to cede to another site within the organization. Secondly, XME Australia had several different professional groups establishing subcultures and lobbying for power within the organization. XME Ireland, on the other hand, was focused on becoming the production center for the XME group.

The Australian Influence: "there was a lot of administrative work in sending everything to Australia"

XME Ireland was created as a subsidiary of the Australian company, and this influence had a significant effect in shaping the knowledge retention structures, particularly the organizational structures, ICT implementation, accounting requirements, and other issues. A persistent theme in XME Ireland was one of proving themselves and gaining respect from the people in XME Australia. There was a perception among the XME Ireland managers that XME Australia was suspicious of what was happening in their subsidiary.

The ICT Applications

According to Marquardt and Reynolds (1994, p. 7): "Information technology changes the way work is done." ICT has been lauded as a way for people within organizations to be connected and to take control of their own workspace; others, however, see ICT as a way of increased organizational monitoring (Shulman, 1996). Where an individual utilizes the ICT infrastructure to retain the knowledge, the knowledge can usually be accessed by other agents of the organization, including the managers of the individual. ICT has also been cited as an influence on organizational structure. Marquandt and Reynolds (1994) have credited ICT with flatter organization structures. XME Ireland used DO_IT and Microsoft Office as the main computer applications. DO_IT, as mentioned in the XME Australia discussion, is an integrated application that deals with materials resource planning, accounts, inventory, and so on. It was used in XME Australia, and XME USA, and XME Ireland had to adopt it for compatibility when consolidating records.

In XME Ireland, few new staff had had experience with DO_IT before it was implemented in Ireland. The Irish distributor of DO_IT was also reported to be unfamiliar with DO_IT functionality, which meant that the external training and the consultancy services offered were not of a uniformly high standard. Despite these drawbacks, DO_IT was a significant knowledge retention structure in the company. There was a perception among several staff that if they had had more knowledge of DO_IT, they could have used it to better effect. Staff had observed deficiencies in the functionality, such as lack of comment fields in transaction functions, which impeded easy notation of special circumstances. Another drawback to the system was that XME in Australia had created descriptions and so on, that people in XME Ireland did not find meaningful or found confusing. There was no apparent mechanism for communicating these problems back to the people in Australia.

A significant moment occurred, however, when XME Ireland took over its own financial monitoring by bringing DO_IT online. Although DO_IT was imposed on XME Ireland by XME Australia, its implementation in Ireland signaled increasing autonomy, as shown in this interview quote:

> We were working on a manual system where XME Australia maintained all the data in DO_IT files, there was a lot of administrative work in sending everything to Australia and the entry of everything there so it was a bit frustrating, annoying because there was a lot of work at their end so it made sense then that we develop a system here so I think it was September 1999, [Australian Accounting Manager] came over to train me up for two weeks and I think that was a defining moment because it kind of, it became independent in that whole area, DO_IT, the system which was crucial to our future.
>
> Interview

Because of the heavy emphasis on production, and the different expertise present within XME Ireland, XME Ireland sometimes used DO_IT functionality differently from XME Australia. On a visit to XME Australia, a person from XME Ireland was able to give advice and the benefit of her experience in a problem-solving session, thus supporting the conclusion in the next chapter concerning the value of multiple sites as knowledge retention structures for the rest of the organization.

XME Australia provided XME Ireland with copies of databases such as a customer warranty database. These databases were created by the Operations Manager who enjoyed working with Microsoft Access and had a lot of experience with databases. XME Ireland, however, found that when they requested changes to the databases from the Australian XME creators, the changes were very slow to occur, as there was no allocated responsibility for keeping these databases current. It was planned that two Irish engineers would be trained in database software so that any future changes could be made in Ireland. Thus XME Ireland was taking steps to increase knowledge retention to compensate for deficiencies in the service from Australia.

Reporting to Australia

XME Ireland, as required with any subsidiary company, had to retain knowledge to be sent to its parent company. This enabled XME Australia to monitor performance as well as to fulfill legislative, taxation, and government grant requirements. There was also a need to prove the production capability of XME Ireland to facilitate the transfer of production to XME Ireland. A large part of these reporting requirements was fulfilled by the use of the DO_IT system to retain information, which was then consolidated with XME USA's information in the form of intracompany accounts.

The organization chart for XME Ireland clearly shows the influence and impact of the Australian operation on the company. It shows that individuals located in the Australian operation are deemed to have direct power over XME Ireland. Not only is the Managing Director located in Australia, but the manager of the military representatives is also named and noted as an individual on the chart. This manager's position on the organization chart clearly shows him to be a person of direct power. The way that the Irish organization chart was designed, showing important power relationships with Australia, supports the conclusion that explicit knowledge retention structures often reflect the culture and structure of the organization in an implicit way. This can be compared to the treatment of XME Ireland on the XME Australian organizational charts where XME Ireland and XME USA were not shown on some of the charts and displayed at the foot of others.

The Nature of Production

XME Ireland was becoming the production center of the organization. This focus had a significant impact on how XME Ireland developed, and how the knowledge retention structures emerged within the site. The production area and warehouse of the building dominated the floor plan of XME Ireland. The impressive production facilities in XME Ireland were partly attributed to a visit of an Irish engineer who was able to ask questions of Australian production people and use the Australian experience as a foundation upon which to build Irish knowledge. Because XME Ireland needed to supply Europe, Canada, Africa, and the USA with various products, there was a requirement to know how much stock and how many components were on hand at any given time. Inventory management and control was a very important issue, and the processes and procedures relating to inventory management developed more than XME Australia. The number of production lines in XME Ireland meant that a significant number of components were out of the warehouse and on the production lines, and these also had to be counted. It was also clear that, in the case of the military units, the organization took pains to ensure that individual units were allocated serial numbers, which were recorded together with their destinations on the DO_IT databases. There was also a need to know the situation with supplies and suppliers and to be able to forecast sales and market demand in the future.

Because XME Ireland was becoming the main production center of XME, there was a strong push to refine production so that products could be assembled quickly in large quantities. With the large quantity requirements came the push for standardization and streamlining. Thus procedures became formalized and documented as part of ISO9000 accreditation, and were followed to reduce variance in the quality of the product. This also meant that the production operators needed no special qualifications except soldering skills. All else required could be taught on the job through the use of procedures. This was in direct contrast to the small Australian production unit, where individuals generally had a high level of technical skill, and often initiated problem-solving sessions to correct the deficiencies in developing products.

The Dominant Knowledge Retention Structures

The dominant knowledge retention structures emerged from a situation of having to report to a distant corporate center, and being engaged in production. The emphasis was thus on one core function that required standardization and explicit ways of working. The dominant knowledge retention structures were thus the physical environment, the explicit knowledge retention structures of ICT and paper documents, and the processes and routines.

The Physical Environment

The focus on production was apparent upon entry to XME Ireland. Opening the front door, a passageway led to a large open space that appeared to encompass most of the building. This was the production area. The production area formed the core around which were arranged the engineers, managers, manufacturing support, and, one floor up, the accounting, administration and military people. Manufacturing was the reason for XME Ireland's existence and the production area was the center of its being.

The building was constructed to achieve the core purpose of production, and the configuration of the building reinforces the message that other activities are peripheral to that of production. This interview quotation shows how the people of XME Ireland in its early days perceived the new building.

> Well, I suppose the first memorable event would have been obviously the building here. We came from very humble beginnings [did you?] yeah, yeah. And having moved our stuff in January, the building here was finished, we moved down in May and sort of..., unbelievable because we were working out of a very small office and Sandra, Bill and then Agnes, the four of us in quite a small office and then we moved here and with all the space here, we just saw the potential straight away and, you know, could look to the future, it was a defining moment. I think the second defining moment would be the extension then, which allowed production.
>
> Interview

Van Maanen and Barley (1985) maintained that a group's physical territory and material world are a primary catalyst for the group's cultural formation. The next chapter will show how the physical environment reinforced cultural and structural knowledge that shaped communication patterns within XME Ireland.

Explicit Knowledge Retention

XME Ireland used a networked server, with documented backup procedures. The DAT tapes, however, were not taken off-site. Possession of a computer was dependent on the position held in the company. Production operators and warehouse assistants did not have their own computers, although they probably could have used their supervisors' if necessary. Because they did not have access, their explicit means of retention was based on the paper documents that were accessible. The assembly procedures used, therefore, were passed to the operator on paper. There were also forms such as the stores material movement form that were placed in the warehouse. By placing this form in a position where people walked past, they were inclined to see it, and therefore to remember to make notes upon it. A computer monitor with the same form on display would not be as easy to see. The policy manual, an important reference for all staff, was a paper document that was given to each staff member, rather than captured on the electronic system.

Paper documents were seen constantly throughout XME Ireland. The warehouse took charge of delivery documents, the production area had printed procedures, signs, and checklists; the manufacturing support people and engineers had a variety of forms, printed emails and charts. Accounts and administration, of course, had invoices, receipts, and so on. The use of the paper documents meant that offices also had in-trays, folders, and cabinets in which to store them.

Finally, the most prevalent use of paper came from external entities. These papers were stored due to requirements from auditors, and to help the XME Ireland staff communicate with these external entities in case of problems. Often these papers would contain reference numbers or suppliers' parts numbers, which would be needed to facilitate the enquiry. The storage of these paper documents seemed to depend on the number of people who needed access to them. In the warehouse, documents were centrally stored because both the Warehouse Supervisor and his assistants needed to be able to refer to them. Similarly, much of the accounting and administration documentation was stored in central filing banks because several managers and their assistants needed to be able to access them. On the other hand, there was only one Purchasing Officer, and thus the documents relating to purchasing were essentially part of his personal files retained in his office.

Procedures and Processes

The formalization and streamlining that was part of XME Ireland had facilitated the adoption of the QMS, which became a significant part of the Irish operation. The QMS provided a framework for procedures relating to communication as well as the manufacturing of the product.

As will be shown in the next chapter, XME Ireland was much more hierarchical in nature than XME Australia, and the QMS gave the staff an opportunity to get internal problems addressed in a structured and effective way, as shown by this quotation from an XME Ireland employee.

> ISO has pulled us up, I must admit. Filling in the paperwork means that someone has to take action, which means that we don't have to waste time always following up.
>
> Field notes

Thus the QMS did not just require the explicit capture of knowledge about processes. The QMS served to create processes and procedures that enabled people to document and transmit any concerns about the way the work was done. The staff believed that the leaders of the company were required to pay heed to the staff's concerns, provided that they were properly documented according to the QMS procedure.

The processes and procedures that related to production operators started with XME Australia providing the Irish engineers with exploded drawings and detailed procedures derived from the engineering action reports. The Irish engineers would instruct the production supervisor and perhaps some operators in the procedure. The people learning the procedure would listen to the engineers and view the procedure. They would assemble products in the presence of the engineers and/or their production supervisor until judged proficient. As they became more proficient, they would use the procedure as a guide. Meanwhile, the engineers would turn the written procedures into checklists. As the production operators became yet more proficient and the correct procedure became automatic, the checklists would often become a prompt and guide as required. Meanwhile, the relevant documentation consisted of documented procedures, exploded drawings, engineering action reports, and checklists. It was apparently rare for the production operators to instigate changes to the product processes. One engineer confided that "we probably wouldn't want a lot of changes at this stage." If the process changed, then this raft of documentation had to reflect the change.

Production operators were expected to be able to solder when they started work at XME. They would still need to be taught the procedure, however, and the procedure would consist of both the documentation and personal instruction, which is described in this excerpt from field notes:

> She tells me that new people have to be able to solder before they start, but Joyce has to teach them things like waiting for the solder to go down the hole and other refinements. She teaches in conjunction with the procedure.
>
> Field notes

The new production operator must also gain the embodied knowledge, which is related to certain physical strength and agility:

> Watching Joyce and seeing the strong wiriness in her hands and fingers, I ask her about the physical side. She says that she had stiff hands at the start, but got used to it.
>
> Field notes

If a production operator were placed on a different production line, and then returned to his/her original production line, she/he would often review the procedures until the process become automatic once again. The training records of the production operators and the warehouse staff were captured as part of the QMS system on the network.

The Role of the Individual in XME Ireland

In XME Ireland, the staff could be classified as managers, technical people, and production operators, who were the most numerous. The managers and technical people had some degree of autonomy, and the discussion relating to the individual in XME Australia also applies to these members of XME Ireland. The production operators, however, had much less autonomy and had less need to know about the products they were assembling, as shown in this excerpt:

> Derek is working on the alkaline assembly. He shows me the pressure tank where the testing is done at 600 "whatevers" (no one seems sure what the "whatevers" are).
>
> Field notes

Despite the lack of technical knowledge, the production operators found the "best" ways of working with experience on a particular production line. It seemed that the definition of the best way of working was to assemble the product to minimize the amount of rework that had to be done, which is reminiscent of Scribner's least-effort solutions (Scribner, 1986, 1997a, b). It was also clear that the production operator came up with their own procedures to fix the problem as quickly as possible, as shown in this excerpt:

> There are usual trouble spots in the [product] assembly. If the assembly does leak, Derek knows where to look, e.g. dust in O-ring, part not screwed on properly. They agreed that rework was a pain. Experience has shown Derek to start with the easiest options first.
>
> Field notes

The systematic processes meant that less knowledge was retained within the individual production operators on the production line. However, the individual learnt more than the procedures taught. The dislike of rework meant that the individual sought ways to avoid or minimize it. The inability of the procedures to capture everything that the production operator needed to know meant that personal instruction had to supplement the learning process. As the individual became more skilled, however, the procedure was relied on less, and the checklist became simply a prompt for action. It should be also acknowledged that, while knowledge was embedded within the procedures, there was a highly significant role played by the engineers. The engineers were responsible for ensuring that the procedures were current, that problems were solved and that the assembly of new products was understood by the production supervisor and the production operators.

The roles of the production operators and the engineers highlight an interesting perspective on Fordism. Epple, Argote and Devadas (1996) maintained that knowledge could not be entirely embedded in organizational artifacts separately from people. This, however, was precisely what the Fordist movement attempted to do. This example shows that, although the procedures, drawings, and tools encompassed a great deal of knowledge, the production operators still found it necessary to formulate their own rules of thumb. In addition, the engineers were necessary to review the processes and coordinate problem solving. Using engineers, however, means that the organization can rely on consistent approaches engendered by the engineers' training. Thus the knowledge of the engineers is at least partially accessible through the body of knowledge relevant to the engineers' profession.

XME Ireland's Knowledge Retention Structures

XME Ireland, with the focus on production, had far greater formalization than XME Australia. This formalization meant that a degree of knowledge could be separated from the individual in the form of explicit procedures, but the explicit procedures could not completely retain all the knowledge required on the production line. Production operators needed both the procedure and the personal instruction to understand what they had to do to properly assemble a product. Procedures did not cover, for example, the best way to approach reworking products that did not meet the testing specifications. Explicit knowledge retention structures, such as the procedures, also need reviewing and updating. Where the explicit knowledge retention structure belongs to an individual, this responsibility forms part of the possession. Procedures, however, are a collective knowledge retention structure, and if the organization fails to assign responsibility for review, the procedure becomes obsolete and therefore useless. In XME Ireland, the engineers were assigned with the responsibility of updating the procedures. This responsibility was approached in a way consistent with the engineers' training, which meant that knowledge required to review the procedures was at least partially available to XME Ireland on a collective basis (through the engineering profession) rather than being based purely on individual local knowledge. In contrast, databases and the DO_IT system were collective explicit knowledge retention structures that were received from Australia, and Australia did not assign responsibility to their people to ensure that these structures were appropriate and usable in the Irish context. XME Ireland, therefore, had to make its own arrangements, with varying success, to use these structures imposed on them from the parent company.

On an organizational level, however, the imposition of DO_IT also had an implication of autonomy. DO_IT may have been imposed on XME Ireland, but at the same time, when XME Ireland received its own version and was able to manage its own accounts, this signaled a turning point for the site. Senior staff recognized that XME Ireland was more than an appendage of XME Australia, and could work toward increasing autonomy. XME Australia, besides being the parent company, was also a knowledge retention structure for XME Ireland. The Irish used the Australians' knowledge as a starting point for two of their own major knowledge retention structures, the design of the production area and the QMS, as well as receiving technical information on products from the Australian engineers. Some training in DO_IT was also provided by the Australians.

In XME Ireland, there were also fewer computers per person, because of the numbers of production operators. The significance of this was that XME Ireland depended much more on paper documents and records than XME Australia did. The QMS also seemed much more embedded within XME Ireland than in XME Australia. One would expect that increased formalization and the creation of procedures would lessen the autonomy of individuals; however, this was shown, in some cases at least, to be incorrect. In XME Australia the advent of performance review procedures meant that employees were given an opportunity to discuss their remuneration, performance, and other tricky issues. In XME Ireland, the QMS as a whole was credited with giving employees a voice that managers would heed. The production operators did have less autonomy than their Australian counterparts in terms of problem solving and making changes to procedures; however, this decreased autonomy was related to the nature and stage of the business. Changes could not be justified at the end of the development and production cycle unless there was sufficient reason, and the production operators generally did not have the technical knowledge required to formulate such changes. Production operators, however, were able to come up with their own solutions within the confines of the procedures to counter the problems of deficient goods and rework.

XME Ireland was intended primarily as a production site for the XME group. The core business was mass production of technological products for global distribution. XME USA, on the other hand, had no production or R&D facilities. XME USA was purely involved in penetrating the lucrative American markets.

XME USA: A Site for Selling

In 1994, after XME had been in operation for 5 years, the corporate management and the board of directors decided that the Australian market was close to saturation. They elected to turn to the North American markets for new selling opportunities. XME USA, as an entity, commenced when a couple of people from Australia were sent to Phoenix, Arizona, to set up a service center. In 1998, the current General Manager was given the challenge of setting up a more extensive operation in the USA. He made the decision to move operations to Las Vegas on the grounds that it was a cheap city to live in, Nevada was a state where considerable sales could be realized and the Nevada Development Corporation was encouraging non-gambling industry and commercial operations to move to Las Vegas through generous concessions. He also allowed contracts with distributors to expire as they came up for renewal, so that the commission which was formerly paid to distributors could be diverted to marketing activity, and salaries for the future XME USA staff.

XME USA was situated in a light industrial area of Las Vegas, Nevada, USA. The premises were set in a complex of single-storey buildings that surrounded a tarmac carpark.

At least half the 12 staff members were knowledgeable on different aspects of what could be called marketing/contextual knowledge relating to the USA. Although marketing/sales is necessary in most corporate organizations, in XME USA this focus permeated all aspects of the organization.

The Development of Knowledge Retention Structures

Like XME Ireland, part of the emergence of the knowledge retention structures was attributable to being a subsidiary of XME Australia. The employment of the accounting and administration staff was partly to fulfill the requirements of XME Australia's accounting/administration area who had to consolidate the group accounts. Like XME Ireland, XME USA was required to use certain software to facilitate the consolidation of Accounts and to make data transfers possible through ICT.

ICT Documents

XME USA, like other XME sites, had a networked server and used Microsoft Office as well as DO_IT. The ICT system was an opportunity not only to communicate with each other and with clients, but to facilitate communication with the other two sites in XME. It seemed, however, that the hardware used by XME USA was sometimes incompatible with the software provided by Australia. In particular, an important warranty database could not be loaded on the network. This meant that the administration manager was obliged to do manual backups via diskette to ensure the changes to the database were properly secured.

As a means of retaining knowledge, the ICT system in XME USA was the most poorly functioning in the study. The deficiencies in the system meant more work for the Administration Manager and accounting staff to ensure that the volume and quality of information available was up to the standard required by the General Manager and the other company offices and safe from data corruption and/or destruction.

The Structure

The XME USA structure had recently changed as the numbers of people and occupations within the organization grew, changing the way knowledge was retained and communicated. The organization recently had become more formally structured with reporting relationships as follows (see Fig. 3.4).

The adoption of a formal structure by XME USA meant that a knowledge-channeling process had begun. The three middle managers were the obvious communication point for the people who reported to them, the General Manager and each other. For the organization, this knowledge backup was important, as the General Manager often travelled around the country. As the company grew, more people were employed to specialize in accounting, marketing and sales, and customer service. XME USA appeared to be the first operation in XME to separate the customer service and technical repair functions, even though it was the smallest operation in terms of staff numbers. This change to the organizational structure reflected the focus on sales and customer relations.

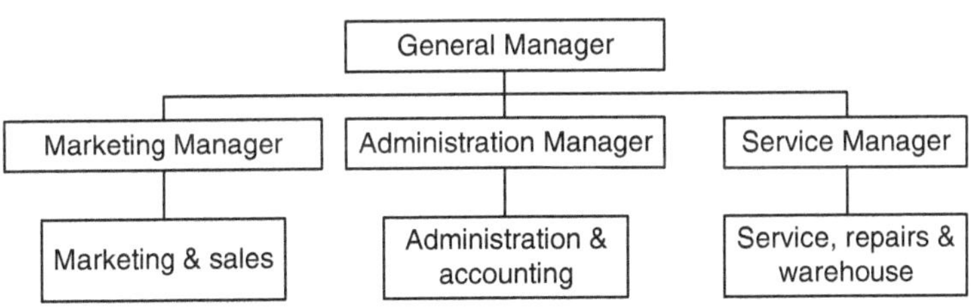

Fig. 3.4 Organizational structure of XME USA

The General Manager also followed a practice of asking questions of staff on a regular basis. These questions caused an expectation of having to report quickly on a number of specific issues. People made an effort to anticipate the questions, and gather information that they thought would be requested. Although this also happened in other sites, it was particularly significant in XME USA, and caused people to develop ways of preempting the questions. They did this by insuring that they had easy access to knowledge retention structures that could provide what was required.

XME USA did not have documented job descriptions. If these were needed, they were borrowed from either Australia or Ireland and adapted. Each person, however, seemed to have a distinct job title, and a clear idea of their own responsibilities and that of their department.

The Dominant Knowledge Retention Structures

The most obvious cultural themes involved marketing/selling/customer service. Most of the employees, although they had diverse backgrounds, had considerable experience in either customer service or some other field that required a high level of people skills. At least one third of the staff described themselves as having "customer service" backgrounds. Although marketing and selling also occurred in Australia and Ireland, both sites had other activities as well, and hence at least some of the staff in those sites were not directly involved in marketing/selling. In XME USA, all the staff seemed to regard their role as part of the marketing/selling process.

The Influence of the Physical Environment: "it gives a very organized feel to the place"

The growth of XME USA meant that the premises occupied by the organization were crowded. The General Manager was obliged to share an office with the Marketing Manager. The two Regional Sales Managers shared an office, as well as the three Accounting/Administration people.

The crowded physical environment meant that people were always in fairly close proximity to each other, which facilitated the retention and flow of knowledge to more than one person. In a practical sense, the current physical proximity of the General Manager to all staff made it almost as easy for all staff to talk to the General Manager as it was to talk to a middle manager. The growth of the company meant also that the physical environment kept changing to accommodate the new staff.

In addition, the display of the company products and the maps of the USA with the dealers reinforced the notion of the company business and the way the company did business. On the walls were framed posters with slogans relating to achievement. Also displayed were various organizing objects, such as envelopes filled with leave and other forms attached to the staff notice board, and various trays were placed to facilitate the smooth operation of a process. The placing and labeling of trays meant that processes for the new recruit especially were very easy to follow. By using the visual cues, it was simple to find the proper place for a particular form at a given stage in a process. By making it easy to follow the processes, the compliance with the process was reinforced. I recorded this comment in the field notes:

> There is a system of perspex filing slots on walls and things. It gives a very organized feel to the place. The slots in Accounts are all labelled.
>
> Field notes

The service repair area had various jigs, cupboards, and racks to facilitate the repairs of returned products. Many of these had been constructed on the premises by the staff. The filing, jigs, and racks were evidence of the way that XME USA would act to create an affordance to facilitate the implementation and compliance with processes (Gibson, 1979).

Paper Documents

The paper records of a company are usually a major area of vulnerability with regard to accidental destruction or sabotage. It was marked that few people within the XME USA operation had records or documents that were not backed up on the server. The major exception to this was the records kept on repair and service that were provided by customers. The service manager, however, had previous experience with the problems associated with destroyed records, as recorded in the field notes:

> [Service Manager] has a repair history on all customers. This is what could not be replaced in the fire test. He has experience in a service centre that got burnt to the ground. They simply had to rely on customers for new records.
>
> Field notes

Some of the staff had hard copies of Microsoft Outlook calendars displayed to stay aware of commitments. These types of paper records display information in a way that is instantly meaningful. The display of appointments in a visual form meant that the people who referred to these records could see at a glance how busy they were on a particular day. Although these calendars were easy to print, XME USA was the only office where they were in evidence in a paper format. This relates to the "contagion of usefulness" notion explained previously. The individual capacity for visual information is much greater than for verbal information (Anderson, 1995); the image of text taking up space in a calendar segment represents a busier day. Other examples used in XME USA were checklists and forms, which can also enable retention via visual as well as verbal representation.

XME USA used some recording processes that were not paper or electronic. For example, when a product was repaired a dot was placed on the metal label of the product to indicate that it had been in the repair shop. This was a simple marker that would mean nothing to the client, but would save time for the repair staff if the product ever re-entered the repair shop.

Creating and Using Processes: "someone new would not know to pack the part"

The processes were dominant knowledge retention systems of XME USA, as something that had to be learned, and a way of retaining the learning. There was evidence that if one member left the organization, other members would, between them, have sufficient knowledge to coach the replacement in what he/she needed to know to become an effective contributor to the organization's goals.

I observed the identification of a problem and the creation with a new process to deal with it, and this is described in the section dealing with meetings. Processes were implemented where a gap between desired outcomes and actual outcomes was identified. Thus, processes did not seem to become obsolete. This outcomes orientation meant that processes tended to be in a continuous state of review. The processes and procedures, however, were not documented in a format such as that required by the QMSs in Australia and Ireland. In XME USA, existing documentation (often originating in XME Australia) was amended as needed, staff would be apprised, and a general agreement to work in the desired way would be made. An example of a change of a process is shown below.

> There is a problem with a product. The dealer has rung through, there is no [part] with the rest of the product. It turns out that it is packed separately. This product is confusing. The USA has a person on sick leave, and a temporary person is taking his place temporarily. This is an example of product knowledge that hasn't been written down. Because the pack-list just says the product name, someone new would not know to pack the part. Deanne looks through shipping documents. It appears that the part hasn't been packed. This reinforces how the system needs to compensate for changes in staff.
>
> Field notes

> Deanne comes in and asks Arnold to change DO_IT description to show that [parts] need to be packed separately.
>
> Field notes

XME USA had one manager who was interested in processes and "elegant" solutions. This manager had, in the past, created systems for the review of his/her peers. Another manager would attempt to restrict the paperwork to the minimum. Between these two differences of style, and with the input of the third manager and the arbitration of the General Manager, the processes that were put into place generally were what all parties could live with, and would then become institutionalized. People would be instructed in the processes via meetings, face-to-face interactions, or emails. The physical environment would be changed to include in-trays, envelopes, new forms and whatever else was required to create an affordance that facilitated the progress of the process. It was clear that the General Manager required people to follow the processes set by the organization. It is also true to say that people had their own ways of working where it did not impinge on the organization's processes.

As the raft of processes was growing and changing with the expansion of the organization, the lack of documentation actually seemed to contribute to the flexibility in the process review. The fact that processes were engaged in by a number of people meant in effect that participants to the process could enforce its compliance. The small number of people within XME USA made it easy to communicate changes. The affordance created for the process meant that it often became easier to follow the process than not to follow it.

The Place of Individuals Within the XME USA Knowledge Retention Structures

The individuals of XME USA each had their own professional and personal expertise; for example, human resource administration, marketing and sales, as well as expertise that was part of the individual's personal interests, such as proficiency in process and form design, and product knowledge. Three of the staff had extensive product knowledge because they used the products in their leisure time. The degree of experience of many of the staff members meant that they had knowledge of a wide range of issues, and where necessary could act as knowledge resources for any issues that arose.

An interesting knowledge retention structure was manifested in the person who worked on the XME USA reception desk. In addition to acting as first point of contact for callers, the receptionist of XME USA also held a big black file of various documents at her desk, and had personal knowledge relating to office administration. Thus she was sometimes called upon by others in the operation to provide price lists and other documents for reference.

> Reg tells me that Bonnie has everything out here. The large black file has Bonnie's important stuff like trouble-shooting guides, price lists, etc. It doesn't have all of it on the IT system. The new system is coming in by the end of the month.
>
> Field notes

There were various reasons for the evolution of the person on the reception desk as a keeper of various documents and other media of knowledge. There is an affordance issue (Gibson, 1979), where the physical location of reception areas is generally accessible and often on the way to some other place the person has to go, for example, the fax machine or a manager's office. The duties of a receptionist tend to mean that he/she will usually be present at his/her desk. The enquirer will rarely telephone or call by to find the receptionist absent. The receptionist also is often employed because of a pleasant personality, and thus will often endure cheerfully being continually asked for various forms, how to work the fax machine and other items of information.

XME USA's Knowledge Retention Structures

XME USA had undergone a transition where it had started out as a flat structure and had then been formally organized along department lines of accounts and administration, marketing and sales, and customer service and repairs. This structure created repositories of knowledge in the person of the managers of each department. The effect of the structure was to create clear responsibilities and hence clear definitions of the knowledge that was expected. By appointing managers, the General Manager effectively gave a signal that the managers held certain knowledge and could act upon it in his absence by making decisions. It also signaled that these managers had equal rights to negotiate new processes and that negotiation needed to happen.

Another significant retention system was the emphasis on processes. XME USA, when a problem was identified, tended to focus on longer-term solutions. These processes would bring together people's activities, ICT and paper forms, and changes in the physical environment so that a particular outcome was realized. When processes were created, the physical manifestations of the process accompanied its implementation: thus perspex trays were placed for the ensuing paperwork and filing systems were updated. Where a checklist was often used, the position of items on the list started to become familiar, and thus it was easy to see whether a check mark had been placed against them. The manifestations of a process, as far as the doer is concerned, are the visual cues that prompt them to act in a certain way. Thus, the plastic tray stays in one position, the checklist is maintained in a certain order and the electronic shortcut stays in the same position on the PC desktop. The individual's contribution gradually converts to a procedural response, and, where several people work together, to an organizational routine (Cohen, 1991; Cohen & Bacdayan, 1994). The involvement of several people in the process also seemed to be a factor in promoting compliance. Often, at the end of the process, the accountant would be obliged to check the paperwork and highlight any deficiencies. The feedback from others involved in the process also promoted compliance.

The individuals who had been recruited to XME USA often had a great deal of experience in various situations, and were thus knowledge retention structures for the organization. This experience could be drawn on in a variety of situations, and their experience also influenced the positions that were assumed in negotiations and discussions regarding various aspects of the operation. In addition, the XME USA receptionist was a knowledge retention structure due to her practice of retaining knowledge in the form of lists, forms, and so on.

The significance of ICT was best shown for the efforts that the people in XME USA made to try to make it work. The ICT functioned poorly, but was still a dominant retention structure for the explicit knowledge of the organization. The ICT systems were largely imposed by XME Australia, and the parent company needed the system to work. Thus XME USA used what means they could to make it work so that the organization as a whole could benefit.

Conclusions

The XME group demonstrated differences in the influences forming retention structures within each site, and how these influences are associated with power in the organization. Within XME Australia, the effects of dominant groups and organizational leaders over time can be observed. The R&D people have caused an emphasis on knowledge retention structures that is local and individual. The mark of the accountant Managing Director is firmly made with the use of DO_IT throughout the group. DO_IT, in fact, reinforces the dominance of the accounting people because the software determines the need for monitoring and training through the organization by the accounting staff. The influences are also determined by the stage of life and the business of the organization. As XME grew, more units had to be produced, which caused the entry of the engineers and production people into the company. These professionals brought with them needed skills in terms of formalization, control and discipline, forming another influence on the way knowledge was retained. XME is bound to heed the requirements of the environment in which it operates; thus knowledge retention structures must be created to fulfill the requirements of the taxation, company and other authorities and stakeholders. In XME Ireland and XME USA, knowledge retention structures have emerged as a result of the environment, the influence of XME Australia and the demands of the core business, that is, production and selling respectively. These influences are thus top-down and strategic in nature and filtered by the decisions and demands of the organization's leaders.

The budgetary power of the organizational leaders meant that besides investing in technology, they could invest in training and education for staff members, focus on recruiting in particular ways and purchase resources such as reference books and journals. The influence of the leaders could also be ascertained in their own knowledge requirements. The act of asking for specified information, at specified times and in specified formats contributed to the establishment and maintenance of information-gathering structures in the organization. At the organizational level, it appeared that knowledge was indirectly but powerfully communicated by the leaders of the organization in terms of the questions that they asked the staff. Staff made an effort to learn the type of questions that would be asked so that they could anticipate what was required. This meant that these questions acted to focus knowledge retrieval and thus the staff made sure that the knowledge was easily accessible, either in their own heads or in records that they had close by. Where a leader routinely asked about the number of product types in transit, the person being asked would take care to have this information prepared. Where the request was repeated, the person would find ways and means to prepare this information in a way that was both accurate and efficient with regard to time and effort. This would become a routine. However, a new leader requires new information, in a different format at different times, and thus the routine was no longer effective. The people must then establish new information-gathering structures to fulfill the requirements of the new leader. Although these requirements differed in each organization, the requirement for compliance was a major factor in knowledge being embedded in the organizations through their procedures and routines.

In XME USA, for example, the General Manager's method of gathering information that he needed was to ask questions of various staff members. The staff in turn would make efforts to facilitate the storage and easy retention of this knowledge so that they could provide answers in a fast and efficient manner. This meant that the staff discerned patterns to the questions so that they could anticipate what sort of questions would be asked. Hence the retention and retrieval of this information became in time a semiautomatic activity for the staff members, as they set up electronic means of managing the required knowledge.

Collective knowledge retention structures may be imposed by the organization's leaders or emerge out of necessity (or record knowledge contrary to the endorsed culture, but this is covered in the next chapter). DO_IT was an example of an explicit, mainly semantic, collective knowledge retention structure, which, despite its drawbacks, served to act as a common language for the XME group. Processes and routines are examples of collective, often tacit, mainly procedural knowledge retention structures. Procedures often represent a merging of individuals' ways of working as well as some imposed activity. Processes are a complex combination of individuals' practice, documents, physical artifacts, and activity, and will usually only become embedded within the organization provided that these components are aligned. Processes may achieve outcomes that are difficult for individuals to manage by themselves. Thus collective knowledge retention structures formed within the organization will themselves have an impact on the group, and will incorporate other knowledge retention structures of the organization.

Individuals within organizations are subject to the top-down influences, and are required to use the knowledge retention structures imposed on them. Individuals, however, are knowledge retention structures in their own right, and use physical artifacts and cultural constructions as knowledge retention structures as well. The organizational structure will, however, determine the individual's ability to change their physical environment, retain knowledge via paper or electronic means and introduce their own knowledge retained relating to their practice. Previous experience teaches the individuals least-effort solutions, rules of thumb as well as standards and values relating to their own practice. The practice of the individual may require the use of local, individual knowledge retention structures that could be considered quite humble and trivial. These individual knowledge retention structures, however, contribute to the achievement of the organization's objectives, particularly because these humble, local structures may make up for the deficiencies in resources provided by the organization's leaders. In some cases, these individual knowledge retention structures will be adopted by others and become collective structures. Although many individuals, unlike their leaders, will not have the power to impose collective knowledge retention structures upon the organization, the structures will be adopted as others recognize their usefulness and contribution to better practice. Where enough individuals believe in the usefulness of the knowledge retention structure, the leadership may be lobbied to agree to the adoption, and the practice of using the knowledge retention structures will itself be embedded in the knowledge retention structures of the organization.

In contrast to XME Australia and XME USA, autonomy for certain members of XME Ireland is limited: production operators could only formulate least-effort solutions within the confines of the approved procedures. Engineers, on the other hand, had the power to change procedures and other knowledge retention structures, and this autonomy enabled innovation. In XME Australia and XME USA, the universal autonomy meant that innovation could occur at any level of the organization, causing changes to both actual knowledge retention structures and the forms of knowledge retention structures. Innovation is often considered a desirable trait for organizations, but innovation is allied to the structural autonomy of individuals within the organization. Clearly, the individual needs to be recognized as an active agent of the collective, with the ability to refine, adapt, and create practices that contribute to organizational effectiveness.

Thus, the influences of top-down and bottom-up factors on organizations may cause a shifting dominance in knowledge retention structures over time. The one stable factor in the dominance of knowledge retention structures is the central role played by the individual, both as a unit of knowledge retention and as a component in a wider knowledge retention system.

This chapter has concentrated mainly on the knowledge retention structures that contribute to organizational performance and effectiveness. Knowledge, however, being a human construct can be emotional and subjective in nature. The next chapter deals with knowledge retention through communication, and this emotional, subjective side of organizational knowledge retention is clearly exposed.

Chapter 4
Retaining Knowledge Through Communication

A howl of outrage bounces around the partitions. Two visitors from another department look at each other, and quietly leave the area. A door slams, and the new recruit is confronted by the red, angry face of the Manager. "Have you seen what those idiots are saying now?" he splutters. "Umm, yeah, it doesn't seem very logical." "Logical, what would those morons know about logic! Look, I have to go to that meeting and there will be hell to pay if I don't – for heaven's sake get onto them and tell them to stop dreaming." The Manager spins on his heel and hurries out of the department. The new recruit looks at the clock. If she telephones now all she will get is the answering machine. She logs onto her email and starts to type...

Dear James,

Good 2 hear from u. Glad to get your email, we do have a few concerns about some of the things in your proposal, though…

Introduction

At an organizational level, communication is a significant part of knowledge retention. For knowledge to be usefully retained at an organizational level, it must be accessible to a significant number of people in the organization. The knowledge, however, is retained more widely as it is communicated. This means that communication mechanisms are also collective knowledge retention structures.

Communication may be formal, such as the distributed minutes of a meeting, or informal such as a chat over lunch. Communication may be endorsed by the organization's leaders, such as the address to employees by the Managing Director or counter to the accepted messages of the leaders, such as irreverent stories told in the leaders' absence. Communication is directly affected by whether the knowledge being communicated is primarily tacit or explicit (Davenport & Prusak, 1998; Garud, Jain, & Kumaraswamy, 1999). Tacit knowledge requires far richer means of communication than explicit knowledge such as face-to-face contact rather than a set of directions in a manual. Tacit knowledge has sometimes been described as being "difficult, if not impossible, to transfer" (Burton-Jones, 1999, p. 7). If transfer implies that the knowledge is disseminated unchanged from person to person, then

P. O'Toole, *How Organizations Remember: Retaining Knowledge through Organizational Action*, Organizational Change and Innovation 2, DOI 10.1007/978-1-4419-7524-9_4,

this contention is valid. Tacit knowledge can be communicated but the knowledge will be filtered in different ways by each person according to their own schema. Tacit knowledge requires different mechanisms to promote communication, such as the apprenticeship system where a craftsperson can communicate tacit knowledge to an apprentice, using tacit demonstration rather than a document to impart what needs to be known.

In addition, there needs to be the resources and the practical detail available for the implementation. It can be difficult to communicate tacit knowledge, and it can be difficult to predict what information is needed to make something work (Szulanski, 1996; von Hippel, 1994). Von Hippel quoted an interview to illustrate the difficulties in communicating knowledge:

> It's very difficult to make a carbon copy [of a gravity wave detector]. You can make a near one, but if it turns out that what's critical is the way he glued his transducers, and he forgets to tell you that the technician always puts a copy of Physical Review on top of them for weight, well, it could make all the difference. (p. 431).

Explicit knowledge, on the other hand, is relatively easily disseminated and relies on the ability of the receiver to properly understand and utilize it (Grant, 1996, p. 379). Although information technology is often cited as the main medium for knowledge management projects, it is difficult for information technology, by itself, to contain the richness required for much of the knowledge required by organizations (Davenport & Prusak, 1998). Although authors have advocated the conversion of tacit knowledge to explicit knowledge in order to facilitate communication (Nonaka, 1991, 1994), the inherent characteristic of tacitness means that attempts to affect such a conversion generally result in substantial knowledge loss (Burton-Jones, 1999; Davenport & Prusak, 1998; Grant, 1996; Polanyi, 1967). It is now realized that tacit knowledge needs to be recognized as such; efforts to communicate knowledge taking account of this dimension, such as apprenticeships and mentoring programs, will generally have more success (von Krogh, Ichijo, & Nonaka, 2000). This chapter deals firstly with the communication within each XME site, the communication structure of stories and then the communication among the sites. The communication structures referred to in this chapter are mainly informal and incidental to day-to-day work and practice.

Communication in XME Australia: "you have to do the walking"

The previous chapter described the growth of XME Australia. From a small number of research and development (R&D) professionals with accounting and management support, XME Australia grew to encompass a series of function- and market-based departments, with appointed managers and staff located in specific areas within the buildings. Organizational structure, that is, the nature of authority, reward, and hierarchy within an organization, will determine the extent and nature of knowledge retention in terms of restricting knowledge access and circumscribing the extent of communication.

Communication and Organizational Structure

XME Australia had a structure organized on a hybrid of function- and market-based departments. Communication across hierarchical levels within departments seemed effective. Most departments had regular meetings, and staff commonly waylaid their manager to ask questions or have a chat. As most managers sat in close proximity to their subordinates, this was quite easy to do. There was evidence that people lower down in the hierarchy frequently asked questions of their managers about things that puzzled or concerned them. I heard of or saw unsolicited reports and papers written by three different staff members, giving the staff members' views and knowledge to management on particular issues within the site.

People who wanted to know about what was going on outside of their department, were generally obliged to get out of their chairs and walk around, as the following quotations illustrate:

> Fred answers a customer query. As part of the talk he describes the new products in mining and industry. I asked him about his knowledge later, and he said he just hears it, walking about. He sees a group of R&D people doing something and asks what they are up to.
>
> Field notes

> Researcher: Would, sort of, your perception be that ... if you sat at your desk, if you were a little robot and didn't need to go to the toilet, would you hear as much stuff as when you get up ...?
>
> Respondent: No, no, you wouldn't hear anything, no. There would be a couple of people that walk past and maybe stop at my station but not a lot. No, you have to do the walking.
>
> Interview

Most of the managers of the company did not have secretaries or personal assistants. This facilitated communication as the managers were obliged to walk around the premises more in order to send faxes, find other people they wanted to speak to and so on. It is probable that XME Australia in the past, as a small, tightly knit group, relied on informal communication networks to underpin much of the work-related communication, which was supported by anecdotes related by longer serving employees. These informal communication networks, being based on continuous face-to-face contact, enabled individuals to communicate rich, tacit knowledge and reinforce the social relationships that promoted such communication. It was also much easier for a majority within this smaller organization to share experiences, which contributed to a stronger collective episodic memory. As the site became larger, these informal communication networks were struggling to cope with structural boundaries and a large building. This has led to informal communication networks that were based on departments and geographical location. Clearly, as XME Australia had grown, and the departments became physically separated, there was a greater requirement to walk around to find out what was going on.

The Physical Environment

The physical layout of workplaces can affect the behavior of organizational members (Oldham & Rotchford, 1983; Strati, 1990) and show the structure of an organization (Giddens, 1984; Rosen, Orlikowski, & Schmahmann, 1990). The physical separation of offices insulates each member and gives a measure of autonomy to those within them, and also serves as a powerful marker of hierarchy (Fischer, 1997; Giddens, 1984; Rosen et al., 1990). Technological objects are also manifestations of culture, both of the organization and of the broader social system. According to Kingery (1993, p. 207):

> In a factory, for example, there is a system of discipline, of rules, of politics in the traditional sense. The forms of machines help enforce these rules: they suggest the easiest possibilities to those who use them. They mediate between the people who make the rules and the people who have to follow them.

A place is the nexus of things and space within a given boundary, and has imputed values and interpretations (Van Maanen & Barley, 1985; Gagliardi, 1990; Gieryn, 2000; O'Toole & Were, 2008; O'Toole, 2010). The physical environment had a large impact on communication within XME Australia. This impact is teased out in the following discussions on proximity and accessibility, visibility, and audibility.

Proximity and Accessibility

A particular example of geographic separation promoting a lack of communication occurred with regard to the production area. The production area was located at the very end of the main building, behind the warehouse stores and the box dumpster. There were only two computers in the area, one of which was generally switched off, and the other that was in the supervisor's area. The production team had its own tea urn, coffee, and entrance to the building. The production people were thus separated from many of their work colleagues outside of production and did not socialize much with others from XME Australia. Their supervisor was active on a variety of organizational committees and acted as a communication channel between production and the rest of the organization: she was effectively the "face" of production. Many of the other people in production were not known even by name to others in XME Australia.

On the other hand, where people were moved closer to others with the same functional requirements, a very positive effect on the communication was observed. In one case in particular, two employees of the site with similar roles mentioned that their new physical proximity meant that they could compare notes, teach one another aspects of systems, and get a greater understanding of how each other worked, which was to the ultimate benefit of the company. Doz, Santos and Williamson (2001) noted this effect, where co-location achieved positive effects in innovation and communication.

In one case, however, too much accessibility was a problem. In the Accounting/Administration area, the payroll clerk sat in a cubicle, as did the rest of her peers. Others told me that they had witnessed real problems for the payroll clerk when she was handling confidential records. People would unknowingly encroach on her area and she would be forced to tell them to go away. On the other hand, the security lock on the R&D door has led to more difficulty for people outside R&D to access the area, and therefore probably a decrease in the diversity of traffic.

Visibility

Allied to the accessibility aspect of the physical environment is that of visibility. Visibility enables people to see where other people are and what other people are doing. In XME, visibility in terms of both the internal and external environment was used as a tool to learn more by the people of XME as shown in the examples below.

In XME Australia, most of the managers had glass doors and glass dividers separating them from staff. This meant that people could see what the managers were doing and who they were meeting. When changes were happening in the leadership of the company, the people who worked for the managers involved were aware that *something* was happening. They knew that there was a secret because of the level of activity that the managers would not discuss, even though they did not know the nature of the secret:

> When Jane went back to her office, Alana and the Managing Director were waiting for her. I could hear her say "This is frightening."Alana came out and collected 2 files. Gemma said to me "Something's going on."
>
> *** Note the knowledge that there are secrets in open plan offices, even if you don't know what the secret is ***
>
> Field notes

The open plan offices also allowed the more experienced people to judge whether newer staff members were correctly performing activities and give feedback where there were problems, as happened in the case below. In the excerpt below, Alana was passing by Betty's work area when:

> Alana glances at Betty's screen and sees something wrong. She takes her back through the transaction and shows her how to confirm by pressing F2. She shows her how to do a shortcut. Alana tells her to read procedures. Christine says you never know whether to press F2 or Esc. Alana says it's a matter of practice.
>
> Betty does another one and feels she understands now. She goes back and checks some she has done previously because she is "not confident" they are done correctly.
>
> Field notes

The management car park was clearly visible to the people in accounting and R&D. The nonmanagement staff could ascertain the presence or absence of management staff from the presence or absence of a car in the car park. This experience at

XME Australia seems to be an inversion of Foucault's (1977) notions on the panopticon and surveillance. The trapping of status, that is, the managers' car park, enabled the lower-status workers to observe the activities of the higher-status managers. It also meant that people new to the company were noticed by the accounts/administration people, which acted as a check against managers forgetting to apprise them of a new employee commencing with the company.

> [Payroll clerk] mentions that she might see someone walking across a car park, so she e-mails their manager asking if they want that person to be paid.
>
> Field notes

Audibility

Although visibility of people in their work areas contributed to increased communication and knowledge of what was going on, it is speculated that the audibility of activity was just as significant.

Many of the departments were segmented by means of partitions, which meant that the people sitting in the cubicles could not be seen by people nearby. Conversations, then, were often held without much regard for others present; if they could not be seen they were not involved. To someone sitting behind the partition who could hear the conservation, it was their choice whether they wished to move around the partition and join in, or remain where they were and keep working.

People who overheard conversations would often join in if it seemed appropriate or if they had something to contribute. Noise was a symptom of the energetic interaction that was a feature of the R&D area; however, it could also be a problem when R&D members needed to concentrate on complex and/or dangerous work. In some cases the noise, as well as the accessibility of the people, was considered a distraction to completing a task.

> As Zane counts the number of threads around the ring, he mentions that he has developed his own counting system over the years.
>
> Mathew walks past. He is going with Len and Yves on an excursion of some sort.
>
> Timothy asks Zane about solder pots, Zane replies and keeps counting…
>
> Len comes over and asks Zane for something. Zane says "Hang on – 15" then tells him that Timothy has had a cleanup and it is likely to be [somewhere]. He then resumes counting. Denis says "I have it on full power now." Zane replies "Full power" and keeps counting. Zane finishes counting. Muses "what chance have I got that that's right – almost none." He dons magnifying visor and starts recounting…
>
> I ask Zane about the difference in reaction between Timothy's and Len's interruptions. Zane could answer Timothy's statement on automatic where Len's required thought. Also, Zane was expecting Timothy to talk to him BUT wasn't expecting Len's interruption.
>
> Field notes

Thus, although proximity heightened communication, it also caused problems with regard to privacy, confidentiality, and close attention. The sort of communication encouraged or limited by the physical environment just discussed tended to center on the informal. The informal interaction is the basis of a significant amount of work-related communication interwoven with the playful and the personal. Nonaka and other authors (e.g., see Nonaka, 2002; Nonaka & Konno, 1998; Nonaka & Reinmoeller, 2000; Nonaka, Toyama, & Konno, 2000; Nonaka, von Krogh, & Voelpel, 2006) have argued that there must be a shared context (*Ba*) before knowledge creation can take place. *Ba* does not have to be a physical place, but is a context where interactions take place that lead to new knowledge being created. Shared contexts also contribute to knowledge retention: shared contexts, including physical spaces, enable people to find out what is going on, different ways of working and a greater understanding of colleagues.

Interaction and Communities of Practice

In XME Australia, as mentioned previously, there was considerable communication within departments. This communication, however, rarely took the form of personal criticisms of other individuals. Where people indulged in criticism, they generally criticized whole departments. This criticism most commonly revealed itself in comments about the lack of understanding of other departments, for example, Accounting does not understand Operations, Operations does not understand R&D, R&D does not understand anything pertaining to the real world. These comments reflected, of course, a perspective, not necessarily a truth. Accounting probably did understand as much as it needed to know about Operations, Operations probably did understand as much as it needed to know about R&D, and R&D probably did understand as much as it needed to know about the real world. Each department, however, had different objectives and sometimes people within those departments failed to recognize the differing objectives of someone from another department. Sometimes, confusion and misunderstandings could arise because of differences in language and terminology, which also contributed to this belief of lack of understanding. Van Maanen and Barley (1985) noted that cultures lead to perceptions of differences of others outside the group as well as similarities within the group, and this was discernible in the occupational subcultures within XME Australia. These subcultures formed what were essentially communities of practice (Wenger, 2000). Communities of practice seem to present the more "human" face of knowledge management. Organizations are sometimes viewed as simply "collections of communities" (Lant, 1999, p. 178) where the boundaries of the communities overlap.

A community of practice may be described as an informal and emergent network created over time by the need for joint learning and support in the process of activity (Lant, 1999; Seely Brown & Duguid, 1996; Wenger, 1999, 2000). Communities of practice are not dependent on structuring activities by the organization, although they may share the same boundaries (Wenger, 1999). A community of practice may coexist within a team, it may be dispersed throughout an organization and it may have members completely external to the organization.

Wenger (2000) identified three elements pertaining to communities of practice:

- A sense of joint enterprise around a topic, which in a sense defines membership, as the members understand what is important to the community and what is not
- Mutual engagement that facilitates calls to other members for help, and admitting ignorance. The interactions over time serve to build trust among the community (see also Adler, 2002) and
- A shared repertoire, which essentially means that the members share assumptions and a language that streamlines the communication process

Members of a community of practice share a worldview about what they practice. Hence Orr's (1990) photocopy technicians, who evolved into a community of practice, saw themselves and their world from the perspective of being a "rep" (repair technician). Wenger's (1999) claims processors saw themselves as separate from management and other parts of the company; they considered that their problems were different; and they thought the information they were given was different. Essentially, therefore, a community of practice is a network of practitioners who are prepared to share experience, pass on tips and hints and often help each other cope with life as a practitioner (Orr, 1990; Seely Brown & Duguid, 1996; Wenger, 1999). The power of subculture and communities of practice as knowledge retention structures, drawn on by the participants in a particular domain, was demonstrated by my own experience. One of the most disconcerting effects of the data collection was the influence of the departmental subculture of the respondents on me. The accounts area of XME had extremely high standards of neatness and order that were endorsed by all the staff. During my time with the Accounts staff, my home environment reached pinnacles of tidiness that were never before (or since) achieved. While working in Operations with engineers, I started to record personal and postgraduate tasks that needed to be done with ruthless efficiency. Thankfully, these temporary aberrations soon relaxed after joining another department, but they did illustrate how a subculture permeates the activities of the people exposed to it.

The knowledge that is shared among the members is generally what is termed by Seely Brown and Duguid (1996) as "non-canonical knowledge," which is knowledge that, although not endorsed by the organization's leaders, gets the job done. In the case of Orr's technicians, they found that the company training was simplistic and generally unhelpful, and thus they would share "war stories" that would educate each other about what to do in certain situations. Similarly, in Wenger's (1999) account of a claims processing department, the claims processors were given insufficient training to deal with complex claims, and learnt to rely on their own experience. The experience of the communities of practice identified by Wenger and Orr, and the observation of XME Australia point to communities of practice forming out of a certain tensions within the environment. Orr's photocopy technicians and Wenger's claims processors had feelings of alienation from other parts of the company. The community of practice formed through the need to support and learn from each other. In XME Australia, this tension was evident as each subculture indicated a lack of understanding from other groups, including the leadership group.

In these communities, the use of narrative through stories is a key factor in the communication of knowledge. The worldview or culture that underlies these stories and collaboration confirms the identity of the member as a contributing practitioner. Several of Orr's (1990, p. 172) technicians quoted a slogan – "Don't fix the machine: fix the customer!" – which reflects a perspective that is unlikely to be endorsed by organizational leaders, but that probably would be endorsed on at least some occasions by the practitioners. Similarly, Wenger (1999, p. 97) commented: "About the claims processors, for instance, an interesting rumor will spread very fast and get everyone talking." The knowledge retention structure/communication mechanism of stories is dealt with in a later section.

Because communities of practice are informal and emergent, organizations may contain several or many such communities, and individuals may be members of more than one community, with different roles and levels of participation. Where this is the case they can attempt to broker knowledge across community boundaries, which may not always be effective because of differing worldviews and differing interests of the communities of practice (Schein, 1996; Wenger, 1999). Wenger (2000) noted that organizations can foster communities of practice, but some care had to be taken not to stifle them. Communities of practice can occur within teams, across organizations, and even across industries. There are times, however, when the members of the community of practice need to interact with members of other communities. Because most of the departments were obliged to use the DO_IT system, however, the people of XME Australia shared a common language related to the DO_IT system when they needed to work together. When individuals from different communities did work together, this common base language enabled them to gauge each other's knowledge and competence and work together toward a common goal.

Sociability

Sociability in organizations means that people are more inclined to seek out face-to-face communication for companionship as well as to perform the task at hand.

XME Australia had grown from a small tightly knit group of people who habitually socialized together, and there were efforts to retain that culture to some degree. A manager at XME Australia noted that some of the managers became concerned that, with the growth of the organization, people were not interacting throughout the site as much as they used to, and the monthly lunches were instituted to promote interaction. These lunches were organized so that each department took a turn to buy, prepare, and serve food that was paid for by the organization. Sometime after 12:00 noon, usually on the last Friday of the month, an email would announce that lunch was ready and the staff would line up in the downstairs tearoom. After serving themselves, people would then proceed to the outdoor lunch area to sit, eat, and chat. The monthly lunch was an occasion where all the people from XME Australia gathered together in a small area to exchange news and catch up with events. This was the most regular and widely attended event; however, there were other functions at which staff gathered together to find out the news, and sometimes to enjoy themselves.

The broader physical surroundings also helped the sociability. The premises were located near enough to a café to enable people to walk there. On Fridays, a nearby market was open which encouraged a number of people to walk there to take advantage of the food kiosks and the eating area. In addition, there was an outdoor area with chairs and tables at the company that accommodated a large number of people. On fine days in particular, people would be lured out to join others at lunch. These social interactions were the site of comprehensive discussion and debates about work issues, the scene for storytelling (see page 89), as well as exchanging information about home life and family. The social atmosphere contributed to the social trust that people developed toward each other, which also facilitated the level of communication. This face-to-face communication and social trust were also supported by the way the email system was used.

One of the advantages of most email software is the ability to set up distribution lists to save time entering each person's name where a certain group of people are regularly sent emails. Global email lists are standard distribution lists that are available to all users of a particular location. In XME Australia the global list for all Australian staff was used extensively. Emails sent via this global list were collected and classified over a 6-month period. Thirty-seven percent of emails were on social matters such as social events, buying and selling personal items and so forth. Clearly the Australian staff used their email system as a community notice board, which in fact is probably quicker than writing out a notice and placing it on a real notice board. There was an underlying assumption that people had email access on a continual basis. Notes such as "Barbecue's on" assumed that a large number of people would be looking at their monitors at any given time, and would alert their colleagues that the event was about to commence.

Members of staff planned social functions that encouraged sociability. Sometimes these occasions were caused by a special event such as a wedding; sometimes just because someone thought a get-together would be pleasant. One example was a "Hawaiian day," where all the staff dressed in various costumes that were meant to convey a tropical theme (with varying success). "Secret bridesmaid's business" occurred on the eve of a staff member's wedding, and there were several "girls' night outs" to which I was invited. R&D often seemed to arrange after-work drinks at a local hotel.

Banter

The friendliness that permeated the organization colored interactions between people when they were obliged to meet. It seemed that, while this may not have been the intention, the task-focused contact was expedited by the use of harmonious social interaction. The people in Accounts, for example, were often perceived in pleasant social interactions, which made the people from other departments more positively disposed to answer queries, check records and generally assist in resolving problematic issues.

Social communication, such as gossip, is thought of as separate from the business of getting the job done. Where gossip was related, however, it did not seem to be with the primary intention of "spreading gossip" as such, but rather to spare colleagues the embarrassment of speaking out of turn, and thus preventing distress to the central figure in the story. Where people interacted, often an element of banter would form part of the interaction. Banter, or playful raillery (Delbridge et al., 1997), is dealt with as a way of facilitating communication, both within teams and across organizations, usually in face-to-face communications. Banter can be used in either a conflict or cooperative context, to praise or blame (Anolli, Ciceri, & Infantino, 2002). Trice (1993) pointed out that people in dangerous occupations often utilize banter as a way of managing the emotions associated with this dangerous work.

Banter was a significant part of the interactions in XME Australia. It sometimes was registered on the computer system. The V:\ drive on the server, also called the Vault, displayed the legend "Abandon hope all ye who enter here." A computer path, typed on minutes that were distributed to Department heads and to XME Ireland and XME USA, was C:\WINNT\Profiles\bosscocky\Desktop\Docs\.... These playful texts contributed to a culture where it was permissible to joke during meetings and other interactions. The email system, as will be discussed below, was also used to communicate jokes and playfulness.

The banter was seen to have several intentions. Railing against fate could be done provided it was witty, as shown below:

> Malcolm fetches Fanny to take a call from Bunnings [a large hardware store]. Malcolm says "I am waiting for a call from the US to talk about a 1.2 million dollar contract, but no, it is Bunnings with the plumbing fixtures."
>
> Field notes

The banter could be also used to diffuse tension and was a signal for what could happen. In one case, an R&D staff member asked me not to shadow him for a few days as the unit he was working on had exploded on the weekend, and he did not want me getting hurt, with which sentiment I was in total agreement. I later heard him laughing with his colleagues, as follows:

> Douglas quips "If you hear a big explosion, it means you have more time for other things."
>
> Field notes

Banter was also an effective method for giving opinions or describing a situation in a nonthreatening way. Below is an example of banter occurring in a meeting:

> Alana – Now this other thing. Need to start with a list of tasks for each area.
>
> Voula – When dealing with cables, it's difficult to cut complaints about thumbs and muscles.
>
> Alana – Good, I thought we could start with [staff member at meeting] so that we don't have to make total fools of ourselves in front of the others. [laughter]
>
> Field notes

Banter contributed to the level and quality of communication between people. Banter facilitated the communication by enabling people to talk about issues in a nonthreatening humorous way.

Conclusions Concerning the Communication of Knowledge in XME Australia

Much of the knowledge management literature concentrates on the transfer of technical and functional knowledge without taking into account the human aspect of knowledge. Some of the exceptions are Szulanski (1996), who discusses problems caused by arduous relationships; the work of Cross and Baird (2000), who note the importance of social trust in knowledge management and particularly in communities of practice and the consideration of care in terms of knowledge outcomes (von Krogh, 1998; Zarraga & Bonache, 2005). For the most part, however, knowledge management literature is based on a rationalist Cartesian model that either understates, ignores, or deplores the human element of knowledge.

In XME Australia, people valued the climate of friendliness and egalitarianism. The friendliness often took the form of banter, which acted as a process to facilitate communication. Concerns, frustrations and criticisms couched in this form were accepted by the listener and rarely led to conflict. Banter, in fact, was often used to diffuse conflict and tensions. People were generally comfortable interacting with their managers, and some even prepared reports that were critical of company practice. The egalitarianism also contributed to the socialization in that staff were comfortable suggesting such events as the "Hawaiian day" without obtaining permission from the leaders of the company. Thus there was little hierarchical division within XME Australia. Lack of communication tended to be more of an issue where there was geographical distance between people. People who are near other people could see, hear and experience what was happening in their immediate area. Even if the matters were confidential, they would still know that something is going on. Proximity, however, is not an unmixed blessing. There is a trade-off to be made in terms of enabling communication at the expense of minimizing distractions and impeding restricted communication where the restriction is deemed necessary.

In XME Australia proximity and a shared physical context enabled people to develop relationships and trust through working together, friendly banter, and social interaction. The common use of DO_IT meant that people from different subcultures had a common language that helped them at least partially overcome the differences wrought by the differing perspectives inherent in each subculture. However, for the most part, communication was substantial within departments, and at the higher levels of the organization.

Communication is an important part of knowledge retention on an organizational level. The next section of this chapter deals with the ways that knowledge was communicated in XME Ireland.

Communication in XME Ireland: "Management doesn't tell us much"

XME Ireland differed from XME Australia in terms of the relationship between communication and structural groupings. Within XME Ireland, as well as the formal vertical structure as denoted by departments, there was a discernible horizontal structure, with the staff belonging to one of three discernible hierarchical groups. These groups could be described as:

- Managers
- Technicians/supervisors and
- Production operators and others

The members of each group tended to spend time together during lunch hours and tea breaks. The distance of the industrial estate housing XME Ireland from shops where lunches could be bought meant that if people had not brought their lunch with them, they had to drive, and they often took passengers. These passengers tended to be people in their own level of the organization. The production operators were a particularly cohesive group. They tended to socialize at work only with other production operators, and after work they went out together in a group to enjoy some "craic." Interestingly, the tools that the production operators used were a barrier to socialization. Other staff who were not involved in production confided that they were reluctant to disturb the intent production people, particularly as they wielded tools that were potentially dangerous. In XME Ireland, there was some physical separation from other staff, but also adversarial relations with the managers. Managers commented to each other and to me on the complaints heard from production, and there was an attitude of having to placate the production people. The relationship was such that a staff manual was created by one of the managers so that the rights of the workers could be clearly specified with a view to reducing the number of complaints and queries. Specific negative feedback that I had gathered in the organization was attributed by the leaders to specific individuals within production. It was clear that individuals within production were well known to all the managers, and it was equally clear that the production area harbored individuals that were "trouble-makers" in the eyes of management.

The managers, on the other hand, formed their own hierarchical group. The General Manager was often absent, performing his marketing role; however, the other managers often had lunch together and seemed to socialize outside of work as well. People from the other structural groups seemed generally not invited to these social activities.

These hierarchical groups were also promoted by the organization of the tea room. Because the organization was growing in staff numbers, the occupants of the tea room tended to form into the previously mentioned groups (i.e., manager, technician/supervisor, production operators, and others). Because the production operators had set times for tea breaks, other staff tended to avoid the crowds, and stay away. The technical/professional people would thus have a break at a different time, and when others saw a couple of colleagues in the tea room, they would join them, and a crowd of technical/professional staff would often share a tea break, promoting communication within the hierarchical group, as shown by this quote:

> Researcher: Good. Now who do you find out about things from in a sort of social sense in the company.
>
> Interviewee: Tea break! Tea break mainly, information on the company can be very scattered like. [X], now, yesterday getting hot, I had inclination, you know, when I went down making tea with the lads, but you'll be still in the dark, you know you'll hear different ways like, but tea break is a good one.
>
> Interview

Banter, or good-humored teasing and raillery, was commonly heard in XME Ireland and was occasionally mentioned as an enjoyable aspect of the company. This seemed to be part of having "good craic" or a good time, and the annual Christmas party seemed to generally be regarded as a highlight of the year. Everyone who mentioned the Christmas party obviously enjoyed these occasions immensely.

It was during occasions of banter that some of the cultural differences between Australia and Ireland were observed, as follows:

> Cultural differences enhance this misinterpretation as the manners of the Irish clash with the conciseness of the Australians. Interesting – note I have been told a couple of times "You Australians, you have no sense of humor."
>
> Field notes

One or two people mentioned that banter was more often heard than stories.

> Researcher: What about … you know how people tell stories, there is sort of a point to it, you know. Have you ever heard someone tell a story about an event or something that has happened in XME to illustrate a point?
>
> Interviewee 4: Yeah, tea break [laughter] but I get lost half the times because of the coils and plugs and all that. It might be just generally banter about what happened last week.
>
> Interview

Like XME Australia, banter was a feature of communication. It was interesting to note that the Irish recognized and valued their banter with each other, where the Australians, although they enjoyed it, did not acknowledge it explicitly.

Although communication and learning occurred within the hierarchical groups, there did seem to be dissatisfaction with the level of communication between management and the other groups, as shown below:

> Communications, they [management] pick and choose what they want to tell you sometimes and other times they're full of information, so much so you don't want to hear anymore, you know.
>
> Interview

Complaints were heard from staff that visitors from Australia were not introduced to them, and that generally

> management doesn't tell us much.
>
> Field notes

It did seem, however, that when XME Ireland introduced formal, explicit measures of communication, they worked quite well. The Quality Management System (QMS) mentioned in the previous chapter is one example. Another example was a personnel policy manual as a reference for staff on human resource issues such as benefits, leave, pay, and so on. It was stated that this reference had led to fewer concerns and questions among the staff. This manual was seen on a large number of desks in the organization, where people could refer to it very easily. There was an emphasis on paper as mentioned previously. Email was not prevalent as a communication mechanism within XME Ireland as it was in the other sites. Generally, email seemed to be used as a vehicle to which reports and other documents could be attached. Occasionally emails took the place of telephone calls or face-to-face communication if the receiver was absent or situated on another floor. With the emphasis on production, however, a far greater proportion of staff members, that is, the production operators, had no access to email. Thus other means of communication were utilized.

In summary, XME Ireland's communication mechanisms were very different to XME Australia's. XME Ireland possessed a different structure and culture to XME Australia and the hierarchical divisions seemed to impede communications. In contrast to XME Australia, hierarchical distance rather than geographic distance impeded XME Ireland's communications, and socializing was bounded by the hierarchical group to which the individual belonged. The physical environment was seen to reinforce the structural boundaries by the limited space in the tea room and the separation of the three out of four of the managers from the production operators. Perhaps because of these hierarchical divisions, formal processes, and documents were useful in overcoming communication problems.

Communicating Knowledge: XME USA

In contrast to XME Australia, XME USA was a small, physically crowded site, where individuals with marketing/selling backgrounds were employed. There was universal access to email, and email was used extensively as a communication device.

In XME USA, knowledge was communicated across various levels in a variety of ways. The emphasis on process in the organization acted to bring together the managers to discuss and approve how a process could and should be implemented or updated. This discussion acted not only as a forum to voice ideas but to increase the managers' knowledge of the issues at hand. As the discussion proceeded, each manager became more aware of issues that would affect the other managers, and in turn could reflect on the impact of his/her own area. Each manager then communicated the agreed process to the relevant people in his/her own department as part of the implementation process. During these discussions, managers drew on previous experience and assessed how well the tools available to them would work to achieve the desired outcomes.

Part of the ease with which these discussions took place reflected the crowded conditions of the work space. It was not difficult to reach everyone who needed to know about a decision because if they were not present, then they would be less than 10 metres away. Hence messages tended to be communicated with the richness of face-to-face contact, instead of being converted into a text or voice-only medium. In this environment, it was also easy to perceive when a peer was having trouble understanding or coping with a particular issue, which would result in action to assist with the problem.

Occasionally, I witnessed interactions where a manager would pass on knowledge to a staff member who needed it. The level of the interaction would depend on the degree of knowledge held by the staff member. Where a staff member needed intensive instruction (e.g., in a DO_IT function), the manager would sit beside them and focus on the instructional event. Where a knowledgeable staff member needed clarification only, the manager would simply pause, make a remark, and then continue with his/her own tasks.

Instances were witnessed where an organizational member, seeing another in difficulty, would pass on a tip or tool to make life a little easier. This took place across departmental boundaries, which in fact seemed fairly permeable. There did not seem to be a great deal of after-hours social interaction among the members, and the most frequented spot for gatherings was the reception desk when lunches were delivered. There seemed to be a discernible amount of banter among members, which perhaps facilitated the offers of help and feedback that were witnessed among staff.

In spite of the structure of managers, the General Manager directly approached all staff when he believed that they needed to know something, or when he needed to know something from them. Thus all staff were aware of the knowledge that the General Manager considered important. This was emphasized by the fact that the General Manager attended and chaired all meetings held.

There was no issue with lack of communication discernible within XME USA. There was, however, a communication issue in terms of lack of privacy, engendered by the physical environment. The premises did not have a meeting room: instead, a warehouse was furnished with a table and chairs. Unfortunately, the warehouse was also used to store products. On several occasions, I witnessed accidental interruptions to private meetings. Conversely, where two people were simply having a conversation that anyone could join, a person walking in had to be reassured that the occasion was not a private one. Occasionally, the General Manager would use his own office as a meeting place. His office, however, was shared by the Marketing Manager who would have to be included in the discussion, or find somewhere else to sit. Thus, although privacy relating to the content of these meetings was gained, there was little privacy in relation to the occurrence of these meetings.

Despite other differences between the sites, however, stories were a common communication mechanism. Stories were used to teach, to make people laugh, and to make a point. The following discussion of stories and storytelling draws from the experience of all three XME sites.

Stories: "He makes up a story about how the new CEO's car sticks out ..."

Stories are structured according to a framework and sequence determined by the teller with the benefit of hindsight (Weick, 1995). The facts of the event are fitted into the story to simplify and amplify the cause–effect sequence and outcome desired by the teller to communicate a given meaning (Weick, 1995; Gabriel, 1998). In essence, stories are representations of meaning where a past event or action becomes connected to something else in the teller's experience.

The stories told by the employees of XME revealed a central connection with the teller. The stories were usually told because they contained a moral or underlying message that the teller thought was of interest or significance. An example of this was the "paint story," which was found to have various versions that depended on the perspective and interests of the teller.

> Alana related a story of how the wrong paint was put on units. It damaged them. Tried to get it off but the damage was done. A very expensive mistake.
>
> Field notes

Alana had responsibility in relations to the accounts of the company. Her perspective on the incident was "a very expensive mistake," which was not shared by other respondents.

> Fred [who repaired the machines] was very uncomfortable talking about it. Said it had to do with problems with warranties. He thought XME might be sensitive to it because they didn't perhaps do the right thing as much as they might, and they wouldn't want customers to hear about it.
>
> I asked Kevin [the Marketing Manager] about it, and he said he had no shame about it at all. ... The paint was fine at the time, but 2 years later, a competitor produced products that customers attached to the XME product. They wouldn't work because of the conductivity of the paint, and some customers were cranky because of it.
>
> Note here how the story changed. The only thing similar was the paint!
>
> Field notes

An interesting factor here was the focus of each of the stories with regard to each of the tellers. In each of the instances, the theme of the story – an expensive mistake/not honoring warranties/dealing with unreasonable customers – was a central concern of the teller, and the story changed accordingly. This indicated that the themes captured had particular meaning for the teller and these were the themes that became the main point of the story told in each case. It is likely that the story is a composite of several events, and this again reflects the concerns of the teller, in that they remember a construction of the events that were of most significance to themselves.

A story told in Ireland clearly illustrates that for stories to be remembered, they must have a personal connection/significance. The following story relates to an event, verging on the slapstick, where mishap followed mishap:

> There was one where we had an urgent, urgent requirement to get [a product] out by the end of the month to the US ... and the only thing is that they needed was the [product]

> charger, the appropriate US one to go in the box, so they went up there to Cork anyway, it was Tuesday afternoon, Andy came back down because he had brought the wrong charger. So he got new chargers and went back up to the airport and I got a call here at quarter to five, or quarter past five, and he had brought up the wrong charger [oh, no!], so they're saying "it's not going to happen, it's not going to happen, it's not going to happen." We were like at war in the old warehouse near the airport. I was the last one here, so I left, it was the old building so I drove up to the door and I didn't know a charger from a hole in the ground so I threw whatever was vaguely similar-looking into the boot and took off up to the airport. And I drove thinking, you know, the flight would be leaving in an hour. And I was saying I am in the grounds and I was at the gate. It was all this kind of stuff, so I remember, ramping the speed control little barrier thing that they had at the airport and drove up and umm – the lads, of course everybody was not talking at that time, and Andy particularly, he was so quiet, because they were all on edge, anyway, I drove up and they pulled the chargers from the car and I just drove quietly away. And they left, but that was the day of complete and utter … and Andy was just catatonic over it. … The day we fecked up the chargers. Yeah. Yeah.
>
> Interview

Each of the participants in this event who were still working at XME Ireland related this event when asked about stories. It was also indirectly referred to by another manager who was working at the company at the time and who mentioned that it had been told by the participants at social gatherings. However, no one else in the company recalled it when asked to think of examples of stories or company folklore. Although it is an amusing story, it is dealing with issues that are of central concern to only a few people within the organization. Andy repeated this story to me with the rider that his manager had never allowed him to forget it. The people who participated were generally involved due to the peculiar circumstances. Few people in the organization were normally directly involved in shipping goods to other countries and thus only a few people could really empathize with the story as told. Although, for the participants, the story approached folklore status, for the majority of listeners, it was soon forgotten. It appeared that the need for stories to connect with a concern or view of the listener was supported in light of the failure of the "day we fecked up the chargers" to enter the organizational folklore for the majority of organization members.

This issue of significance in what the story represents is repeated in further stories in succeeding sections. There were, however, stories that were generally known and remembered, and these were stories that communicated the culture endorsed by the organization's leaders.

Stories That Communicate the Endorsed Culture

XME was a relatively new company, where approximately 70% of people had been employed for less than 3 years. In Australia and Ireland, each operation had stories that related to the beginnings of the operations. In addition, XME Australia had stories related to the success of the operation. These stories amounted to sanctioned narratives that were related to new staff at the time of joining the organization as part of their induction. A typical quotation elicited is below:

> a story about the success of the place, I mean very quickly after I started here you hear a lot of them and you are aware of it. There's a lot of pictures around the place as well, and there's a lot of people working here who have been part of it so you do hear about that…
>
> Interview

These stories were reinforced by various physical artifacts such as photographs and framed awards testifying the success of the organization. These artifacts were prominently displayed in places that were main thoroughfares or meeting rooms for the organization. The new chief executive officer (CEO) also told stories. These stories communicated his experience of the international business scene, as well as being a way of illustrating his point of view and justifying changes in the organization. This genre of storytelling has been recommended by various authors (e.g., Boje, 1991; Denning, 2007; Gargiulo, 2005; Snowden, 2000b) as an effective management practice. Stories were also told to the new CEO about past events within XME. These stories, which were supported in the higher levels of the organization, are notable for the mechanisms reinforcing them. In the case of the stories of the organization's commencement, these stories are told as part of the induction procedures of the company. The recruit then sees the physical objects confirming the representation of the organization as a vital growing force in its market sectors, and intended to instill in the staff some feeling of pride in the organization's achievements. The stories of the new CEO were reinforced by the procedures that he introduced and also by the continued telling of the stories.

Stories Counter to the Endorsed Culture

Stories were also heard in the lower levels of the organization. Many of the stories were fragmentary, designed only to illustrate a point or to teach a concept. It was also recognized, however, that one group within the organization represented an alternative view regarding the actions of the leaders. Stories that were a form of resistance against the organizational leaders were generally told during breaks or when people worked together. These stories had a general theme of "see what we have to contend with," "if only management would listen" and "you can't trust them to behave appropriately." There was a clear memory of retrenchments that occurred approximately 18 months prior to my discovery of this genre that influenced this group's perspectives and reaction to events within the company. An example of this related to my presence in the organization, and gave rise to an interesting rumor:

> [Graham] mentions that someone said that I was a management spy. … Note that this is the third time that has been mentioned.
>
> Field notes

The stories that related specifically to the retrenchments are notable for several reasons. Firstly, despite extensive briefings and conversations with managers of XME,

I had no knowledge of the retrenchments until I interacted with the group of "cynics." Although I had heard about earlier retrenchments, many years ago, of which the former Managing Directors and the current Accounting Manager were the only survivors, no one had related anything about the more recent events in the organization's history. For me as a researcher, then, the "cynics" and their stories were an important and alternative source of knowledge that gave insights both on the organization's subcultures and past history. Secondly, the retrenchments were an extreme historical event that was remembered with some distress by those who lived through it. The stories told gave form to this distress and provided reasons for their distrust of and unhappiness with the organization's leaders. Each time a story was told, the pain of the retrenchment program could be remembered. Finally, as with the stories endorsing the culture, the stories were reinforced in two ways. Firstly, most of the people involved in storytelling, along with others, displayed Dilbert cartoons on their walls. Dilbert cartoons were created by an American cartoonist, Scott Adams, and feature life in the cubicles for a software engineer. The cartoons comment irreverently on the foibles of aspects of organizational life such as marketing, accounting, managerial practice, team dynamics, quality and special projects, and information technology. According to Kessler (2001, p. 285): "In contrast to ivory-tower conceptions of management, Adam's commentary is one of the few perspectives on organizations that is practitioner driven." Secondly, the group of "cynics" each retold the stories, reinforcing them for each other. This also occurred with the product stories, described below.

Another series of resistance stories that were frequently heard were the problems with the products. Although the technology of the products was superior, according to employees the leaders did not allow sufficient time for testing and quality checks, and, as a result, there were a high number of defective products returned by customers. The employees allegedly reported these problems to the organizational leaders, who refused to countenance any action to resolve the problems. Nothing was done, and nothing was recorded in the formal collective knowledge retention structures of the organization. The individuals who attempted to resolve the situation, however, still had the knowledge of events in their own memory, and these events were added to a genre of stories involving the theme "management won't listen/the problems with our leaders." The organizational leadership prevented knowledge from entering the formal knowledge structures of the organization, but failed to prevent an interpretation of the event from entering the informal collective structures.

Stories that become part of the cultural fabric of the organization, whether the espoused culture or an alternative subculture, are generally a representation of past events that are relevant and have some emotional connection with the listeners. A specific story may be retold because of the power of the message and circumstances surrounding it. Alternatively, a story may form a part of a repeated genre. Although individual stories may be forgotten, the central message may remain with the listener. A key determinant in the message being remembered, however, is the skill of the storyteller. Although many individuals related anecdotes and fragments of events to other individuals, there were specific individuals who would relate longer narratives to groups of people. According to Livio and Rietz (1986, p. 20), the storyteller can be considered as the "other"; someone who enters into another reality and introduces that reality to their audience.

The people described as "storytellers" were adept at narrating stories so that they had an emotional connection for many of the listeners and from which a clear message could be drawn. An example of this was when a member of XME Australia told a series of irreverent stories about events revolving around the managers' car park. Most of the individual stories related were quite trivial, but engaged the listeners' sense of humor:

> I ... sat down at the tables with people from R&D. [Jeremy] apparently has a view of the car park [from his workstation]. He makes up a story about how the new CEO's car sticks out beyond anyone else's and looks sheepish about it because it is such a monster. It keeps trying to tuck its bottom in without success! There is an underlying theme here that the CEO must think very well of himself because the car is so large; it seems that even the car is embarrassed.
>
> Field notes

This form of storytelling illustrated two things. Firstly, as with the success stories of the organization, these stories had tangible artifacts that reinforced the stories. As I walked past the CEO's car in the car park, the story came to mind, trivial though it was, and I had to smile. Secondly, although these stories were not about dramatic events or crises, they formed part of a theme of stories constantly repeated. When the acknowledged storytellers told the stories, they were retelling and reinforcing a theme that had cultural implications for the company. The CEO and managers may have felt that the new CEO could give value to the organization through his expertise in international markets; other staff knew that he thought so well of himself that even his car was embarrassed.

Boje (1991: 124) acknowledged that "people who are more skilled as storytellers and story interpreters seem to be more effective communicators than those that are less skilled" and he wondered at the lack of storytelling training in management education. The new CEO of the XME group regularly told stories of his experience to explain his desired culture and ways of working. If framed and narrated to engage the attention of the listener, even a trivial event could stick in the mind of the listener, such as the stories about the managers' car park. In many cases, the details of the story may be lost, but the meaning is retained and strengthened as more related stories serve to reinforce it. Where the storyteller is skilfull, it is not one particular story that sends a message counter to those desired by the organization's leaders. A skilfull storyteller tells many stories, and multiple stories around one motif clearly can contribute to cultural beliefs built on specific perceptions of the organization, as happened in XME with the multiple stories about the products and the car park.

The Communication of Knowledge Across Sites: "they don't think the same way we do"

Doz et al. (2001) suggested that, in the past, organizations were structured around the principles of co-location and projection. Co-location refers to locating people and resources to form nodes of competence in one particular place. Doz et al.

gave the example of the Microsoft corporate campus outside Seattle, USA, which is the site for all major developmental activities. In XME Australia, it has already been demonstrated that proximity facilitates communication and learning, while geographic distance, even in a different building, impedes communication in learning. In XME Australia, a strategy of walking around could serve to overcome the problems of distance, but when dealing with sites in other countries, clearly other strategies were needed to overcome these issues. Doz et al. (2001) warned that organizations would have to learn how to compensate for an increasing inability to co-locate in the face of increasing globalization. The projection strategy involved organizations projecting knowledge from the "home base" to other sites, which would adapt the knowledge to local conditions. In the XME group, much of the knowledge projected related to the technology used. A significant reason for establishing XME Ireland related to the location of component suppliers in Ireland, which meant that production could be achieved at a much lower cost than within Australia, using components that reflected leading-edge technology.

The advent of global telecommunications capabilities, however, has led to a perception of global interconnectedness for international organizations. Email has become a prevalent means of communication in the developed parts of the world. In organizations, it is used to transfer messages within teams, within organizations and to external entities. Shulman (1996) stated that, while some researchers hypothesized that emails were used only for certain sorts of communication, other researchers concluded that there was no clear pattern. In XME, email was a significant communication mechanism among the XME sites, although there were different usage patterns discernible within the sites.

According to Roberts and Grabowski (1996), international and organizational boundaries may become blurred as organizations seek to pursue mutually beneficial opportunities. This trend toward globalization creates issues with communication between associated organizational sites. Sole and Edmondson (2002) related how contextual and local knowledge sources were valuable for distant colleagues participating in projects that involved a different site. This study showed that multiple sites may act as a knowledge resource for an organization as each site develops a different operational and cultural focus, and develops different types of expertise.

In XME communications difficulties were exacerbated by the time differences between countries. In addition, there were difficulties with regard to the logistics of communications. XME Australia, for example, could not hold teleconferences with XME Ireland due to the deficiencies of the Irish telephone lines. Email and other software functionality in XME USA were often curtailed due to problems in the XME USA computer networks. These logistical problems were accepted and dealt with by the people within the XME group. The issues relating to perceptions and constructions of individuals within each site were more problematic. The major sources of difficulty related to the misunderstandings that were often sociocultural in nature and the lack of feedback mechanisms across the sites.

Connecting via Information and Communications Technology (ICT)

A major factor in the XME group communications was the ICT requirements imposed on the group by XME Australia. The use of this network, and the need for compatibility in terms of software used, meant that XME Australia required other sites to use certain software packages such as DO_IT, Microsoft Office applications and Microsoft Access, and specified CAD software.

Email and other ICT-type methods of communication were far more commonly used than telephone calls. Although it seems logical to attribute this to the cost of telephone calls, in fact a substantial communication problem was the time difference between the countries. Although the managers of both sites seem to accept phone calls at odd hours, for the professionals and technicians, the time difference was a headache. If a problem occurred in Ireland in the late afternoon that needed to be discussed with an Australian, the Australian would not be in the office until close to midnight Irish time. The only really practicable time to call within office hours was early morning Irish time/late afternoon Australian time. Although the managers in XME seemed to accept the need for out-of-hours telephone calls, teleconferences were not viable in that part of Ireland due to the inability of the telephone lines to maintain the picture resolution.

XME USA had continual problems with ICT in terms of staying consistent and connected to the other sites. This requirement as part of the XME group meant that XME USA experienced compatibility problems between software and hardware; problems with software; and an inability to connect with the Australian network. The ICT problems were at least partially caused by XME USA's subordination to XME Australia, and the need to use XME Australia's resources, being such a small organization themselves. XME Australia needed XME USA to use the DO_IT software; XME Australia also provided various Access databases that were not quite compatible with the XME USA network. The problems that were experienced in the XME group highlight that the need for sites to stay connected can sometimes cause productivity losses in terms of computer downtime, and increase the need for considerable investment in terms of compatible hardware and software and ongoing support. Where the site, such as XME USA is a young, growing operation, this investment may form a considerable burden.

Using Email

Although email is essentially ICT software that is meant to communicate explicit knowledge, emails also contain tacit knowledge that can cause problems in terms of relations between sites of different cultural backgrounds. In XME, the manifestation of these problems took place in terms of XME Australia and XME Ireland. Each site had its own characteristics that were unsettling and sometimes awkward for the other site. To the Australians, the Irish communications sometimes seemed a little bit too overblown and wordy. The Irish seemed to the Australians to demand answers in an unrealistically short time frame. One person in XME Australia explained her viewpoint:

> Joy doesn't think the Irish and Americans think the same way we [Australians] do. In their emails the Irish use funny contractions such as "ye" instead of "the." ... In the USA, it seems to happen that when Australia asks them to hold off action while Australia finds the answer to a problem, the USA will forge ahead and take action that is incorrect and has to be rectified.
>
> Field notes

Gaver (1996) stated that different perceptions of what email was (i.e., a note, a letter, a memorandum) tended to affect the way people regarded its use. The Irish and the Australians had very different perspectives about the way email should be used, and this had an impact on their communications and perceptions of each other.

The Irish emails seemed to have much more supportive narrative, more like a letter or a conversation, rather than the short, fact-driven communications generally seen in Australia. Email seemed to be an instrument of conflict as much as communication. Further investigation showed that the Irish often found the Australians abrupt (and not just through emails). A further problem was that the Irish often depended on an answer from Australia before they could take any action. Many Australians did not acknowledge receipt of emails while they were investigating; hence the Irish had no idea whether their problem had been heard and understood or not. When the answer did come, the Irish sometimes found the style directive and terse. On a contrasting note, one XME Australia staff member was perceived to be including some social chat in his/her emails to other sites. When I asked about it, he mentioned that he believed that things were easier if you developed some sort of relationship with the people you were dealing with. This person was spoken of highly by his counterparts in other sites.

It is possible that, as email entered XME Australia, people became used to email being an adjunct of personal conversations, and had not really become used to using it as a primary mode of communication. It appeared that there had been no concerted attempt to achieve a consensus on the role that email should have within the company. Instead, people used email according to their own beliefs, which tended to be consistent within each site.

International Processes

XME Ireland seemed to communicate a great deal with XME Australia, because of the process of transferring product assembly from Australia to Ireland. The change from producing relatively small batches in Australia to mass-producing them in Ireland tended to highlight problems that had not before been identified, and which caused a great deal of communication between the production people. In addition, XME Ireland sometimes needed to obtain parts from Australia suppliers through

XME Australia. This was in addition to the communications concerning marketing and financial accounting reporting.

XME Ireland was a comparatively young company and thus its procedures and processes were still evolving. In addition, as more products were transferred to XME Ireland for assembly, procedures from Australia had to be assimilated and occasionally altered to take local conditions into account. Although XME Ireland contributed to the consolidation of accounts for the XME group, the engineering action reports (EAR) seemed to have far greater dominance. One of the reasons for this perceived dominance was that far more people were directly affected by the EAR, while the accounting cycle occurred in the background, managed by the two accounting staff. In Ireland, the EAR was a source document for initial product assembly and product changes. It therefore affected the dominant part of XME Ireland's activities. XME Ireland, however, had to contend with delays in receiving the EARs, procedures and drawings from XME in Australia. There were also problems with the product structures created in Australia, again without consultation from Ireland or XME USA.

Although the QMS system may have given the staff members a voice within the Irish operation, there seemed to be no mechanisms to communicate problems that came across the water, that is, from Australia or the USA.

In XME USA, a large portion of the interactions between XME USA and other offices were routine and part of a standardized cycle. The most obvious examples of this pertained to the accounting area, where figures had to be reconciled, then amalgamated with Ireland and then forwarded to Australia. In addition, there were processes designed to regulate product development that involved the EAR. This report was distributed to all the XME sites and was used to retain and communicate product changes and their various approvals. The EARs were mainly referred to by the service technician and manager, who needed them as a reference in repairing returned product, and by the person in charge of customer service. XME USA also received the minutes from meetings conducted in XME Australia and XME Ireland that were distributed to all offices. Some of these minutes were useful references where decisions were made that could affect the other sites, such as the research and development meeting and the engineering meeting.

Sociocultural Relationships with Other Operations

Levitt and March (1996) discussed the nature of superstitious learning, where people would know an erroneous fact, from a mistaken cause and effect. In XME Australia, this superstitious knowledge was very apparent in terms of the people's knowledge of other sites, because of a tendency for some people in each site to construct meanings from events that perhaps were not entirely justified. There was evidence of people in one site taking offence at an action or words of a person in another site, and then blaming the entire site for it. An example may be where a member of Site A is heard to be critical of a department in Site B, and staff in Site B will thereafter attribute these comments to everyone employed in Site A. On occasion, staff would make statements with perfect confidence, sometimes in front of small groups of other employees, about other locations that were either untrue or distorted to a significant degree. Unfortunately, these statements generally were negative about the other sites.

There was a clear perception in Ireland and the USA that Australia did not communicate enough. It is suggested that this could be an effect of only recently having been a small company that relied a lot on face-to-face relationships. In the case of sites located internationally, any form of personal verbal communication was difficult to achieve due to the time difference between countries. It was interesting to note that the negative feeling engendered by misunderstandings of the tone of emails largely seemed to dissipate when the Irish met the Australians on visits. Oddly enough, individual Australians would be quarantined from the negative rhetoric against XME Australia as a whole. On one occasion in XME Ireland, one individual described almost the entire Australian management team in a positive way as individuals, while XME Australia as a whole suffered serious denunciation in the same breath. A number of staff cited the effectiveness of visits of staff among the three operations in facilitating communication and understanding between the operations. Certainly, an example of the effectiveness of at least one trip could be seen in the impressive production facilities in Ireland. Significant credit was given to an Irish engineer spending time in Australia's production area, gathering information, ideas and feedback from the Australian staff.

In XME USA, the operation was sometimes described as the "redheaded stepchild" by members of staff, a description that evokes an image of an outsider attached to the family, but not quite part of it. Part of the situation was caused by a lack of response from XME Australia concerning XME USA-reported problems with products and/or marketing. This lack of response by XME Australia to XME USA feedback caused a discernible level of frustration. There was also some frustration because it was evident that the cultures of the two organizations had significant differences. XME USA was much more attuned to a marketing focus, where XME Australia was perceived by XME USA to have a technology focus. It is also speculated that the habit of circulating minutes from XME Australia to other sites about corporate issues projected a message that decisions had been made without reference to the other sites.

Despite this, communications between the USA and Ireland, and the USA and Australia seemed to be fairly cordial. Most of the staff in XME USA who communicated with overseas sites telephoned Ireland more often because it was easier to cope with the time difference. The problems that arose from the time difference were delays in communication while waiting for offices to open and people to arrive. These delays meant that XME USA was essentially nearly a day behind important decisions that had been made in the XME Australia headquarters.

The XME USA staff believed that the XME Australia staff ("the Australians") were more informal than the Americans, and that generally Americans did things in a different way to Australians. There were few reported problems with email communications. Although XME USA staff believed that they were the red-haired stepchild of the XME group, there was evidence of cordial relations between staff at XME USA and specific staff in XME Ireland and XME Australia. These cordial relations between people of different nations but the same company group were useful when oversights occurred. It was reported that occasionally one of the sites would be unable to find records relating to shipments: when this occurred the people involved would contact their counterparts in the other sites and ask for copies of the records. Thus the sites acted as knowledge retention structures for each other in the case of missing paper documents. Despite the cultural differences that caused problems within the XME group, there still was a sense that all three sites belonged to one group.

Both XME Australia and XME Ireland dealt extensively with external suppliers. In both sites there was considerable evidence suggesting that the XME Ireland site was closer and communicated more extensively with their externally suppliers than with the other XME sites. XME engineers would hear about the illness of a worker in the production line of a local supplier, or new staff employed, which could affect the quality and/or quantity of supplied components. On the other hand, it was clear that XME Ireland had no idea of problems in XME Australia that could affect the supplies from that source. Similarly, in XME Australia, the staff would often know, in advance and with a high level of detail, of issues with external suppliers. On the other hand, where substandard deliveries were made or some other problem was discovered in relation to goods produced by XME Ireland, the staff in XME Australia would be critical of XME Ireland with no knowledge of what caused this situation to occur. It would be rare for either site to attempt to investigate the causes of the problems, and feedback did not appear to be consistently given.

Feedback Mechanisms Across the Sites

The processes of a company retain a huge amount of knowledge in a collective sense. Many processes rely on more than one staff member for completion and usually have some form of monitoring or feedback mechanism to ensure that the sequence of activity is properly accomplished. Although the company did have feedback mechanisms in place, the further the distance from where the process was initiated, the less feedback seemed to take place. There was not a great deal of evidence of people who had to handle the created outputs being given an opportunity to comment on the effectiveness of the outputs, with a view to further improvement, although the situation did seem to be getting better over time.

The communication and ability to obtain information in XME Australia was variable. Within departments, information seemed fairly easily obtained. Across departments, it was often more problematic. There were various instances where decisions were not communicated to other departments until the decisions were put in effect. As mentioned previously, there were also problems in trying to track back to past products and issues due to poor or nonexistent documentation practices.

There were also issues where it was believed that decisions were made without access to reasonable supporting information. It was reported that changes to projects and product development would be made at the behest of business managers without proper business cases being prepared, although the instances of these omissions had apparently decreased with the implementation of new practices by the new CEO.

There were also issues with feedback mechanisms with regard to the QMS that was designed to formalize and document processes within the site. Both XME Australia and XME Ireland had established QMS and XME Ireland had used some of the Australian resources to help develop their system. It was observed that the QMS had positive effects in both sites, in that deficiencies within each site were identified and addressed. Although the QMS was active within each site, however, there did not appear to be mechanisms to transcend the site boundaries. It is acknowledged that a couple of supplier corrective action reports were received by XME Australia from XME Ireland, but at the same time there did not appear to be formal mechanisms to promote feedback loops from XME Ireland to XME Australia or vice versa. At the management level, the managers have generally visited other sites and established friendly relationships with other managers, which makes giving feedback perhaps a little easier. It was, however, a far more daunting prospect for a staff member who had not established friendly relations with people in other sites to generate feedback. Although it is acknowledged that people could have worked through their manager, it was easy to see situations where a staff member may have been wary of being seen to cause "trouble." This was particularly the case in XME Ireland, where a rigid hierarchical structure was evident.

The exception to these communication problems was in the military division. The military division was comprised of four people, two in XME Australia and two in XME Ireland. Three of the four members had served in the Australian armed forces; the managers had formerly been officers. They were responsible for marketing and administration relating to the specific XME products sold to government and humanitarian organizations. It was clear that all four members of the military division had knowledge of its operations at their fingertips due to the discipline and protocols that ensured explicit storage of communications. The common military background of three out of the four members meant that they had common perspectives and ways of working and thus were able to initiate the communication protocols and retention arrangements to meet similar goals. The fourth member without a military background was the most junior person in the group who was easily socialized into the "military" way of operating. There was, however, considerable hostility shown between the military staff of XME Ireland and the military staff of XME Australia. The shared cultural background, however, which facilitated a disciplined way of communication meant that this hostility rarely interfered with communication. In fact, in some ways, the combination of military discipline and hostility meant that communication was facilitated even more due to a reluctance to be "caught out" by the military staff of the other site.

Despite the communication issues that arose among the sites, there was evidence that having multiple sites meant that one site could build on the knowledge of another site. In XME there was one site with a technology focus, one site with a production focus and one site with a selling focus. When a new task had to be undertaken, the work and knowledgeable individuals of the other sites acted as a reference and a resource from which a new, relevant and sometimes better resource could be developed. This was the case with the production lines in XME Ireland, marketing resources developed by XME USA and in the different ways each site used the DO_IT system.

Conclusions

The last chapter dealt with the formal knowledge retention structures of the XME group. This chapter demonstrates the importance of the informal in the communication of knowledge. Communication is facilitated by banter, socializing, and the ability to see others face to face. In XME Australia, communications became more difficult as the site grew and the functions of the organization were separated into departments that housed groups of the same or similar occupations. The growth of XME Australia, then, immediately caused geographical and structural distance as well as cultural distance caused by the formation of occupational subcultures. In contrast, XME Ireland suffered from hierarchical distance as the physical environment in the shape of the tea room arrangements fostered the adversarial relationships between the production operators and management. Communication issues involve, however, a trade-off between promoting communication and enabling privacy, as was noted in XME USA where the cramped accommodation facilitated communication wonderfully, but made it difficult to hold a private conversation.

Communication may also have either positive or negative consequences for the organization as shown by the discussion on storytelling. Stories may be told for any number of reasons, but the power of the story for the listener depends on the strength of the connection, how it resonates with the listener. This in turn may depend on the inherent power of the story or on the skill of the storyteller in framing it to connect with the listeners through elicitation of an emotional response. Stories, however, can keep knowledge current that organizational leaders may wish forgotten.

Communication centers on commonality. This commonality may be missing where different sites in different countries come under one organizational banner. The national and occupational cultures contribute to the sense of difference, which is compounded by a lack of face-to-face communication and by differences in styles and forms of written communication as well as different understandings of what the written communications represent. This was particularly apparent in the email communication between XME Australia and XME Ireland, who used different words, had different understandings about what an email was and different understandings of how people should behave. The challenge for organizational leaders is to introduce and foster commonality. XME did this by arranging social occasions, enabling a culture that fostered banter and having an organization-wide ICT network. More could have been done to promote effective communication, though, particularly in the area of having processes that spanned the borders of each site and an organization-wide intranet. The XME experience shows that organizations need to review both explicit and tacit communication mechanisms to judge their effectiveness in overcoming the problems of distance that beset organizations that cross international boundaries. Organizations also need to monitor the informal communications both as a potential issue to be addressed and, perhaps even more importantly, as a form of feedback on the effectiveness of the communication that is disseminated from the leaders.

Chapter 5
Managing Knowledge Retention Structures

"So, how do we stack up against the last place that you worked at?" The new recruit screws up her eyes and makes out the grinning face of Brenton, the IT administrator, against the glare of the sun. She gathers her thoughts as she swallows her mouthful of sandwich. "Umm, well, I like it a lot better so far. Everyone is friendly, and I haven't found any nutters in power, like at the last place" she comments, somewhat caustically. "So, more like 'Everyone Loves Raymond' than 'Apocalypse Now', you think!" he comments. They both laugh. "Some things stay the same though. Why did the computer system go down this morning?" the new recruit asks. "Oh, just a worm, you know, over the Internet. Someone got an attachment on an email and was silly enough to open it," replies Brenton through his pitta wrap. "We need to get a protocol about things like that." The new recruit looks a little surprised. "Isn't there one? My last place was fanatical about things like that."

Introduction

So far, knowledge retention structures have been dealt with in terms of how they develop within organizations, and how communication mechanisms act as knowledge retention structures. This chapter examines how the different characteristics of different knowledge retention structures affect their protection and management. Management implies control, and the field of knowledge management has thus tended to focus on the knowledge that can be controlled and is valuable to the organization. Knowledge within organizations, however, despite the efforts of knowledge management adherents, is limited in its capacity to be integrated and managed (Gabriel, 1995). This limitation, however, has not prevented the creation of useful models of knowledge retention and typologies of knowledge within organizations. In Chap. 2, the constructs of explicit and tacit knowledge and collective and individual knowledge were introduced, in addition to Tulving's model of episodic, procedural, and semantic memory. In this chapter, knowledge retention structures within the XME group are examined in terms of a model of knowledge retention that includes these constructs. By examining knowledge retention structures in terms of this model, different characteristics are highlighted that have significant implications for organizational leaders. This chapter also explores the

P. O'Toole, *How Organizations Remember: Retaining Knowledge through Organizational Action*, Organizational Change and Innovation 2, DOI 10.1007/978-1-4419-7524-9_5,

issue of the protection of knowledge, and the knowledge that evolves into core competencies and core rigidities of the organization, thereby affecting organizational performance.

A Model of Knowledge Retention Structures

Spender (1996a, b) extended the distinctions between explicit and tacit (termed "implicit") knowledge and individual and collective (termed "social") knowledge by proposing dialectical relationships which are illustrated by the following matrix (Table 5.1).

According to Spender (1996b), each quadrant represents a different model of the interaction between knowledge, learning and memory or knowledge retention. The conscious knowledge retention may be in the form of personal notebooks, for example, that may be available to others but are possessed by the individual. Spender also refers to conscious knowledge as being the articulable knowledge that the individual holds in his/her mind, which may depart with the individual or be forgotten. Objectified knowledge, in contrast, is available and belongs to the organization. It may be in the form of books, databases, and procedures. The notion of objectified knowledge illustrates how knowledge can be abstracted and separated from human cognitive structures, and how the activity of the individuals within the firm is required for the acquisition of new knowledge and the discarding of obsolete knowledge from the retention structures harboring this form of knowledge. This points to the need to have objectified knowledge firmly placed within the organization's accountability structures so that there is responsibility allocated with regard to its management and review. The automatic knowledge refers to the individual's skill base and the collective refers to the tacit knowledge of the organization, which is retained in the culture, the stories, and the routines of the organization. The automatic knowledge is the most easily lost to the organization, as it resides within the individual, and is lost on the individual's departure from the organization.

Spender and other authors (see, e.g., Bogner, Thomas, & McGee, 1999; Lei, Hitt, & Bettis, 1996; Prahalad & Hamel, 1990) described the collective knowledge as the most powerful within the organization because it was difficult to communicate across organizations. Although collective knowledge includes the organization's core competencies, it also includes the convergence of sensemaking activities of the organization's members which may not always conform to the sensemaking activities of the organization's leaders. It should be noted that,

Table 5.1 Spender's (1996b, p. 70) matrix of different types of organizational knowledge

	Individual	Social
Explicit	Conscious	Objectified
Implicit	Automatic	Collective

although Spender defined the collective knowledge to mean only the organization's tacit knowledge, in this work collective knowledge refers to either tacit or explicit knowledge provided it is available to or part of the organization or a group within the organization.

Spender's (1996b) matrix accounts for the role of experience and activity in the making and retention of knowledge. Although he stated that "the attachment of meaning" (p. 71) is part of the development of knowledge, somehow the emotional and the subjective which is part of the making of meaning is omitted. An effective model of knowledge retention needs to account for this all too often overlooked element of organizational life. In Chap. 2, Tulving's model of human memory incorporating semantic, procedural, and episodic memory was discussed. When classifying organizational knowledge according to the typology used by Tulving, common organizational retention structures can be classified as shown in Table 5.2.

This typology is based on the ideas of El Sawy, Gomes and Gonzalez (1986), and is problematic in that the fundamentally different dimensions of tacit and explicit knowledge are included in the same categories. The inclusion of explicit knowledge retention structures raises some issues. Knowledge retention structures have been implicitly classified as either tacit or explicit in the preceding analysis. Is it valid to further classify semantic, episodic, and procedural knowledge retention structures in terms of explicit and tacit dimensions when Tulving bounded his model to the cognitive structures of the individual? The need to extend Tulving's classification to include explicit forms of knowledge retention structures relates to the nature of organizations. Organizations are not simply groups of people working toward goals within an authority structure. Organizations are comprised of buildings, equipment, and other infrastructure such as computers, files and the humble pen and notebook, as well as the individuals who interact with them. To ignore the knowledge retention structures that are represented by the physical and the virtual environments means that a considerable part of the organization's knowledge is also ignored. The members of an organization are not just individuals; they are

Table 5.2 Examples of declarative and procedural knowledge retained by individuals and organizations

	Semantic	Episodic	Procedural
Individual	Known facts	The memories of experienced past events	Skills
	Personally owned reference books	Log books	Habits
Collective	Financial and numerical records	Stories	Processes/routines
	Databases	Artifacts relating to past events	Procedures
	Reference books and journals	Learning histories	
		Annual reports	

present in a particular time and space, active in particular ways. Part of this activity involves creating and drawing upon other knowledge retention structures to enhance the degree or depth of knowledge available to individuals. Polanyi's notion of "indwelling" is relevant here – individuals have a subsidiary awareness of the retention structure with which they interact. To exclude these other knowledge retention structures would be to exclude a vital part of both the organization and of the way individuals remember. It should also be remembered that Tulving is a cognitive psychologist, with no reason to formulate a model that extends further than the cognitive structures of the brain.

Other authors in the field of organizational studies have investigated semantic, episodic, and procedural knowledge retention structures at a collective level, for example, Moorman and Miner (1998), with their discussion of declarative and procedural knowledge structures in relation to organizational improvisation. El Sawy et al. (1986) discussed the value of collective semantic and episodic memory. Cyert and March (1963), Cohen (1991) and Cohen and Bacdayan (1994) explored the notion of organizational routines, which emerge from individual procedural memory; Kim (1993) discussed the merging of individual mental models (schemas) into collective mental models. A detailed exploration of this model of knowledge retention structures on a collective and individual basis, however, is lacking in the literature, although such an exploration would be of considerable value. A model of knowledge retention structures within organizations, based on Spender and Tulving's work, is conceptualized in Fig. 5.1.

This model is conceived not to set these knowledge retention structures in opposition so much as to acknowledge differing characteristics. In this framework, tacit knowledge retention structures are depicted in the underlying layer of the diagram.

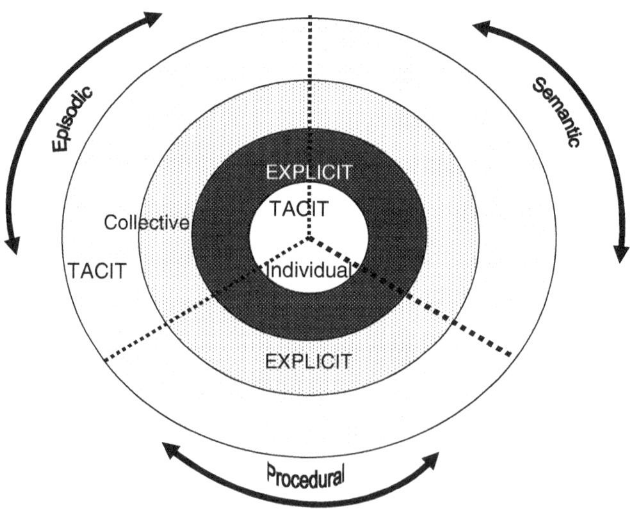

Fig. 5.1 A framework of knowledge retention structures in organizations

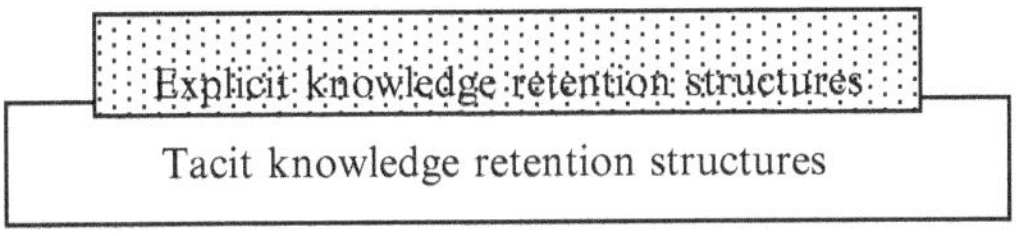

Fig. 5.2 The knowledge retention model from a different perspective

The collective tacit knowledge retention structures are shown on the outer rim, while individual tacit knowledge retention structures are shown on the inner circle. Although explicit knowledge retention structures are labeled thus because the knowledge retained is verbalized, this knowledge also has a tacit element. If the model is displayed from a different perspective, the explicit knowledge retention is shown as an addition to the tacit knowledge retention, illustrating that explicit knowledge retention emerges out of tacit knowledge retention (see Fig. 5.2).

The individual tacit knowledge retention structures are shown on the inner circle showing that the individual is critical to knowledge retention. As the individual records part of their knowledge, individual explicit structures are created (shown by the heavily shaded circle) that may become collective explicit structures if adopted by others in the organization (shown by the lightly shaded circle). Collective explicit knowledge retention structures may be created from the documentation of the collective tacit knowledge that is articulable and/or the individual explicit knowledge retention structures that are adopted at a collective level.

These knowledge retention structures have a semantic, procedural or episodic nature, or can be combinations of the three. The broken lines show that knowledge retention structures may not have firm boundaries among what is semantic, procedural, or episodic. It is important in a discussion involving explicit knowledge retention structures to determine the differences between the semantic, episodic, and procedural. Based on Tulving's work, as above, the semantic, as mentioned previously, relates to facts and figures. Thus a price list or a product structure would be a semantic explicit knowledge retention structure. The procedural is involved with action. Hence a procedure relating to a production process is an example of a procedural explicit knowledge retention structure. A technical manual that contains information relating to parts and information relating to assembly thus contains elements of both semantic and procedural knowledge. To be of an episodic nature, a knowledge retention structure requires two things: firstly to be a record of the past, and secondly, to have a subjective nature intended by the writer. Thus annual reports will often have an episodic element as the organizational leaders attempt to set an emotional tone for their past performance, although much of the content will be semantic to comply with regulatory requirements and the demands of shareholders.

When an organization's knowledge retention structures are applied against the framework, a depiction is built that highlights issues within the organization's knowledge retention structures. The individual, besides being critical for knowledge retention in the organization, is also the possessor of the individual tacit knowledge retention structures.

The Tacit Knowledge Retention Structures of the Individual

The tacit knowledge retention structures of the individual pertain to the individual's own memory as theorized by Tulving (see Tulving, 1972, 1985a, b, 2001; Tulving & Donaldson, 1972). Thus, the center of the model depicts Tulving's theory of memory for the individual in a diagrammatical form.

In the diagram shown in Fig. 5.3, the individual tacit structures shown for procedural, semantic, and episodic memory may be usefully relabeled as the individual's skills and habits, facts, and figures, and subjective past experience respectively. These knowledge retention structures, of course, make up the memory of the person, the individual who has been continually cited as the center of knowledge retention activities. When observing individuals working by themselves on a task, it becomes clear that the knowledge retention structures, that is, episodic, procedural, and semantic memory systems researched by Tulving (1972) and Singley and Anderson (1989), work in unison.

For example, in XME Australia, an accounts person was observed checking transactions for the monthly balance. Her eyes scanned a list of invoice numbers, amounts, transaction numbers, company names, cost of goods sold, and sale price. Her fingers automatically pressed the <down> key. When she saw a value that "doesn't look right," she stopped and looked more closely. She remembered that she had spoken to the accountant of that company, and that transaction was a special case. She knew from her knowledge and experience that this special case was allowable. If she recorded this conversation, this would be an explicit knowledge retention structure. She returned to the listing and continued checking.

If individuals can be conceptualized as structures of knowledge retention within the organizations, it follows that the ability and free will of individuals in terms of their continued employment with the organization put the knowledge retained within their heads at risk of loss to the organization. Although some knowledge may be converted to explicit knowledge retention structures, the unique knowledge that training, education, and experience gives each individual, and the unique interaction of semantic, episodic, and procedural memory can make organizations vulnerable to the individual's departure. This is particularly the case where no effort has been

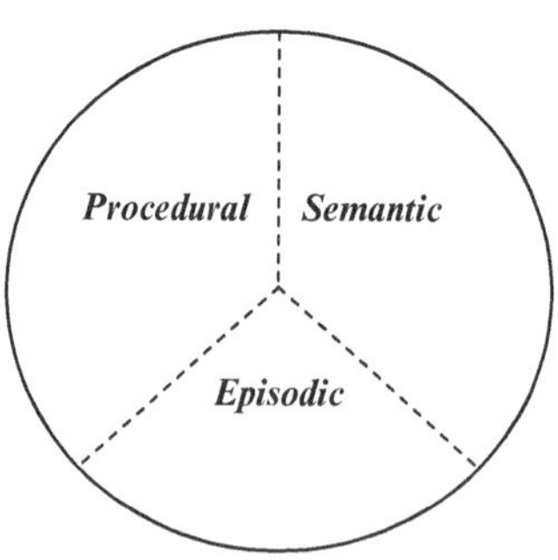

Fig. 5.3 Individual tacit knowledge retention structures

made to target and train other individuals to take over an important role in times of absence or unforeseen departure.

In XME Ireland, the managers reporting to the General Manager obviously had considerable task responsibilities. The Operations Manager was in charge of the manufacturing and assembly of the product. This meant that he was in charge of the majority of people employed in XME Ireland, as the production operators accounted for almost half of the total staff of XME Ireland. The Administration Manager, however, was in charge of all the supporting services that enabled the operations area to function, such as human resources, industrial relations and information and communications technology (ICT). She was also in charge of signing off the shipping of products to customers and dealers. The Accountant had a monitoring role in terms of the financial records of the firm, and also had an informal teaching function in helping people in the organization understand the financial systems and tasks for which they had responsibility. None of these managers, with the exception of the General Manager, had people reporting to them who could take over for extended periods of time in an emergency. Structurally, there was a significant level of difference in experience and expertise between at least two of the managers and the people assisting them. Thus the individual knowledge retention structures that these managers represented were a significant vulnerability for XME Ireland.

Another perspective on this vulnerability of the knowledge held by individuals is illustrated in the case of the Operations Manager in XME Australia who created databases that were then used by XME Ireland. This issue is slightly different to that described above relating to the XME Ireland managers in that the Operations Manager had no structural responsibility for the creation of databases. It was a skill that he enjoyed practicing, but his responsibility lay in the area of overseeing the transformation of inventions into production goods. This lack of structural responsibility meant that databases were more or less his hobby within the organization, something that the Operations Manager picked up when he had some time to spare. It was not his fault that XME Ireland needed changes to those databases, and he had to make his normal duties his highest priority. Thus Ireland did not have databases (knowledge within knowledge retention structures) that suited their specific needs. In this case then, the individual with a valued skill did not depart from the organization, but in essence was not required to practice the skill when needed, and the knowledge remained inside his head. There was no structural responsibility imposed by the organization to ensure that the collective knowledge, in the shape of the databases, was reviewed and updated.

There are several possible courses of action to reduce this vulnerability represented by the diagram.

Figure 5.4 illustrates that the tacit knowledge of the individual, which is vulnerable to the departure of the individual, may be transformed into collective tacit knowledge or collective explicit knowledge or a combination of the two. This is consistent with the identification by Mentzas et al. (2001) of the product-centered approach and process-centered approach to knowledge management, where the former involves the conversion of knowledge to an explicit medium and the latter involves social communication. Although these approaches have an "either–or"

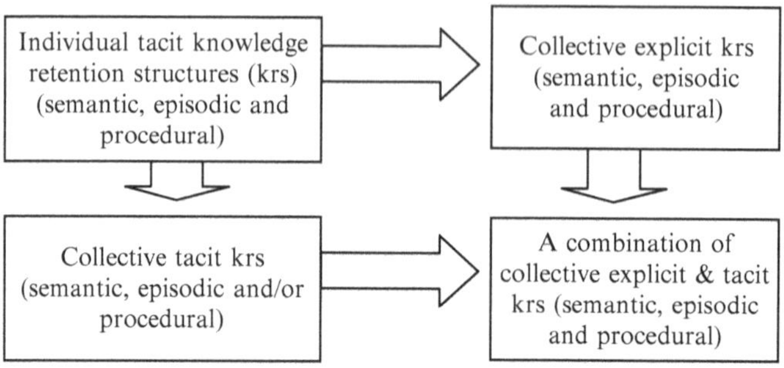

Fig. 5.4 Converting individual tacit knowledge retention structures to reduce vulnerability

flavor to them, the XME group used both to reduce their vulnerability to the departure of individuals. The choice of approach was consistent with the subculture of the relevant department.

An example in XME Australia related to an individual who had been with the organization less than a year. She used the procedures developed in her area to compensate for the lack of her organization-specific knowledge and to assist her to perform the required tasks. Thus her professional semantic knowledge was supplemented by the explicit procedural knowledge retention structures that outlined the organization-specific activity. This product-centered approach helped her work effectively while building her own procedural knowledge as her experience increased.

The strong collective in the research and development (R&D) department fostered more of a process-centered approach. XME was fortunate enough to have as their technical consultant one of the world's leading experts in the technology. He had been associated with the organization since its inception. He was a prime example of someone holding a degree of expertise that probably could not be duplicated in any other person. In XME Australia, there was a perception, however, that this central expertise was not a major vulnerability. Although acknowledging the contribution made by this person, there was a belief that the staff of the R&D area had sufficient expertise to carry on, if for any reason this leading expert could not continue with the organization. One person, when asked whether the expert's absence would be a problem, replied:

> Oh no, we have a lot of clever people here in XME.
>
> Field notes

The management team of the organization structured the work relating to R&D so that there was not a dependence on the technical consultant, although his expertise certainly contributed to the knowledge of the collective, and to the other individuals within R&D. He added significant value to the products, but the products' development was in the hands of the R&D department. Thus the collective tacit knowledge retention structures of the R&D department reduced the vulnerability to the departure of one individual.

Finally, in instances such as that shown in the case of the XME Australia Operations Manager, a combination of these two strategies is needed. In XME Ireland, they took steps to have the engineers trained in Microsoft Access so that the expertise of the Operations Manager in another operation was no longer required. In addition to this, the responsibility for the review and updating of the databases was being incorporated in the explicit authority structures of the organization. This underlines the necessity of recognizing the valuable knowledge retention structures in organizations and taking steps to reduce the risk of departure in the case of individuals or destruction in the case of explicit knowledge retention structures. A problem here is that in many cases, organizations may not perceive the value of what people do until those people leave.

Where knowledge is retained in individual explicit structures or collective structures, the distinctions among the dimensions of semantic, procedural, and episodic become more marked.

Procedural Knowledge Retention Structures: Automatic Action

Procedural knowledge retention structures are related to action. Tacit procedural knowledge may be usefully thought of as skill and/or habit and underpin much of the notion of core competency (Prahalad & Hamel, 1990). The individual interacts with the physical environment, creating and/or taking advantage of physical affordances, and establishing objects as procedural knowledge cues to streamline the process and reduce the amount of attention required for a standard action. As people contribute to different stages of the process, their knowledge of people before and after them in the process also becomes automatic. The collection of individuals' procedural knowledge merges to become an organizational routine (Cohen, 1991; Cohen & Bacdayan, 1994; Cyert & March, 1963). Successful outcomes will establish the routine in the organization; unsuccessful outcomes will cause the routines to be discarded. According to Levitt and March (1996, p. 520):

> [A] competency trap can occur when favorable performance with an inferior procedure leads an organization to accumulate more experience with it, thus keeping experience with a superior procedure inadequate to make it rewarding to use.

In XME Australia, the technical superiority of the product technology meant that some less-than-satisfactory procedures relating to inadequate testing did not appreciably affect the revenue, and therefore these procedures were retained. Routines could also cause problems at a more individual level, although these could be dealt with by effective checking measures.

Where an individual performs a part of a routine, her procedural knowledge may mean that the learned associations can be difficult to break. Individual tasks that have nonroutine features may be processed inappropriately in a routine way. A process underlying a routine may be described as a system of actions that leads to a result. In a corporate environment, processes have a variety of implications. Most, if not all, processes need to leave a trail that can be scrutinized for various purposes;

for example, processes relating to purchases must be recorded to facilitate financial reporting to the board of directors and to the various governmental regulatory bodies.

In XME checking mechanisms were embedded in the processes that encompassed the close involvement of the accounts area. Accounts staff contacted various people throughout the organization, tracking down paperwork, and seeing that the paperwork was properly filed for later retrieval when necessary.

Although checking stages and results of a process can expose inappropriate actions, it is possible that an accepted process can itself contain inappropriate or irrelevant stages as work becomes habitual and not thought about, as stated below:

> [T]he chain of causality of the experience is often lost, therefore routines may contain knowledge that is no longer appropriate to the present. Cohen and Bacdayan (1994) gave the example of a routine where motorized artillery crews were continually pausing for three seconds before firing. This pause was traced back to the time where horses were used to transport the guns; the pause was needed to hold the horses before firing.
>
> (O'Toole, 1999, p. 64)

Procedural knowledge retention structures, although automatic in nature, could be converted to an explicit form by observing individuals perform work, or visualizing individuals performing work in the case of procedures relating to new processes.

As procedural knowledge involves the learned associations between stimuli and response, this means that the explicit knowledge retention structures must document these learned associations. Documented procedures are not simply accounts of activities, such as meeting minutes or project plans. Meeting minutes are records of an activity that has passed. Project plans are documents that set out the perceived future of a planned activity. What is missing from both these examples is the account of how work should be done on a regular basis when particular stimuli occur. Explicit procedural knowledge retention structures are generally procedures and associated documents, that is, documents that show how a set of activities should progress that make up a regularly performed task. The individual who is new to the task uses the procedure as an enabling mechanism to learn the correct associations between the stimulus in the environment and his/her response. As the correct associations are learned, the explicit procedure is used less until it can be discarded.

The increasing dominance of the engineers and the implementation of ISO9000 meant that XME Australia and XME Ireland had extensive documented procedures, the explicit form of procedural knowledge. The explicit knowledge retention structures, however, could not describe every facet of the tasks. According to Nelson and Winter (1982, p. 82) "language can communicate a framework, but a great deal of filling-in remains to be done after the resources of the language are exhausted." The procedures served to make a small part of the knowledge of the Australian and Irish engineers available to the Irish production operators. In XME Ireland, as mentioned previously, the explicit knowledge retention structures, that is, the production procedures, often acted as teaching aids and then cues to stimulate the tacit procedural knowledge of individuals. An individual would start by reading the procedure carefully;

as the individual becomes more skilled, she/he may need only to glance at certain sections, to then use only an abbreviated cheat sheet to stimulate the correct response. In XME USA, there was more emphasis on verbal procedures. A more complex procedure might be quickly noted and issued via email, but the small number of people meant that it was easier to verbally communicate the intention, background, and substance of a procedure than in the larger sites in Australia and Ireland. The proximity of the people meant that checking the progress of the process was easy to accomplish.

At an individual level explicit procedural knowledge retention structures were less common, probably because they have a built-in obsolescence. Individuals tend to prepare such documents so that they remember how to perform an activity. If the document is generally useful, it will tend to become converted to a collectively available document. If it is useful only to the individual, it will often be discarded or lost as the individual's tacit procedural knowledge develops, making the document unnecessary. Although a new person starting with the organization may find such a document useful, in a dynamic organization such a document may be found to be out-of-date by the time the new recruit arrives. In XME Australia, the Accounting/Administration staff took pains to document ways of working and new processes. The staff, however, were strongly encouraged to retain these documents in suitable format on the XME Australia server so that the documents would be available to the whole department, thus becoming a collective resource.

Procedural knowledge retention structures are strongly associated with the episodic knowledge retention structures of cultures and subcultures. The perception of culture as part of episodic knowledge retention is discussed in the next section.

Episodic Knowledge Retention Structures: The Subjective Past

Episodic knowledge is not simply knowledge of the past. Tulving (2001, p. 20) described episodic memory as "making possible mental 'time travel' through subjective time," and this distinction is important. An individual's episodic knowledge is the past recalled as it happened to the individual, often with an emotional element. This subjective nature is critical to the understanding of episodic knowledge, and contributes to the individual's sense of self. Chap. 2 outlined how the sense of "I" of the individual can merge with others to become the collective sense of "We" that underpins group cultures. The collective episodic knowledge retention structures within an organization can mean that a new recruit may "remember" events that occurred before they commenced. Stories and artifacts, such as awards and pictures, are significant knowledge retention structures for collective episodic knowledge. The power of tacit episodic knowledge can be seen in the power of stories to carry emotions through time. Because of the richness of the cues, and emotional resonance of some stories, it can be futile to attempt to counteract stories with, for example, directives or memoranda. Snowden's (2000b) strategy of countering stories with other, management-endorsed, stories illustrates a situation in which one knowledge structure is pitted against another knowledge structure, where the structure with the most emotional resonance for the listener will be accepted. This resonance can be conceptualized in terms of the richness of the story for the listener. If the cues (see Huber, 1996, p. 145) in one story resonate with the past experience of a listener more than another story, then it is argued that more credence will be given to the first story. This conceptualization illustrates why silence on the part of the leaders, or an issued directive, has less power with a given audience than a resonating story.

Collective explicit episodic knowledge retention structures seem to be relatively rare within organizations. Many documents will elicit emotions in the reader, often emotions not sought by the writer. Explicit episodic knowledge retention structures, however, are documents that explicitly record subjective accounts. Thus, although the meeting minutes of XME Australia may have caused emotional reactions on the parts of the managers of XME Ireland and XME USA, these reactions were not intended by the writer and therefore the documents were not generally episodic in nature. Marketing materials, on the other hand, often contain small case studies that show the positive emotions of buyers of products. Annual reports generally include accounts of the pride, satisfaction, disappointment, and so on relating to organizational results, although also containing a significant amount of semantic knowledge. One source of explicit episodic knowledge retention structures would be emails, where the writer communicates his/her point of view or reaction to an event to the reader. This form of knowledge retention structures, although technically accessible to the organization, is generally unlikely to become practically accessible unless the writer or reader has a specific reason for further dissemination.

There are several implications relating to the lack of explicit episodic knowledge retention structures in organizations. Firstly, the subjective, emotional element of episodic knowledge may serve to set actions and consequences in a context. A small profit from a project may be disappointing or it may be far more than the project team expected. The figures alone will not enable a reader to understand the reactions of the participants. Secondly, where leaders take actions that cause dismay and distress in the organization, semantic communications from the organization's leaders are not sufficient to meet the emotional reaction of the workforce. In XME Australia, for example, while the leaders seemed to ignore the history of retrenchments several years previously, the relevant departments had a subcultural understanding that was communicated in the form of stories and banter. Another perspective on the case just described is that the semantic knowledge of the event was not retained, but a collective tacit episodic interpretation survived. Snowden (2000a, b) argued that effective knowledge management included the recognition of the sociocultural knowledge and networks that are present in organizations. Effectively, then, Snowden advocated that organizational leaders recognize the knowledge that pertains to the collective "We," that is, the episodic knowledge, as well as the semantic and the procedural. Although Gabriel (1993, 1995) argued that cultural manifestations such as stories are inherently unmanageable, Snowden viewed the fostering of stories within the organization as a significant part of the organizational knowledge management. Although, according to Snowden (2000b) organizational leaders cannot prevent people from telling stories, they can arrange to have other stories told that generate messages desirable to the organization. Alternatively, organizational leaders could also regard stories as an opportunity to obtain an alternative feedback about their actions. Whether the feedback is justified or not is irrelevant; the important point is that it is believed. Walsh and Ungson (1991) noted that causality for an event can be distorted through time. An adaptation of Snowden's thesis could therefore be used to ensure that the leaders' rationale for action is included in the episodic interpretations of the organization.

In the R&D department, for example, there was little or no evidence of explicit knowledge structures that captured the experience, or sense of what "We" did within the area. Thus the R&D department depended on the knowledge retention structures of the individuals, such as their own cognitive structures and personal logbooks to provide the emotional experience of the past. In XME Australia, the formalization and documentation of semantic and procedural knowledge retention systems was being implemented as part of the quality management system (QMS).

However, the considerable knowledge of the longer-serving employees, although utilized, was not being recorded in the form of a collective explicit episodic memory, with the exception of the military division, which retained all significant emails in both locations (i.e., Australia and Ireland). It was noted that employees were being promoted and moved around the organization, and a significant number of new employees were being recruited. It seemed that some form of episodic memory would have considerable value to the organization, but at the time of my leaving the site there appeared to be no plans in place to develop such a resource.

Semantic Knowledge Retention Structures: The Facts and Figures

The semantic knowledge retention structures are essentially encyclopedias of facts. Of the three memory systems formulated by Tulving, semantic knowledge most closely aligns with the conceptualizations of Burton-Jones (1999) and Davenport and Prusak (1998) relating to data as semantic knowledge retention structures that retain knowledge that is low in subjective meanings. Semantic knowledge, however, includes directory knowledge. Anand et al. (1998) argued that directory knowledge, that is, knowing who retains particular knowledge or where it is retained, was an important part of organizational knowledge retrieval. Semantic knowledge retention is also important in terms of how it interacts with other dimensions of knowledge. As an individual engages in practice, the semantic knowledge retention structures interact with the procedural knowledge retention structures. As subjectivity and emotions are engaged, the semantic knowledge retention structures interact with the episodic knowledge retention structures. Semantic knowledge abounds in organizations. The explicit knowledge retention structures may generally be more geared to the semantic simply because the procedural and the episodic can be filtered out during the documentation process. It is generally easier to formulate semantic documents than to include procedural and episodic information.

For example, a price list may be relatively easy to formulate. A history of the organization's development of the product and the procedure of selling included in the same document, however, would require more effort and makes the information on pricing more difficult to find. Episodic knowledge may also be deliberately omitted from explicit knowledge retention structures because of connotations concerning a lack of professionalism that seem to accompany emotional displays, particularly in the corporate sector.

In XME Australia, the individual explicit semantic knowledge retention structures retained knowledge that was valuable to the organization, particularly in the R&D area. This is a risky way of retaining knowledge. The vulnerability of explicit knowledge retention structures was highlighted in the accounts of the organizational disruption after the terrorist attacks on the New York World Trade Center on September 11, 2001. Individual explicit knowledge retention structures were found to have a new importance:

> Mr. Dadakis is now working temporarily out of the company's Greenwich office. "Every task that would normally take 10 minutes now takes me an hour because I've lost everything," he said. "When you lose your Rolodex and all the things you do business with, it's hard."
>
> (Newman, 2001, B9)

Where explicit knowledge retention structures are captured on paper, the use by a small collective does not reduce the vulnerability of the assets. Where there is only one copy of paper resources that are relied on by a group, the risk to the organization increases. In XME Australia, for example, the R&D department had a collection of references that people had built up over the years. It was mentioned by an R&D member that it would be extremely difficult to replace the reference books. According to Newman (2001, B9), after the September 11 disaster, one businessman found that

> he has to get used to ... getting by without some of his essential research materials, like a collection of academic texts that researchers in his group relied on in planning financial strategy.

In the XME group, there were extensive semantic memory systems using both ICT and paper media. Factual knowledge such as contact details, product structures, prices, financial transactions, and scientific notations were retained in either paper or ICT retention structures accessible by individuals, groups, and the organization.

The Protection of Explicit Knowledge Retention Structures

Explicit knowledge retention structures are tangible and usually in the form of signage, electronic, or paper media. Signs are usually easily replaced, and will not be further discussed. Electronic and paper media, however, often retain knowledge that is not easily replaced and can cause serious organizational dysfunction.

Although all the research sites practiced some degree of server backup, onsite storage still rendered the data sensitive. In the case of XME Australia in particular, the practice of using paper logbooks in the R&D area meant that a significant amount of valuable data was vulnerable to loss, theft, or damage.

Protection of knowledge is often not regarded as a strategic issue by organizational leaders and is delegated to the ICT staff (Anonymous, 2001). According to Gasparino and Smith (2001, C1), the damage caused by the September 11 attacks illustrated the low level of preparation and planning by organizations to meet such disasters. In one instance, "the plan left out an essential component: the firm's backup computer system, which also was damaged in the attack's aftermath." Explicit memory structures often revolve around the ICT capability of the company. As shown previously, in XME even the paper records were often simply printouts of electronic records. The ICT capability, however, was impeded due to viruses imported from external sources and with ICT problems suffered by XME Ireland and XME USA. The loss of functionality not only reduced productivity, it took up the time that could have been used for strategic ICT planning. In XME Australia, the information technology consultant used by the organization was a contractor who was kept extremely busy by the day-to-day problems of the users within XME Australia, and by problems experienced with connectivity in XME USA, and sometimes XME Ireland. Despite the fact that the XME group would have benefited enormously from the establishment of an intranet, this had not occurred.

In Australia, Ireland and the USA, there were various examples of documents that would have been useful to the other sites had they known about them. A well-organized, hyperlinked intranet or equivalent was obviously needed and would have acted as an XME group resource and reference. An intranet would have prevented duplication of knowledge creation and enabled the accumulation and display of information from all three sites. Although I was told that an intranet would be introduced eventually, it was clearly not a high priority for the company. Most of the senior managers of the company did not understand the value or functionality of an intranet, and part of this lack of understanding was attributable to the ICT contractor not having time to provide them with relevant information. Although the General Manager of XME USA seemed to support the establishment of an internet quite strongly, this support was a lone voice in the darkness.

The Australian site was commencing disaster prevention and recovery planning, which also included elements of succession planning. It was interesting to note, however, that in the months prior to this planning, some managers believed that such planning was unnecessary in an organization of their size.

The actions of the XME group illustrate how the decisions and mental models of the organization's leaders filter and affect the forces of the external environment. In XME USA, generally the backup provisions of the explicit knowledge retention structures were satisfactory for a site of that size. Even the possibility of destruction to the paper documents had been acknowledged and planned for. In other sites, ICT backup procedures had been put into place, but there had been little planning with regard to the important paper documents, especially in the R&D area, although this was being redressed with the arrival of the new Chief Executive Officer (CEO). Despite the potential loss to organizations in terms of loss of goodwill and negative publicity (Trembly, 2002), a significant number of organizations fail to embrace disaster planning and testing (Anonymous, 2001, 2003; Brown, 2003). This appears to be a symptom of a broader issue – a mindset of "it can't happen here" (see Casamayou, 1993; Vaughan, 1990, 1997). The effective protection of explicit knowledge retention structures requires an evaluation of cost of protection compared with the value of the knowledge to be protected. This protection generally entails the allocation of responsibility for protecting the knowledge, which includes a function of review and updating the knowledge, as well as strategies to ensure that the knowledge is accessible to those who need it. This accessibility requires the reproduction of explicit knowledge retention structures, that is, copying via backup DAT tapes, photocopying, and microfilming. Ensuring that there is more than one copy of an explicit knowledge retention structure, held in different locations, means that in the case of disaster the knowledge retained is still available.

The Protection of Tacit Knowledge Retention Structures

The protection of tacit knowledge is more problematic because of its nature. Tacit knowledge, being held in the heads of individuals or groups of individuals cannot be reproduced in the same way. As the cognitive structures of each individual come into play, the meaning differs. Where there is strong cultural agreement, this difference may be quite small, but is still there. Because of the subjective, emotional nature of the human beast, the knowledge held even in one individual may take on different meanings from day to day.

Thus, instead of an approach of reproduction, the protection and management of tacit knowledge requires an approach of communication and learning. If an organization actively manages knowledge, then the creation of opportunities for communication and learning must be part of the organization's culture.

Communicating and Learning: "let's just do it!"

As people within XME acted, they tended to learn; as they interacted with others, this learning was communicated to other people. The learning may have related to other people within XME Australia, it may have related to a new product or it may have related to a pregnancy or social event. The item communicated might have been known to one person and then passed on, or a group might construct the learning where it was needed. Von Krogh et al. (2000) described the ways of sharing tacit knowledge including direct observation, observation and explanation, imitation, experimentation and comparison, and joint execution, where more than one person works on a task and the more experienced may give hints to the less experienced.

Where a task was not completely known by one person in XME Australia, several members would cluster in front of a screen or around a table, each adding their mite of knowledge so that the entire process could be completed. In other words, although a task may not be known by one, it becomes known by the group, and, as the group shares their individual understandings, the whole task becomes known to each individual. Thus one person may contribute their understanding of what the end product needs to be; another may contribute their knowledge of the functionality of the system; yet another might have read about some feature of the task in a reference. By constructing this understanding of the task, a new way of working is created that may be carried on until problems occur, and a better way is constructed.

> Jane comes in. She is involved in the query. Jane says "Alana remembers lots of stuff, she's better than me." Christine says that they have to add in the Australian dealer somewhere so that it links. Jane suggests "I reckon addresses, try, try… Is it customer menus?" Alana says "I've got some notes here, if all else fails…" The three of them are staring at the screen. Alana decides to find her notes. She refers to a folder. Alana looks at each item on the menu. She questions – should they do a build. "Let's just do it!" Alana processes the build. Alana says "now, if we go in and pretend to do a sales order, that will show us if anything has happened." Alana does this "It worked!" There is some celebration. Jane says "now we should do it…," Alana says "I reckon we need to make a note somewhere that a build has to be done. … we don't have to do many new Australian customers. Do you have the procedure on this?"
>
> Field notes

In the case above, Jane, Christine, and Alana each contributes to the process of determining the correct way to process the new customers. The interaction includes a little risk-taking – "let's just do it" – and some celebration when the risk-taking worked. As they construct the correct process, each of the three retains the knowledge, and Alana takes steps to ensure the knowledge is also retained in an explicit knowledge retention structure of the organization – "we need to make a note somewhere … do you have the procedure on this?" Alana is in a leadership position within the organization, and it is clear that she sees the management and protection of knowledge as part of her responsibility. At the same time, the other members of this group actively contribute to the task of construction. In the demeanor of the members of this group, there is mutual respect and no fear of appearing stupid or incompetent. Silins and Mulford (2002) demonstrated the importance of establishing a trusting and collaborative culture to promote organizational learning. The personal autonomy that was part of XME Australia's culture also encouraged experimentation, and the proximity of the group's participants enabled them to come together to try out a new way of doing things.

A person new to an organization also may learn tacitly from a more experienced person. Polanyi (1962) described how an apprentice learns from the master. The apprentice accepts the master's authority and learns through imitation. The master provides corrective feedback, which often is not articulated in detail. Cook and Yanow (1996) described how this feedback may be along the lines of "It doesn't sound quite right," which, although not specific, succeeds with other messages in causing novices to become proficient in their craft.

The previous chapter introduced the issue of proximity as a significant factor in the effectiveness of communication. A problem that a growing company faces when the current sites outgrow the premises is who has to go off-site. When this problem faced XME Australia, it was decided to move approximately five R&D people. At the time, these people were working on industrial projects, but then industrial work was mainly suspended. Three of them came back to the main building but two had to continue work at James Street as it contained the prototypes for other products. This caused dissatisfaction among the R&D people:

> According to Yves, the separation of staff at James Street is problematic. George working on Sam's project and has to come back and forth. Telephoning is not always practicable. The production area was mooted [for the move] but management decided not to because there were too many problems transporting parts. However intellectual transportation is not a problem according to management. Clearly Yves disagrees.
>
> Field notes

The reason for this dissatisfaction was apparent. Of all the departments within XME Australia, R&D was probably the most reliant on informal face-to-face communication. One person within R&D showed me a tongue-in-cheek diagram he had created of R&D's communications network. The diagram resembled a piece of raveled knitting. To remove five people from their network, particularly specialists, was perceived to be detrimental to the working of the department. Thus the protection of tacit knowledge retention structures may take the form of taking account of the effect of changes to the geographical location on the interactions and collaborative learning opportunities of the staff. Will the organization suffer from a decrease in learning caused by geographic distance? The answer to this question will help the organizational leaders to make decisions based on likely implications rather than short-term expediency.

The coming together of Jane, Christine, and Alana was the result of an agreement to meet and resolve one specific problem. These spontaneous gatherings occurred regularly with different participants contributing to the solution of the given problem or task. In common with other organizations, each XME site had a structure of regular, scheduled meetings that created opportunities to share knowledge, albeit in a more formal way.

Meetings: "Well, we won't see you again this week"

In organizations, meetings are a taken-for-granted social practice with a variety of formats and purposes. According to Volkema and Niederman (1995, p. 5) meetings may be defined as

> a gathering of two or more people for purposes of interaction and focused communication.
>
> (Goffman, 1959; Schwartzman, 1989)

In XME, meetings were a social practice involving face-to-face communication. Despite the communication technologies available, face-to-face communication generally facilitates the communication because of the participants' capacity to read nonverbal cues such as voice tone and body language. Lantz (2001) noted in her research on face-to-face, chat, and collaborative virtual environments, that face-to-face contact is important in establishing close cooperation initially, although technology is useful after this cooperation is established. According to Lantz (2001, p. 112), face-to-face meetings have definite benefits:

> Previous research has shown that decisions are reached more rapidly in a face-to-face meeting than when an electronic medium is used.
>
> (Adriansson and Hjelmquist 1991)
>
> Text based communication takes longer time.
>
> (Lebie et al. 1995)

Meetings are more than simply a means of communication. According to Schwartzman (1989), meetings can reflect the organization by representing the organization in miniature and are a significant means of organizing the organization.

In XME USA there was a system of meetings from Monday to Thursday to ensure that people knew the things relevant to them and their position. There were complaints that there were "so many meetings," but this may be related to the fact that the meeting schedule was of fairly recent date, and people were accustomed to less frequent organized meetings. The General Manager was a dominating presence within this site and the General Manager chaired most of the meetings. Much of the interaction took the form of Volkema and Niederman's (1995, p. 5) "hierarchical meeting," where one individual is the primary sender or receiver. The participation of these meetings involved

- The managers' meeting for the General Manager and the middle managers
- The department-level meetings for the General Manager, relevant middle manager and staff of the department for the marketing/sales area and service area
- The staff meeting, where all staff would be included

The meetings confirmed the authority structures of XME USA according to who could participate at what meeting. They could, however, also take on a more organic format, where knowledge was shared freely among the participants (Volkema and Niederman, 1995) and problem solving occurred.

One incident was observed where a member of staff identified a problem, and they raised it with their middle manager. The middle manager and the staff member discussed the issue, from which emerged a recommended course of action. The issue was then raised by the manager at the managers' meeting, where the issue and the course of action was discussed and agreed, with any amendments suggested by the managers. The issue was then raised at the relevant departmental and/or staff meetings to ensure that everyone knew about the new course of action. It was noted at, for example, the staff meeting that

> [t]his meeting seems the major mechanism for promoting communication and issues. The diversity of the group means varying views on matters relevant.
>
> Field notes

The discussion of the issue in these different forums meant that not only were there a diversity of views and knowledge brought to bear on the issue, but that the issue was communicated to all the staff, where they could give their input. In these forums, moreover, the staff could see the reaction of their manager and General Manager and gain an understanding of the significance of the issue as well as its context. Minutes were not taken at these meetings. There was an expectation that people were responsible for taking their own notes and acting on decisions made. These meetings as a social practice were of importance within XME USA, but did not really impact on the rest of the XME group. The General Manager communicated significant decisions to his Managing Director in Australia directly.

In XME Australia, the regular meetings had been a requirement of the former Managing Director, and he had dictated the format. This seemed contradictory when compared to the personal autonomy encouraged by the culture; however, these meetings generally did not just have relevance for the given department or group. The XME Australia meetings often made decisions that had an impact on the rest of the XME group, which meant that a certain formality was needed to ensure that the knowledge communicated represented accurately the decisions made. Like XME USA, XME Australia had general staff meetings, but because of the greater staff numbers involved, these meetings were far less frequent and far less participatory.

In XME Ireland, the meetings were held both on a departmental basis and across XME Ireland for information gathering by specific managers. The participants at nondepartmental meetings were usually the XME managers and some technicians, and the meetings were a valuable way of finding out what was going on in other areas. Although meetings are a way of sharing knowledge, typically they are considered a necessary and sometimes time-wasting evil. In XME Ireland, when I mentioned that I was attending a managers' meeting, a staff member laughed and exclaimed:

> "Well we won't expect to see you again this week!" He was right. It lasted until about 3.10 pm, after starting from 11.00.
>
> Field notes

This managers' meeting was the most formal of the meetings in XME Ireland, with the possible exception of the military meeting. The General Manager, whose function was more marketing than overseeing the site's operations, chaired the managers' meeting. This meeting enabled him to update his knowledge on what was happening on the site and account for it to Australia. The military meeting was the formal update on the availability of military products to meet the markets served by the military manager in Ireland. Like the managers' meeting, the military meeting had minutes prepared and distributed to the XME Australia office. Unlike the other meetings in XME Ireland, these meetings were part of the accountability systems between XME Ireland and XME Australia. Other meetings in XME Ireland were held more frequently and were not considered to make decisions that had an impact on XME Australia; minutes were not prepared. People were expected to take their own notes of the discussion and decisions, and because of the frequency, it was comparatively easy to follow up on the decisions. The meetings were typical of a hierarchical structure. They were strongly chaired by the senior person at the meeting, and decisions were generally the senior person's directives after gathering information from the assembled staff rather than by participants' agreement.

When compared to the gathering of Jane, Christine, and Alana, the regular meetings of each site tended to the more formal, the more hierarchical and more of an information-gathering exercise rather than an opportunity to construct new knowledge. It seems from, for example, the relative organic nature of the XME USA general staff meeting compared to the general staff meeting of XME Australia that the greater the number of staff involved in a meeting, the more the ability to create knowledge is stultified. There are various texts available on how to organize meetings, and the expensive nature of meetings in terms of time is often deplored (e.g., Seekings, 1981). Observations of meetings in the XME group indicate that the number of staff at meetings needs to be carefully managed in terms of the underlying purpose of the meeting. Despite the common dislike of meetings found in organizations, large meetings can be an efficient mechanism for gathering and disseminating knowledge, although not so efficient for creating it.

Blocking the Retention of New Knowledge

Knowledge retention can be an asset to an organization. It can, however, also be the organization's downfall. Knowledge that is deeply entrenched in the organization's culture and structures can cause the blocking of new and valuable knowledge. Where the knowledge relates to a change in the environment, and the old knowledge has previously been a core competency, the results can be disastrous for the organization.

Core competencies, or core capabilities as Leonard-Barton (1992, 1995) called them, are those collective attributes that add significant value to the organization, are not possessed by other organizations, are difficult and costly to imitate and have no real strategic equivalent (Hitt, Ireland, & Hoskisson, 2003). The notion of core competence is used in strategic planning to focus on the knowledge retained within the organization that contributes most to the organization's strategic advantage. When the concept of core competencies is examined within the framework of the knowledge retention model, issues are exposed that highlight the vulnerability of knowledge retention structures, and point to potential or actual knowledge rigidities that inhibit the effectiveness of the organization. Core rigidities, according to Leonard-Barton (1995, p. 30), "are the flip side" of core competencies. Essentially, knowledge rigidity occurs when the knowledge retained in the organization impedes the flow of different knowledge that may be valuable to the organization. Effective knowledge management necessarily meets and overcomes these obstacles to improved organizational effectiveness. A famous example of knowledge rigidity relates to the Xerox company where the organization kept producing photocopiers that had been superseded by their competitors (Henderson, 1996). This section shows how factors in the organization can lead to the blocking of new and valuable knowledge in the organization, and the issue of core competencies and rigidities in the XME group are explored. The factors promoting rigidities, according to Leonard-Barton (1995), are dispositional, political and/or economic.

Dispositional Factors

At an individual level, there are various reasons why existing knowledge may block the retention of new knowledge, which may be classified into reasons relating to trust, habit, and cultural influences.

For people to accept and absorb new knowledge, there is an issue of trust. Generally they need to trust the purveyor of the knowledge. McDowell (2002) classified these issues of trust relating to knowledge into two parts: epistemic trust and social trust. Epistemic trust means that the receiver of the message trusts the communicator to have information that is truthful and accurate. Social trust, however, has more indirect but still powerful effects on whether the receiver will seek out or even accept unsolicited messages from the communicator. Social trust has two facets. One facet is termed by McDowell as "communication worthiness"; in other words: is the communicator socially trustworthy? A common example of this may be the reluctance of people to approach a person who, although an acknowledged expert, may also be obnoxious and unpleasant. The second facet is "inferential effects" where, because the communicator perhaps does not conform to the receiver's notions of socially acceptable behavior, the receiver infers that they are not a trustworthy source of information. An example of this may be when a person is sloppily dressed, and others infer that he is not as competent as someone who wears a business suit. Adler (2002) foresaw that a knowledge-intensive society would need trust as a coordination mechanism, and that this trust would be built upon values of competence and integrity, that is, epistemic trust. Social trust and simple human friendship, however, also facilitate the communication of knowledge throughout the organization.

The mental set of the individual, which they may not be aware of, may sometimes obstruct novel solutions and applications (Sternberg, 1999; Morris, 1988; Birch & Rabinowitz, 1951). When dealing with new approaches to existing concepts, there is a tendency in some people to be unable to see novel applications. This inability is termed by the cognitive psychologists as "functional fixedness." Anderson (1995, p. 264) defined functional fixedness as "people's tendency to represent objects as serving conventional problem-solving functions, thus failing to see their serving novel functions." Functional fixedness is, perhaps, a symptom of the human ability to streamline life. Although it means that no conscious information-processing resources in the brain are needed when they need to use a familiar tool or process to accomplish a routine task, it also means that the individual may suffer a cognitive inability to perceive the novel, which diminishes the ability to formulate creative solutions. This ability to streamline life may also be discerned in organizational routines. Routines can become engrained instead of the organization adopting a better way to accomplish goals (Ashforth & Fried, 1988; Cohen, 1991; Cohen & Bacdayan, 1994; Leonard-Barton, 1992, 1995; Nonaka & Reinmoeller, 2000).

Berman, Down and Hill (2002, p. 17) suggested that, when a group comes together, there is a period of intense learning as the members' learn to work with each other, and group schemas are formed, supported by a store of tacit knowledge. Routines develop as a result, which may mean that the group becomes less open to change. As the ways of working are tacit, and therefore unconscious, unlearning behavior may be very difficult to accomplish. It has been suggested by various authors that, by taking new members in the group, new learning can be increased, through the knowledge of new technology (Berman, Down, & Hill, 2002) and new ways of working (March, 1996).

Cultural elements of an organization or a team may promote knowledge rigidities. The new knowledge may require a new language (von Hippel, 1994), which may be difficult to introduce because organizational language is created and developed over time (von Krogh & Roos, 1995). Cyert and Goodman (1997), for example, discussed how one of the major difficulties with university–industry alliances was that the languages of the two organizations are different, reflecting the different cultures and goals of the parties. Alternatively, organizational stories may foster a culture of rigidity and fear of trying new things as shown in the following example:

> Consider an engineer who wants to convince his group to develop new software for steering a production line. He might be told, "Don't you remember that guy Finch, the one who tried to do stuff like that himself. Well, he's not with us anymore."
>
> (von Krogh et al., 2000, p. 24)

Political Factors

Political factors refer to power, whether it be the individual's power within the organizational hierarchy or the individual's perception of personal power. Where the knowledge that an individual must assimilate is too "new" and does not fit within the scripts or schemas previously assimilated by the individual, the individual will have difficulty in integrating the knowledge and therefore put barriers against it (von Krogh et al., 2000). This conflict will be exacerbated if the individual is viewed as an expert within the organization. This expertise is often critical to the individual's self-image, and if the new knowledge puts this self-image at risk by making this expertise worth less than previously (or even worthless), then the individual will usually have considerable difficulty in accepting the new order.

At an organizational level, organizations have political structures relating to how knowledge is acquired, accessed, and stored. Where these structures are threatened by new ways of operating, the power, status, and influence of individuals may also be threatened (Coopey, 1995, 1996). It may be that the hierarchy of power within an organization is based on knowledge, such as that of old technologies. Where a new technology is promoted by line operators, people at the top of the hierarchy may feel threatened because the reason for their power is being undermined, and therefore they work to block the new technology from being adopted (Leonard-Barton, 1995).

Economic Factors

Core rigidities may be promoted by the underlying economic structures of the organization. The organization, for example, may have product lines that represent rigidity in thinking, for example, IBM's commitment to technology that supported the mainframe business, even though microcomputers were emerging as a potent new force in technology markets (Leonard-Barton, 1995). Where the organization's leaders have made heavy investments in particular directions there is often a marked disinclination to change direction and therefore effectively lose the investment. The disinclination to lose the investment is also tied to the political "face" of the leaders, who are unlikely to want to be associated with a mistake in strategy. In XME, the DO_IT software was a prime example of rigidity caused by economic and political reasoning, albeit not a rigidity that was associated with a core competency. The DO_IT software was expensive to introduce and establish but XME did not invest enough to properly tailor the software to their company. The software was established in all three sites, and the deficiencies of the software were obvious to all who used it. Even the accounting staff, for whom the software was most functional, had to use supplementary Excel spreadsheets that were manually prepared because of the lack of an ad hoc reporting function and the inability to download data. The former Managing Director, having made the investment, would not listen to complaints because of a hefty personal and political stake in the software.

Thus the behavioral, political, and economic factors that impede the retention of new knowledge are usually present to some degree in an interconnected and synergistic way. There is often a bias toward solving problems in well-defined ways; there will be reasons not to innovate; experimentations will often be based on the interests and expertise of existing staff and external knowledge will be ignored and/or discounted (Leonard-Barton, 1995).

Core Competencies and Rigidities in XME Australia

In XME the core competencies enabled the manipulation of the electronic fields that were critical to the effectiveness of the technology. These core competencies sat squarely in the R&D area. The competencies that evolved in Operations, Accounting and other areas were enabling or supplemental competencies, which were not unique to XME or hard to duplicate (Leonard-Barton, 1995, p. 4), although they contributed mightily to the effectiveness of the organization.

Leonard-Barton (1995) argued that core competencies (and rigidities) are comprised of:

- Physical technical systems
- Employee knowledge and skills
- Values and
- Managerial systems

When the XME core competencies are examined in light of these dimensions, the vulnerability of this strategic strength of the organization becomes apparent. The physical technical systems are the ICT and paper systems, the equipment and other tangibles that the R&D use and that become knowledge retention systems over time. As stated previously, much of the explicit knowledge used in R&D was at an individual level, which immediately points to an area of vulnerability. The employee knowledge and skills in the R&D area were a critical part of the core competency. Part of the uniqueness of this resource can be attributed to working with the technical consultant who was a world leader in this form of technology; part can also be attributed to the recruitment strategies of the organization; and part can be attributed to the values of the R&D area. The values that characterized the R&D area revolved around personal autonomy and collaboration. Leonard-Barton emphasized the importance of knowledge flow in fostering core competencies, and this knowledge flow was overtly apparent in the R&D area. There generally seemed to be a high level of epistemic trust, and social trust was encouraged by the playful banter. The R&D area was an open plan area which facilitated communication.

The managerial systems alluded to by Leonard-Barton pertain to the "organized routines guiding resource accumulation and deployment" (p. 23) and include the processes relating to compensation, incentives, and human resource development. The problem in XME Australia was that the managerial systems and some cultural elements (values) promoted core rigidities that stood in the way of organizational effectiveness.

The rigidities in XME Australia in terms of the R&D area were discernible in the tensions experienced between the R&D department and other sections of the site, and result from the schemas or mental models held by the people in R&D and the organizational leaders. Earlier, the dissatisfaction with the management policy toward product testing was outlined. The people in the R&D area complained that they were not given enough time to properly test new products before the product was transferred to the Operations area. This meant that when products were transferred to XME Ireland or released to the public, product returns and complaints would ensue. Part of this problem could be attributed to the tacit values of the R&D area and the organization. XME had experienced dramatic growth because of the technical superiority of its products. Other competitors could not duplicate the technology. Hence a core rigidity evolved that is labeled by Leonard-Barton (1995, p. 32) as "overshooting the target," where organizations "succumb to the simplistic notion that more of a good thing is always better." In XME, the superior performance of the organization had been attributable to the superior technology; hence there was a value to keep producing products that were superior to the competition. Because the former Managing Director was under pressure from the Board of Directors to produce revenue, he was loath to allow the R&D people the time that they thought they needed to properly test the products. The framing of the issue therefore was whether or not the R&D people should be allowed more time for product testing as the products became more technically complex. The new Chief Executive Officer, however, framed the problem in a different way. The new CEO pointed out that improving the products so much in a short time was wasting the chance of having future upgrades based on their current technology. Staggering the upgrades in this way, provided the market permitted, was also a way of keeping critical knowledge within the organization so that its value was retained over a longer period. This in turn would mean that the required testing time for each upgrade would be shorter.

This solution to the issue of testing time, although a fairly simple one, had simply not occurred to the other members of XME Australia. The value of superior technological development had caused them to continually overshoot the target to the detriment of the quality of their products, illustrating the power of habit, as discussed previously, when merged into a cultural value. They had learned to overwhelm the market with technological superiority. This was something that the CEO was going to have to make them unlearn, and it was likely to cause some degree of consternation.

Another core rigidity was fostered because of the success of the organization. Some of the success stories heard in XME Australia related to the reaction of customers when they first tried the XME products. The continued success caused a mindset of not really listening to the customers, which some of the XME people recognized:

> I ask about market research. [R&D staff member] says that doesn't really happen. "The attitude tends to be 'We are going to make a water proof [product] and you're going to love it'. That happens a lot."
>
> Field notes

This mindset also was translated into a dearth of people within the XME group who extensively used the products as consumers. XME Ireland and XME USA had, respectively, one and two avocational experts who were employed for their experience. Although the level of communication had improved, there was still dissatisfaction with the amount of credibility that these experts had with the R&D area. XME was coming to grips with the value of knowledge outside the R&D area, and the new CEO was playing a significant role in introducing new mindsets to the company. But it was taking time. And it needed a new CEO to identify and confront them with the rigidities.

Conclusion

This chapter introduces a holistic model of knowledge retention that draws together the different dimensions and characteristics of knowledge retention and shows their interaction. The critical role played by the individual in knowledge retention is acknowledged by the individual's placement at the center of the model of knowledge retention explored in this chapter. The ubiquitous nature of tacit knowledge is shown by the placement from the outer rim to the center where the individual resides. Explicit knowledge is a product of human activity and is shown as an overlaid component. Organizations involve physical objects and infrastructure as well as people, and an effective model of knowledge retention must take these organizational elements into account.

The dimensions of the tacit/explicit duality and the individual/organizational duality have been explored in the literature; however, the nature of the dualities, rather than a concentration of one or other of the dimensions, may lead to far richer understandings of organizations. The inclusion of Tulving's constructs acknowledges the place of action, subjectivity, and emotion in organizations in addition to the facts which have been traditionally emphasized in the rationalist, functionalist accounts of organizational research (Burrell, 1997; Porac & Garud, 1999).

Explicit knowledge can be protected by reproduction and retention in different sites. Tacit knowledge can be protected by communicating and learning. Communication and learning, however, are human activities and thus require more complex and human mechanisms. The issue of trust and the quality of relationships are necessary facilitators of organizational tacit knowledge retention. At the same time, the explicit knowledge retention structures of an organization can be critical to the performance of the individual, and yet many organizations delegate the responsibility for knowledge protection to the lower levels of the organization. In the case of individual knowledge retention structures, there may be no acknowledgment of their value until disaster occurs.

Knowledge retention is clearly a critical component of organizations; however, the discussion on core competencies and core rigidities shows that this critical component has a darker side. The group mental models that form over time when the organization is successful can blind the organization to deficiencies in practices and opportunities lost. The core competency model of Leonard-Barton, however, can be very useful when applied against the knowledge retention model, to identify vulnerabilities in the retention of the very knowledge that makes the organization successful. Clearly, to protect and manage the knowledge retained within organizations, organizational leaders need to first identify and then understand it.

Chapter 6
How Organizations Retain Knowledge

The new recruit clicks the "send" button, and closes her email. She wonders what they will think of the drawings at the Irish site. She only had to finish a few things off, her predecessor had done most of it, but she has added some notes to the spec as she had learnt to do in her old job.

****

"Did you go to that new pub last night then?" asks the Production Supervisor. "Mmm, great craic there – you should go," replies the Engineer absently as he leafs through the drawings he has just collected from the printer. "Jesus, look at this! The Australians just sent it!" the Engineer exclaims, extracting one paper and holding it at arm's length. The Production Supervisor peers at the spec through her glasses. "My God, what's come over them, then? This will make life easier."

Introduction

Knowledge retention structures in organizations are the result of a range of complex influences both within and outside the organization, and at all levels. This chapter sets out a discussion and conclusions drawn from the study of the XME group. It is based on the assumption that knowledge is constructed in the minds of individuals in interaction with each other and their environment. An individual does not come to the organization as a *tabula rasa*. The individual, however, is more than a unit of knowledge retention: individuals also function as components of complex systems of knowledge retention in the form of structural units, that is, departments within the company, communities of practice, cultures, subcultures and social networks. The complexity of the networks, together with the variety of individuals in the networks, means that knowledge retention within organizations may be managed and deliberate and have the effect of engendering knowledge retention that is unmanaged and informal but still powerful. This chapter focuses on how knowledge retention structures develop; how knowledge is communicated; and issues in the management and protection of knowledge.

P. O'Toole, *How Organizations Remember: Retaining Knowledge through Organizational Action*, Organizational Change and Innovation 2, DOI 10.1007/978-1-4419-7524-9_6,

How Do Knowledge Retention Structures Develop?

The creation and level of use of knowledge retention structures by individuals determine the structures' dominance within the organization. What causes individuals to use the knowledge retention structures that they do? The influences that determine this usage revolve around:

- The culture and occupational subcultures of the organization
- The demands of the regulatory and other entities in the external environment
- The actions and decisions of the organization's leaders and
- The past experience of the staff

The Culture and Occupational Subcultures

The development and usage of knowledge retention structures is heavily influenced by the culture of the organization. The culture itself is in turn influenced by the subjective history of the organization, and the dominant subcultures within it. In XME Australia, for example, the past dominance of the research and development (R&D) people caused a culture of personal autonomy but also meant that a legacy of individual knowledge retention structures and collective tacit knowledge retention structures were significantly used, particularly in the R&D department. This legacy was much more widespread until the entry of the engineers had caused a new focus and use of collective explicit structures, particularly of a procedural nature. The knowledge retention structures were also subject to an accounting influence due to the long service of the two most powerful accountants in the organization, the former Managing Director and the Accounts Manager. The influence of the occupations could particularly be seen in the comparison between XME Ireland and XME Australia. In Australia, the production operators were relatively fewer and more separated from the rest of the organization. In XME Ireland, they were relatively more numerous and their output was the focus for the site. In XME Australia, email was far more widely used as a knowledge retention structure and communication device than in XME Ireland. In XME Ireland, paper documents were more widely used. In both sites, the production operators did not have access to a computer, but in XME Ireland the production operators were far more visible and dominant.

The Demands of External Entities

The raft of legislative and other external requirements caused a heavy investment in explicit knowledge retention structures to capture the required knowledge in formats acceptable to these external entities. According to Anderson (1995), the capture of knowledge by explicit means serves to counteract decay and interference of knowledge. The supply of this knowledge in an explicit, predetermined format by professionals ensured that the meanings embedded in this explicit knowledge would be generally understood by those professionals, so that compliance with the external entity's requirements could be evaluated. Thus, for example, ISO9000 auditors could view the documents and records pertaining to the XME Australia quality management system (QMS), and evaluate whether XME Australia complied with the relevant ISO9000 standard.

The growth of the company and the entry into foreign markets meant that XME had to create systems to collect and retain semantic knowledge in explicit knowledge retention structures to meet the knowledge demands of a host of external entities. DO_IT was the focus of this knowledge retention, but in XME Ireland and XME USA procedures also had to be created to organize the communication of the knowledge to the corporate center, XME Australia, for dissemination to the relevant authorities. The knowledge retention structures created were often not the most efficient or most productive for the site, but what was demanded by XME Australia to ensure consistency. Where the collective knowledge retention structures enforced by XME Australia were deficient, the individuals within XME Ireland and XME USA used their own ingenuity to overcome or live with those deficiencies. Surprisingly, although DO_IT was imposed upon the subsidiaries, it was also a signal of increasing autonomy for the individual site. Thus the knowledge retention structures were accepted far more readily than may have been supposed. Like the employees cited in Scribner's (1986) work, there were numerous instances of individuals finding least-effort solutions to making the knowledge retention structures work, thereby creating yet another set of knowledge retention structures. The implementation of these imposed knowledge retention structures was the result of decisions by the organization's leaders, another major influence on knowledge retention structures.

The Decisions and Actions of the Organization's Leaders

The decisions and actions of the organization's leaders have a significant effect on the knowledge retention structures used across an organization. These decisions and actions, although overtly arrived at through a process of rational decision making, are strongly affected by the leaders' own previous experience, occupational orientation, and by the focus of the business.

In XME, for example, the accounting background of the former managing director influenced the decision to purchase DO_IT, a software application with a strong accounting functionality, but that was less strong on the production side. Similarly, it was clear that the former managing director did not really understand the benefits of intranet technology. The new chief executive officer (CEO) committed to establishing an intranet in the future, as he had experience of an intranet in his previous company.

The organizational leaders have power over the budget, which determines what forms of knowledge retention structures are used by the staff. The organizational leaders also have the power to demand knowledge on particular issues at particular times, which can lead to the staff forming their own routines to meet the needs of the leaders. If these demands, or the leaders themselves, change, then the staff have to change their behavior to cope with the new demands, perhaps leading to new knowledge retention structures.

Past Experience of the Staff

The past experience of individuals meant that they had often formed practices before entering the XME group. These practices were usually based on what they had learned in previous organizations as well as knowledge acquired through professional training. In addition to knowledge in the form of practices, people also brought knowledge in the form of what *should* be done and what results should be achieved, that is, expectations. These expectations were generally of two types. The first type of expectation took the form of a psychological contract (Rousseau & Parks, 1993), where individuals had expectations regarding their rights and duties as employees and the organization's rights and duties as an employer. The second type of expectation related to the values and objectives pertaining to what individuals regarded as good practice, for themselves, their department/occupation and their organization. Where their expectations were not met, a degree of frustration was caused. The culture that enabled some degree of personal autonomy caused them to try to resolve the frustration by changing their workplace in some way to achieve a better result. The example of the engineering action report is noteworthy here, where a form that was used by a person in a previous workplace was successfully implemented in the XME group with the support of other people who also had worked in the former workplace.

The four significant factors outlined, that is, culture and subcultures, demands of external entities, the leaders' actions and the past experience of staff, interact and are themselves a result of two other factors, namely the growth of the business and the focus of the site. The entry of people to XME Australia had an effect on culture and structure as shown in Chap. 3 March (1996) found that when individuals entered an organization there were varying degrees of adaptation to reach an equilibrium by both the organization and the individual. When a large number of individuals enter an organization in a specific window of time, the organization tends to adapt more dramatically, particularly where the individuals entering the organization hold similar values and beliefs. This could be seen in XME Australia, where number of individuals who were trained in the creation and use of collective explicit knowledge retention structures joined the organization, and, as a result, the organization started to become more formalized in the keeping of documentation and procedures. The growth and entry of new subcultures to the company thus created new forms of knowledge retention structures that were in fact quite alien to the dominant culture. As the needs of the business required new forms of knowledge retention structures, they became increasingly dominant within the company. The focus of each site also had a considerable impact on the formation of knowledge retention structures both directly and indirectly. The focus of the site, in the case of the XME group, the central office, the production site and the selling site, affected the employment of specific individuals and the physical infrastructure at the site.

The next section deals with the individual as an organizational knowledge retention structure, and the role of the physical environment in knowledge retention.

The Individual as an Organizational Knowledge Retention Structure

The role of the individual as the driver of action and knowledge retention has been a significant theme throughout this work. In the research sites, human action was a direct influence on the dominance of retention structures. When discussing the dominance of knowledge retention structures, the individual as a structure of the organization has to be identified because knowledge is a function of the interaction with the individual's cognitive structures with the external world. Scribner's (1986, 1997a, 1997) "least-effort solution" has been identified as a major theme in how individuals managed their interaction with the external world. In all of the research sites, the least-effort solution allied to the personal autonomy of the people involved meant that if one person generated a useful knowledge retention structure that was noticed by others, they would adopt the use of the structure, leading to a "contagion of usefulness." In XME USA, it was noticeable that a number of people printed out monthly appointment calendars from Outlook. In XME Australia, people created paper records to facilitate materials handling. If a person decides to display or use a particular document, and others judge that this display is useful or fulfills some other purpose, they are likely to copy the idea. Thus, at a local level, a knowledge retention structure can increase in dominance as its effectiveness is proven. Undeniably, however, there were specific individuals who were sought out by others to act as a knowledge resource.

Boundary spanners, according to Tushman and Scanlan (1981), have strong links both within and outside the organization and are able to communicate information effectively. In XME Australia it was found that the increasing size of the organization encouraged individuals to walk around to discover what was going on. The accounting staff and operations staff in particular needed to continually walk to other areas with queries relating to their own function, and would find out other things going on in the organization. Another role was ascertained within the XME group, which I labeled "knowledge node." These people did not necessarily have to move around the organization to span boundaries; people came to them because they were significant knowledge retention structures. It was apparent in each of the sites that various individuals acted as "knowledge nodes" within their organizations at different levels of the company to fill different needs. When these individuals are compared it seems that, besides having collected the knowledge either through documents or their own cognitive structures, they also shared a cheerful willingness to answer questions and help the enquirer. Questions would be answered comprehensively, without making the enquirer feel that he/she was being a pest. This is an example of building the epistemic and social trust identified by McDowell (2002).

These people were not "knowledge activists" (von Krogh et al., 1999), in the sense of aggressively going out to find out what was happening across organizational boundaries. On the contrary, they attracted people from other areas as they became known for their knowledge and their willingness to help. The knowledge that they retained may have concerned complex organizational issues or simply possess a folder containing every form that anyone would ever need. The knowledge nodes themselves gained knowledge from enquirers about what was taking place in other areas of the organization or the XME group. A problem with the establishment of individuals as knowledge nodes within the organization, however, is whether the individuals who assume these roles are really knowledgeable in the areas of expertise they claim. Stein (1989) noted the instance within an organization of an individual who was reputed to be extremely knowledgeable about accounts. When a person who genuinely was knowledgeable about accounting joined the company and questioned her, he found that her knowledge was sketchy at best.

The sensitivity of the knowledge retained by the "node" was usually dependent on their position on the organizational chart. It was clear in all the sites of the XME group that the knowledge shared depended to a large extent on whether the employee was a manager or not. In XME Ireland, there were some things that the management was reluctant to communicate to the production operators that could be known by the technicians/supervisors. In XME Australia, the payroll clerk was given more access to sensitive information than was usual for her hierarchical level in the organization. In this case, there was a tension between the physical environment and the individual, as the hierarchical status of the individual meant that she/he had to work on the sensitive information in the open floor plan area of the organization instead of in an office. Proshansky et al. (1995) pointed out the confusion and unhappiness that workspace allocation can cause when mismatched by the structural status of the individual. This example illustrates the problems caused when the level of knowledge access is unusual at a particular level in the hierarchy of the organization.

The Individual and Their Work Environment

There were strong indications in the research sites that the existence and placing of physical objects in the workspace of individuals acted as cues for the retrieval of retained procedural memory. Most of the people in the XME group had the autonomy to place their objects as they wished. As individuals became used to the position of objects, this positioning would become part of their procedural processes. Polanyi explained the "indwelling" of the promixal terms with regard to the distal terms. In Chap. 2 an example is given of driving a car (the distal term), and how the competent driver does not consciously attend to braking, steering and indicating (proximal terms). Polanyi (1967), however, did not explicitly deal with the importance of the positioning of the objects related to the proximal terms, such as the steering wheel and the pedals. Where the objects, such as the indicators, differ from what is cued in procedural memory, the driver can proceed to wash the windows instead of signaling a left-hand turn. An example of this was the accounting clerk who, moving to another workspace, needed to order her files and objects in a particular way before she was comfortable working. The object forms a cue to facilitate retrieval of the procedural memory. When the object is missing, the individuals have to change from primarily a procedural mode; they access their declarative memory to think about what they need and where it might be.

Physical objects and place interacted with the individual's procedural knowledge to generate activity. It seems that the intersection of the physical object and the individual is also the intersection of constructivism with cognitive psychological theories, as the local and situated interact with the cognitive structures of the individual. The physical environment thus represents a class of knowledge retention structure with which the individual interacts, often as part of a process. Also of significance was the role that physical cues played in the performance of the processes. This is discussed in the next section.

The Individual as Part of a Process

Knowledge retention structures can emerge and change through the agreement of individuals to formulate processes in order to achieve an outcome. The success of processes in achieving desired outcomes is dependent on a series of factors, such as the feedback mechanisms that are built into the process and the degree of physical affordance for the process. Processes are a particularly dominant knowledge retention structure in organizations as they bring together individuals, the physical environment and documents to enhance an activity. In establishing processes, individuals will usually need to communicate within teams, sites or across the organization.

A process starts as an agreement between the people involved in the activity or responsible for the activity. The activity may lead to explicit knowledge capture regarding the process, that is, a documented procedure and/or a review or alteration of the physical environment to facilitate the process. Individuals perform the process, and as part of the activity, explicit knowledge retention structures such as the completion of forms are created. The individual draws on explicit knowledge retention structures such as the documented procedure, training and reference material, and previous examples of the forms or work orders. In addition, the individual interacts with the physical environment, creating and/or taking advantage of physical affordances and establishing objects as procedural knowledge cues to streamline the process and reduce the amount of attention required for a standard action. Physical objects manifest perceptual cues that act as a message for the participants, for example, the height of papers in an in-tray.

As people contribute to different stages of the process, their knowledge of people before and after them in the process also becomes automatic. The collection of individuals' procedural knowledge merges to become an organizational routine (Cohen, 1991; Cohen & Bacdayan, 1994; Cyert & March, 1963). The routine continues to be supported by the existence and configuration of the objects, equipment and floor space that make up the physical environment.

Knowledge Retained in the Physical Environment

In the workplace, the physical environment retains knowledge relating to both the culture and the way work is done; hence in XME Ireland, the production area is the center of the building, just as it is the center of the activities. The physical environment, by being the site of work activity, becomes a manifestation of culture and structure. The entry sites of the three organizations are examples of these manifestations. Visitors to XME Australia would probably have observed clues to the different subcultures and operations of each department as they viewed the degree of order/disorder, the presence of products and components or not, and the types of desks, workbenches and racks. In XME USA, products and components were present in the workplace, but in a different form than XME Australia. In XME USA, the products were part of a display. Components were kept in the warehouse or in the repair workshop; they were not placed around desks and work benches for the convenience of the engineers working on them, as in XME Australia and XME Ireland: XME USA had no engineers. Thus the day-to-day ways of working and available resources shaped the physical environment, which in turn emanated messages about the ways of working.

In comparing all the XME sites, a persistent theme of structuration (Giddens, 1984, p. 2; Turner, 1986) emerges. Gibson's theory of physical affordance (Gibson, 1979) postulated that the physical environment provides opportunities to the individual. For example, a chair may offer an opportunity to the individual to use the chair for seating, as a bench or as a prop. On the other hand, the individual does not passively accept what the physical environment affords. If the individual feels dissatisfaction with the environment, then, provided that the individual has the power to change things, the physical environment will change. Thus the environment influences the activities of the individual; however, the individual may change the environment for their own purposes.

An organization is organized to perform activity and achieve objectives. An organization's processes then are the manifestations of the performance of organized activity, or according to Delbridge et al. (1997) processes are a systematic series of actions directed toward one end. Processes link with other knowledge retention structures as the process progresses, so that a process will require individuals, physical artifacts, paper and electronic documents, and have elements pertaining to the culture and structure of the organization embedded within them.

In XME USA, a new procedure would stimulate the allocation of plastic trays, envelopes being prepared and so on and being placed as needed. Gibson's (1979) theory of affordance was seen to come into play as the physical environment was altered by the process's participants to make it easier to follow the process. The existence of documentation was dependent on the nature of the process, the stage of the process and the people performing the process. In the XME group, when recently developed products were released to customers, the processes and documentation with regard to production were documented and retained in the vault in XME Australia, theoretically being accessible to all XME sites. In fact, when a product was released, there was an expectation that the product would be accompanied by specifications, drawings, procedures, instruction manuals and brochures. There was a relationship between the development stage of the product and the degree of documentation that could be expected. It is suggested that this was not simply a factor of the time available to document, but an expectation that the amount of change in the product would diminish. This meant that it was more feasible to complete substantial documentation as the development stages progressed. The closer the product was to being provided to the client, the more procedures were implemented to reduce variability, that is, to make the product conform to the standards set by the organization. This was particularly necessary in the case of the XME group because much of the production was removed from the people who created the processes. The clients needed to receive a product that conformed to the specifications in the instructions, on the packaging and in the advertising. Documenting the processes was necessary to produce this degree of conformity, and to comply with the requirements of ISO9000. In XME USA, on the other hand, the membership of the organization was fairly stable, the people involved in the process were generally involved in its formulation and the organization was changing and growing. Thus documentation was considered too onerous at that stage of the organization and not attempted.

It is clear from the preceding discussion that the influences on knowledge retention are dynamic, complex and interact with each other. This points to the need to align knowledge retention structures that are used for a single, particular purpose, for example, where a strategy and/or process needs to be introduced, the physical environment, information and communications technology (ICT) resources, documentation as well as the individuals involved need to be geared toward the same purpose. Where individuals have a deficient knowledge retention structure imposed upon them, they will often create other knowledge retention structures to compensate for this deficiency; however, this will cost time and resources, reducing organizational effectiveness. It has to be remembered, however, that individuals are knowledge retention structures in their own right and work in concert with other individuals. This implies the need for collective tacit knowledge retention structures such as the culture and organizational structure also to be aligned to the organizational goals underlying the processes, as well as to the processes themselves.

An important organizational knowledge retention, particularly in terms of collective tacit knowledge retention, is the communication of knowledge.

Retaining Knowledge Through Communication

The communication of knowledge is a significant factor of organizational knowledge retention. The communication of the knowledge, after all, is essentially the process of converting individual knowledge to collective knowledge. The people involved in the communication need to overcome varying degrees of distance. The distance may be small, and therefore negligible, as when face-to-face interaction occurs, or it may be considerable such as when communication occurs between people in different countries. Distance can be geographical, but it may also be temporal as when communication occurs between people in different time zones, and structural as when people have to communicate across levels within the organization, or cultural as when people from different cultures have to communicate.

Proximity and Distance

In all the sites, proximity enhanced communication for a variety of reasons. Proximity was more likely to enable activities and conversations to be visible and audible to others. Proximity also enabled managers to quickly call meetings of all or some of the people within the area. In XME Ireland, it was easy to call meetings of the staff engaged in production, to plan out issues and activities. In XME Australia, on the other hand, a lack of proximity between production and the other departments contributed to a separation of the staff engaged in production from the staff of other areas. Where two staff members with similar functions moved together, they were seen to compare ways of working to the mutual benefit of both. Doz et al. (2001) maintained that the benefits of proximity were advantages of co-location, where people engaged in a particular feature of work were located in one site. They argued that the richness of face-to-face communication, high frequency of interaction and the chance encounters and shared language that people employed when located at the same site were powerful advantages to having people located at one site. When the communications within XME Australia are compared with, say, the communications between XME Australia and XME Ireland, the statements of Doz et al. (2001) have a certain amount of justification.

Doz et al., however, did not take into account the effects of department/occupational subcultures and the separation that can occur in a large building. Co-location undoubtedly has benefits where people located in one site have a chance to get to know each other. It is possible, however, that people can work in the same building in similar areas and not know of each other's existence. It is also possible that tension between departments can diminish the advantages that proximity brings, as shown by Schein (1996) in his account of misunderstandings and tensions between the three occupational cultures that he identified (see Chap. 3).

Proximity means that the problem of geographical and temporal distance in communications does not arise. Face-to-face interactions are easy and cheap to accomplish. The ability of a person to access the workspace of another also yields contextual knowledge that can be of benefit in making decisions. The observations of a department can be at significant variances with the assurances of the manager of the department, for example. Proximity can be useful in diminishing structural distance, as people work together, exchange banter and interact on a continual basis. The layout of the physical environment, with the implications for more or less visibility and audibility related to people's activity, also affected communication. If people could see and/or hear conversations, they could then choose whether to join in or not.

In XME, the power relations implicit in the Foucauldian notion of the panopticon (Foucault, 1977; Atkins, Simmons, & Roberts, 1998) were reversed in a rather odd way. XME Australia had introduced a system of car parking spaces reserved for management that were situated close to the building. It became apparent that where staff were located close to a window facing the car park, they commonly used the proximity of the car park to discover whether a particular manager was on the premises or not. Ironically, then, a trapping of status actually encouraged surveillance of the higher ranking members by the lower ranking members. This surveillance was not attached to any sinister purpose; rather it was an example of Scribner's (1986) least-effort solutions that individuals formulate to streamline their work. The issue with proximity, visibility and audibility can be a function of too much access to knowledge when not desirable. It can be very difficult to keep confidential events confidential in an open plan office. At times, the distraction of other people's activity can prevent task performance. Proximity and movement of individuals meant that there was continual interaction between individuals in each organization, which is dealt with in the next section.

The Face-to-Face Interaction of Individuals

In all sites investigated, face-to-face interactions were common. It was noticeable that some people new to the organization would make a point of walking around to make enquiries and so on, and after they had been with the organization for a period of time, the degree of walking around would decline. It is speculated that, as their knowledge of people, systems and cultural norms increased, there was less of a need to initiate face-to-face interaction. Understandings between the new people and longer-serving employees were established and could be counted on to fill in any gaps in communication caused by electronic or other media of communication (Gaver, 1996; Lantz, 2001).

One thing that all the sites shared was a certain affability and banter in their interactions. Goffee and Jones (2001) argued that too much sociability was detrimental to the effectiveness of the organization. Anolli et al. (2002) showed that banter could be used to convey blame and other less positive communications. In the XME group, however, it was found that the banter and joking that the people engaged in actually facilitated communication. According to Trice (1993), banter can be a method of dealing with managing emotions, including those caused by dangerous situations.

In the XME group, banter generally served one of three purposes, which were to communicate stress or frustration in a socially acceptable way, comment on a task or a situation and promote cordial work relationships. Chapter 5 explained the subjective element to episodic memory. In the XME group, people talked to each other, empathized and laughed with each other. Conversations were a combination of the work-related, personal pursuits and gossip. As people interacted and shared the jokes, humor and banter, it meant that they shared a moment that became part of an enjoyable past with that group. Banter was part of the social culture of the XME group; another part of the culture is the telling of stories.

Stories

The research of Szulanski (1996) illustrated the importance of absorptive capacity, that is, how some initial knowledge facilitates the absorption of further knowledge, albeit knowledge that is endorsed by the organization. This study showed how, with regard to unmanaged knowledge, the theme of the message needed to resonate with a previously held belief or perspective of the listener before the knowledge would be remembered and communicated. This resonance would serve to overcome efforts by organizational leaders to forget the knowledge.

There were two foci with regard to the episodic memory to be found in the XME group. One focus was the power of the story with regard to the listener. A story would impress a listener only where there was an emotional connection with the underlying message. If a story held a powerful message for the listener, the listener would tend to remember and repeat the story. The other focus was the skill of the storyteller. If the event was framed and narrated to engage the attention of the listener, even a trivial event could stick in the mind of the listener. Snowden (2000b) saw storytelling as an organic tool for organizations to issue cultural messages to employees. It is perhaps the case that where the storyteller is skillful, it may not be one particular story that sends a message counter to those desired by the organization's leaders. If a storyteller is skillful they tend to tell many stories, and multiple stories around one motif clearly can contribute to cultural beliefs built on specific perceptions of the organization. Although the storytellers may not have Snowden's overt agenda, the skilled storytellers may garner support for their views by using their narrative talents. Boje (1991) wondered at the lack of storytelling training in management education. Boje, however, did not explore the role of the storyteller in the organization except at the senior levels of hierarchy. Gabriel (1995, p. 1) posited that storytelling was a manifestation of "grudging material acceptance [of managerial control] accompanied by a symbolic refashioning of events and official status." Certainly the stories told by the storytellers often included a pointing out of human quirks and funny incidents relating to senior members of the company. This also illustrates a facet of organizational knowledge retention – an organizational leader may successfully hinder a particular item of knowledge from entering the formal knowledge retention structures of the organization. This will often, however, simply stimulate the retention of an interpretation of that event in the informal knowledge retention structures of the organization.

Both Boje (1991) and Boyce (1996) illustrated how the leaders of organizations can use stories to promote particular cultural norms. People lower in rank, however, can also use storytelling to present a particular perspective. Stories are essentially, as Boje and Boyce agreed, a manifestation of sensemaking (Weick, 1995), that is, making sense of events that happen within and to the organization and its members. Sensemaking happens at all levels of the organization, and a persuasive storyteller may influence the sensemaking of events so that a type of knowledge about the organization and what happens within it becomes accepted within the organization.

The Knowledge of Difference Retained in Subcultures

Wenger (1999), in his study of claims processors, noted that the processors saw themselves as different to the rest of the organization. Van Manaan and Barley (1985, p. 32) posited that culture "presumes 'consciousness of kind' and 'consciousness of difference'." Subcultures encourage certain ways of thinking that may focus on some things and ignore others. In an organization, where one subculture ignores aspects of the organization central to another subculture, the members of the latter subculture may become convinced of the first subculture's lack of understanding and perhaps lack of competence in the organization's activities. Thus the subculture retains knowledge/perceptions of the other subculture's understanding and competence as well as knowledge related to occupation and task. An engineering subculture, for example, may have a low opinion of another department because of the department's lack of understanding about production processes. There was considerable evidence of lack of understanding between subcultures in XME Australia reminiscent of Schein's (1996) investigation of three subcultures in one organization that had difficulties in communicating and coordinating. The subcultures often spawned communities of practice. It is tempting to speculate that, in light of the evidence seen within the XME group and in the accounts of Orr (1990) and Wenger (1999), communities of practice flourish in an environment where a group perceives a tension between itself and others, which may be a rich area for future research. In addition to the knowledge of difference across occupationally based subcultures, there were issues in communicating across national cultures.

Communicating Across National Cultures

National customs and norms change across boundaries. Actions that are taken for granted within one's own culture can be context-dependent and can thus cause problems when transferred to another culture. In the XME group, the most common forms of communication were email and staff visits. Managers also extensively used the telephone; however, this form of communication tended to build on relationship formed by staff visits, which are dealt with later in this section.

Email was a major communication mechanism for the people in the XME group. Company staff in all three operations extensively used email to communicate with others within the same location, in different company offices and with external parties. Some staff regarded email as a durable means of communication with which to build up an audit trail of communications. Others regarded it as a quick and easy way to send fast communications without having to rise from the chair, and a way of overcoming time and geographical distance.

Email enables individuals to do several things. The obvious is to communicate via text. Often this is said to be instantaneous. This issue of timeliness is less important when overseas operations are involved. Provided the communication reaches its target within, for example, 6–8 h, the communication will be quick enough to be there for people as they arrive at work. When the receiver of a message is likely to be in bed on receipt, the synchronous receipt of the message becomes less important. Email is a composite of both the private and the organizational. Sited within the personal computer on the individual's desk, it is both convenient and private, although this privacy can be an illusion considering that email files are often located on organizational servers, and the ease with which email can be passed on without the permission of the initial sender. On the other hand, to be connected to email means that the individual is part of a group of email users. To not be connected when most of one's peers are, is to be alienated from the group, and to be essentially disabled in terms of communication. This inclusiveness of email is exacerbated when the sociocultural element is introduced. If the email system is used to tell jokes, sell personal goods and announce social events, the unconnected may feel very lonely indeed.

Gaver (1996) pointed out that email has given rise to questions on the social practices that should be observed. An example he gave was: "For instance, how should unanswered E-mail be interpreted? If you send a message to a colleague and receive no reply, should you consider yourself snubbed, assume that it has disappeared en route, or infer that it has been buried under newer messages?" (pp. 120–121). The email communications within XME particularly illustrated the problems as a method of communication. The intention was, when an email was sent, either to inform or to request information. The receiver of the email, however, inferred meaning from the email that may or may not have been intended or meant by the sender. If the sender and receiver did not share similar understandings, the communication may have been interpreted in a manner not intended by the sender. Where the email crossed international borders, this problem was exacerbated. It was noticeable that members of XME Ireland and XME USA perceived that they were the put-upon younger siblings of the group. Although XME Australia communicated with the other sites, the emails often distributed meeting minutes and so forth, which sends a message that decisions have been made without the input of the other sites. This supported Shulman's (1996) contention that email provides faster and more convenient opportunities for communication but "it does not provide us with communication per se, let alone better communication" (p. 368).

Because email is a text, the receiver retains the original in the communication; strange words and sentences are there to be puzzled over, and a blunt request is there to be fumed over. Van Maanen and Barley (1985) posited that culture highlights differences between others and the group as well as similarities within the group. Email was found to provide an opportunity to preserve the manifestations of difference, where a verbal conservation is ephemeral and thus lost as soon as spoken.

Staff visits to other sites, on the other hand, were generally successful in terms of promoting effective knowledge retention. The effects of proximity meant that a better understanding could be reached between colleagues. Visitors could observe the practices of the other site's members working within their own context. This meant that the visitors saw the documents, the systems, the suppliers and the clients and how they interacted to form the other site's context. It was noticeable that members from one site tended to evaluate the actions of another site according to their own context unless they had the knowledge to do the contrary. The face-to-face interaction meant that individuals from both sites could reach mutual understandings while the visitor was on the visited site and also to enhance the use of email, as explained in previous sections.

Many visits incorporated a social element to them that would entail the visitor being taken out to lunch or dinner. I consider this social element an important part of this temporary co-location. Where I witnessed social occasions, the conversations tended to include humor, anecdotes and stories that served to induct the visitor into the culture of the site. The visitor gained an understanding of the past events of the organization that was richer and more detailed than a semantic outline in a report could give.

The visits did have one possible drawback. When a visitor appeared on the scene, there was some effort to schedule events such as meetings and visits to suppliers so that the maximum value could be drawn out of the visit. The problem with this was that it disrupted the normal practice of the site, and sometimes gave the visitor an erroneous impression of the practices of the site.

Although distance impedes communication, there are mechanisms that overcome the effects of distance, which are discussed in the next section.

Mechanisms That Overcome the Effects of Distance

Although the managers traveled to other sites, the other staff were compelled to use other mechanisms to overcome the distances between the three sites. Even where managers met other staff members, this often occurred in a fairly formal way. The majority of staff were not invited to participate in the social occasions out of hours, and thus did not really become acquainted with the visiting manager. As mentioned previously, email was subject to cultural misunderstandings. How, then, can organizations facilitate communication among different sites at levels lower than management. Increased staff visits may seem to be an answer, albeit an expensive one. There are two strategies that emerged through this study. The first strategy to be discussed is ensuring that the sites are linked through organizational processes that overcome problems that arise through distance. The second strategy, used extensively by the XME group, is to have common ICT systems. Finally this section discusses how an organization, by having multiple and varied sites, possesses vast and significant knowledge retention structures as the sites develop specialized and valuable knowledge in their own right.

Formal Processes

In the literature pertaining to organizational knowledge, there is a considerable raft of work pertaining to routines and core competencies (e.g., Cohen, 1991; Cohen & Bacdayan, 1994; Argyris, 1992/1999; Berman, Down, & Hill, 2002; Lei, Hitt, & Bettis, 1996; Spender, 2001; Cyert & March, 1963; Prahalad & Hamel, 1990; Spender, 2001). There is considerably less emphasis on the role of processes in overcoming issues that individuals cannot cope with themselves. Although XME Australia and XME Ireland both had functioning QMS within their organizations, there did not appear to be processes to transcend the operational boundaries. There did not appear to be formal mechanisms to promote feedback loops from Australia to Ireland or vice versa. Issues would arise at one site that were caused by problems at another site. Although the staff visits by managers to various sites promoted better communication, this mechanism usually was not available to individuals lower in status. The people who had to do the accounts, ship and receive the products and handle the customer enquiries and complaints generally had little knowledge of sickness, backlogs and other problems in other sites that affected their own tasks. It was significant that in both XME Australia and XME Ireland, there was more knowledge of the situation and issues faced by local suppliers than by their counterparts in other countries. Also, where a site experimented with knowledge from another site, there would be value in understanding the results of the knowledge being used in a different context.

It was found, however, that a common ICT system did promote communication by providing a common frame of reference.

Common ICT Systems

The ICT market is a global one, and the giants in the field have a global influence. An organization investing in technological systems then may be in a quandary. Does the organization purchase the best software for the purpose, or does the organization purchase the most widely used? If the former path is pursued, the organization may achieve gains in effective utilization of the software, if the new and existing members of the organization can be fully trained in its use. If, however, the latter path is pursued, the organization may be able to exploit the knowledge retained by new and existing staff members, which means that the software may be immediately used to its fullest capacity, with much lower training costs. In addition, members new to the organization may bring higher levels of expertise in the software, which may enable more efficient usage of the software by the organization (Grant, 2000). This illustrates how technological norms and standards in specific arenas facilitate useful memory retention (Garud, Jain, & Kumaraswamy, 1999). When a person has learnt the industry or area software standard, she/he retains and uses that knowledge for a number of years across different companies and situations. At a global level, it may be comparatively easy to find staff who are familiar with the same software despite residing in different parts of the world. XME used two significant software applications throughout the three sites. One of these applications, Microsoft Office, is dominant in the global market and was usually familiar to new staff in each site. The other, DO_IT, is not so well known, and usually had to be learned by people new to the company. The use of the Microsoft applications meant that the sites could share various files such as databases, forms, marketing material and so on. In addition, despite its deficiencies the use of DO_IT throughout the company gave individuals in different occupations and different sites a common language. As the specialized knowledge in each site grew, so did the use of DO_IT in terms of that specialization, and this knowledge was sometimes shared between the sites to great advantage. This is one instance of the advantage of an organization having multiple, diverse sites.

The Advantage of Multiple Sites

Multiple sites enabled each site to build on the knowledge of another site, or access the other site's experience for decision making. Where a new task had to be undertaken, the work of the other offices acted as a reference and a resource from which a new, relevant and sometimes better resource could be developed. This was apparent in the use that the Las Vegas operation made of other operations' job descriptions and employee manuals. There was also evidence that staff in other offices were valued for their expertise and knowledge in particular areas, despite the national boundaries that existed. Doz et al. (2001) noted that many multinational companies needed to adapt their knowledge to the context of the local markets. In XME, the functions of each site were different to the original Australia location, and thus the ways of working and the culture that evolved were also different. Each site acted as a dispersed knowledge retention structure with its competencies and worldviews.

There are clearly advantages to creating new operations beyond cheaper production or access to markets. When an operation such as XME Australia grows over time, the physical environment that forms the company experience and investment generates both an affordance and a constraint. The affordance promotes performing activities in a certain way; the constraint impedes performing activities in another way. When a new operation comes into being, the new members of staff have their own experience to call on, as well as the experience of the people in XME Australia. They can learn about things that the people in XME Australia would change if they could. Thus to create different sites is to create different structures of knowledge acquisition and retention.

Communication is thus the means of retaining both explicit and tacit knowledge on a collective level. Tacit knowledge retention structures, however, are complex, and at times the tacit messages received can be unintended and problematic for the sender. Distance is probably the single most significant impediment to effective communication. Distance can be geographic, structural or cultural. Creating a common language, perhaps through common technology is one way of bridging this distance; another way is to formulate multisite processes that make it easier for individuals to communicate problems and issues across borders. Generally, though, communication flows much easier where a face-to-face relationship has been fostered and where there is a degree of positive emotion associated with the relationship. These positive emotions need to include both social and epistemic trust. Knowledge "nodes" in organizations have also been identified, that is, people who have elicited the degree of social and epistemic trust that has resulted in them being sought out and consulted about various work issues. Emotional connection is also identified with stories. For stories to be remembered they have to have meaning or elicit some degree of emotion in the listener. This could be due to the inherent power of the story or the skill of the storyteller in framing the story. The next section deals with the protection of knowledge retention structures.

Protecting Knowledge Retention Structures

Protecting the knowledge that is valuable to the organization is an essential part of knowledge management. This protection may take several forms, such as changing knowledge retention structures so that the knowledge is held in a less vulnerable form and making the knowledge accessible, through reproduction in the case of explicit knowledge, and communication in the case of tacit knowledge. Organizations that embrace knowledge management need to commit to a program of review and audit so that valuable knowledge can be optimized, and knowledge that is not endorsed by organizational leaders is acknowledged. These aspects of knowledge protection are discussed further in the following sections.

Changing Knowledge Retention Structures

Singley and Anderson (1989) discussed how individual knowledge can change from procedural to declarative and from declarative to procedural. Within organizations, changes can also occur from the individual to the collective and vice versa, and from the tacit to the explicit and vice versa.

Some tacit knowledge may be impossible to explicitly communicate. Much tacit knowledge, however, may be simply unarticulated, and much tacit knowledge may be communicated in a partially tacit and partially explicit form, as occurs frequently in terms of processes. Where knowledge is valuable to the organization, some effort needs to be made to change the knowledge retention structures from the individual to the collective and from the tacit to the explicit where this is possible. In XME USA, for example, the ICT was a supporting mechanism, to record and monitor various processes surrounding the sales of the goods that provided the income. On one occasion, an unusual product caused a problem because a staff member was unaware of the product-specific variation in the normal handling. After the problem was investigated, DO_IT was updated so that the system would warn any new staff of the unusual situation in the future. An alternative course of action would be simply to teach the employee what had to be done with that product. That, however, would be a solution for the individual, not for the company. The solution that was arrived at would hopefully prevent any other new employees from making the same mistake, that is, it was a solution that encouraged the organization, not just the individual, to remember. The knowledge of the unusual product structure had moved from group tacit knowledge to individual tacit knowledge by people leaving the firm. It was tacit knowledge simply because no one had thought to codify it. By including the knowledge in the ICT systems of the firm so that it was accessible when needed, meant that the knowledge became both collective and explicit. If the same problem occurs in the future it is likely to be a one-off oversight rather than a failure of the organizational systems. This type of codification is common in organizations; however, the tacit knowledge that is codified tends to be simple and easily articulated.

In this study, many of the local individual knowledge retention structures of the people in the R&D department were of considerable value to the company, particularly the personal logbooks and the computer files stored on diskettes and local hard drives. Local knowledge retention structures also contributed to the organization's effectiveness on a local tactical level. There has been, in the past, considerable urging in the literature for conversion of individually based knowledge to collective knowledge retention structures. There is, however, little investigation of individual knowledge retention structures that are external to the individual's cognitive retention structures (e.g., Senge, 1992; Senge et al., 1999; Nonaka, 1991). Ackerman and Halverson (2000) noted that some means of knowledge retention had a mixed provenance, that is, simultaneously belonging to the individual and the group or organization. A collective knowledge retention structure may emerge from a knowledge retention structure created and used by one individual, particularly where the structure is evaluated as effective by the individual's peers. In XME Australia and XME USA the personal autonomy enabled individuals to invent and adapt and others were willing to adopt the successful products of these endeavors. This cultural endorsement of individual knowledge retention structures may be an unofficial but powerful strategy for protecting knowledge, provided that the organization is willing to evaluate and convert these individual knowledge retention structures to a collective resource. Other organizational strategies for the protection of knowledge are discussed in the next section.

Organizational Strategies for Protecting Knowledge

How does an organization ensure that the work-related knowledge needed is retained within the organization in such a way that operations are not interrupted where absences or disasters occur? In the research sites, the issue of backup was dealt with in varying degrees of seriousness and varying degrees of success. What the organizations demonstrated was that the backup of personal expertise does not necessarily require the services of a similarly qualified person. Mechanisms such as a team of professionals and staged releases of product development can act to overcome vulnerabilities in backing up core competence. Surprisingly, in this age of technology, the issue of backup of explicit knowledge structures was more problematic. Although all the research sites practiced some degree of server backup, onsite storage still rendered the data vulnerable. In the case of XME Australia in particular, the practice of using paper logbooks in the R&D area meant that a significant amount of valuable data was vulnerable to loss, theft or damage. The protection of explicit knowledge is often not regarded as a strategic issue by organizational leaders, and is delegated to the ICT staff (Anonymous, 2001). In smaller companies, the question of backing up the senior leader/leaders of the organization also may be a problem. In the case of smaller organizations, the specialist knowledge needed is usually outsourced. This means that this specialist knowledge is backed up by the profession to which the specialist belongs. If a chartered accountant can no longer handle the accounts of an organization, the organization can simply take their business to another chartered accountant. As the organization grows and absorbs specialist knowledge into its structure, and the specialist knowledge become intertwined with organizational knowledge, the issue of knowledge protection may become more problematic. Subordinates may be able to cover for organizational leaders, but as the tasks become differentiated and specialized, the managers may not be able to cover for the subordinates. This could be problematic where the subordinate has rare specialist skills needed and valued by the organization.

Spender's identification of objectified knowledge (Spender, 1996a, b) raises also the issue of who looks after objectified knowledge in the organization. Objectified knowledge is the organization's collective explicit knowledge. Because it is not essentially cognitive, it maintains an existence outside the heads of individuals, and because it is not individual, people may feel no obligation to maintain the knowledge retained. In XME, there were differing levels of accountability for objectified knowledge. The function of producing and maintaining product drawings and procedures was embedded in the job descriptions of several people. There was, however, no designated function of maintaining databases: this was done when an expert with another job had time. Because these databases were useful sources of objectified knowledge, XME Ireland and XME USA also used them, but then found that XME Australia was sometimes very slow in making requested changes. In the case of XME Ireland, this resulted in plans to train up two of their engineers in database competencies who would have the responsibility of maintaining the databases in their own site. The failure to allocate responsibility for maintaining collective explicit, or objectified, knowledge retention structures limits their usefulness within the organization. A collective explicit knowledge retention structure is usually the result of an investment of time and/or money; thus to neglect its maintenance seems a waste of organizational resources.

In XME Australia, the knowledge was retained both in the processes and in the people; in R&D, predominantly in the people. In XME Ireland, the knowledge was retained/embedded far more in the process. As Epple et al. (1996) maintained, knowledge cannot become completely embedded in an organization's technology, but the ratio of knowledge retained in technology versus the level of knowledge retained by the people is variable. In XME Australia, the stage of development of the process was much earlier. It was therefore more feasible to bring retained knowledge to bear on its improvement, and there was motivation to deliver to XME Ireland a process that was as trouble-free as possible. In XME Ireland one person confided that "we probably wouldn't want a lot of changes at this stage" in answer to my question relating to whether the production operators improved the processes. This did not mean, however, that the knowledge was embedded solely in the artifacts such as machines and drawings. Some improvement to processes did occur, but it was coordinated by the engineers, who gathered feedback from the production operators on the issues and problems of existing processes. Having the engineers act in this way meant that the mode of problem solving changed from a local way of working to a way of working reflected in an occupational body of knowledge. Thus, although the individual was still the driver of updating the knowledge and knowledge retention structures, this process was done in a way that would probably be recognized by other engineers. Hence, for the organization, a significant degree of knowledge was retained in the external entity of the engineering profession. Thus the protection strategies of reproduction, communication and a degree of standardization through the profession are added to the strategy of conversion which was initially discussed. In the next section, knowledge protection is discussed from the aspect of preventing knowledge rigidities.

Preventing Knowledge Rigidities

An aspect of protecting knowledge valuable to the organization is preventing knowledge rigidities from occurring where retained knowledge obstructs the acquisition of new knowledge (Leonard-Barton, 1992).

In XME, a core knowledge rigidity was apparent in terms of repeating behavior that caused the organization's success. The high level of upgrades to products and the inadequate testing time caused a relatively high number of repairs under warranty. The CEO, being new to the company, did not share the bias toward "overshooting the mark" (Leonard-Barton, 1995) and caused a rethinking of an old entrenched mental model. Argyris and Schön (1978) have been critical of the failure of organizational leaders to accomplish double-loop learning, or to question underlying assumptions related to the organization and its activities. Amburgey and Miner (1992) noted the tendency of organizational leaders to repeat previous successful strategic actions. Although the power of organizational leaders within their own organizations may be considerable, the external pressures of a corporate organization can mean a diminishment of review where the organization performs sufficiently well enough not to draw criticism. In XME, it appeared that the pressure of the Board of Directors on the former Managing Director may have caused some reluctance to meddle with a winning strategy. A regular program of auditing knowledge retention structures may be a way of overcoming organizational knowledge rigidities.

Auditing Knowledge Retention Structures

This book has dealt extensively with how organizations, in particular the XME group, retain knowledge. Understanding how organizations retain knowledge and the different characteristics of those retention structures gives considerable insights into the effective management of knowledge. Each organization, however, is unique. This book illustrates how even different sites within the same organization retain knowledge in markedly different ways.

A knowledge retention framework based on the individual/collective and tacit/explicit dimensions, and the knowledge retention structures identified by Tulving (1972; 1985) and Anderson (1995) would have considerable value in understanding organizations and their means of knowledge retention. It would also be helpful in diagnosing possible deficiencies in the retention structures. Culture, for example, can be problematic to define, as culture is essentially a metaphor for artifacts and behaviors that evoke a shared collective past. If culture is equated with the sense of episodic memory, that is, what has built our collective identity, it creates a powerful understanding and interpretative lens on the possible effects of leadership action. Organizational leaders can then investigate the perceptions of the organizational "We" in the past, and speculate on the perceptions of the organizational "We" in the future. Organizational knowledge retention structures thus can be conceptualized by a framework of semantic, episodic and procedural knowledge retention structures and account for the tacit/explicit dimensions that denote the nature of knowledge. At the same time, this framework acknowledges the significant aspect of knowledge retention pertaining to its accessibility, whether the knowledge is collective or individually retained.

This framework is conceived not to classify the knowledge retention structures so much as to acknowledge them. When an organization's knowledge retention structures are applied against the framework, a depiction is built that highlights deficiencies within the organization's knowledge retention structures. For example, the collective paper and ICT documents from XME Australia R&D department were involved in the retention of semantic information. There was little or no evidence of explicit knowledge structures that captured the experience, or sense of what

"We" did within the area. Thus the R&D department depends on the knowledge retention structures of the individuals, such as their own cognitive structures and personal logbooks to provide the experience of the past. This also means that, as staff are transferred to other sites and departments or leave the company, it is likely that R&D will lose the knowledge of who participated in particular projects, that is, the directory knowledge identified by Anand, Manz, and Glick (1998) as an important part of organizational knowledge. Evident is the dominance of individually kept documentation, particularly with regard to paper documents, rather than collectively retained. This highlights a vulnerability in terms of loss if a staff member leaves or if a localized accident occurs.

Thus it is suggested that audits using the above framework would have considerable value in highlighting such vulnerabilities and deficiencies. Such audits would need to be conducted at regular intervals due to the dynamic nature of knowledge retention structures.

Conclusion

The recognition of knowledge as a factor of production means that knowledge retention is a critical area of organizational performance. Knowledge is itself a problematic term, but must be capable of being encoded in human cognitive structures, as a result of humans interacting with each other or with their environments. Knowledge retention structures then are human cognitive structures, the humans themselves being part of larger organizational or group structures, the patterning of behaviors within these larger structures that we call "culture," "structure" and "processes" and the physical environment, including documents and records.

Communication within organizations changes knowledge from an individual or team resource to an organizational resource. Before effective communication can occur, there needs to be some degree of shared understanding or commonality so that there is less chance of the receiver of the communication inferring meaning different to that intended by the sender. In XME, the growth of the company meant that the members of the organization could no longer rely on the face-to-face interactions with their richness in tacit communication to facilitate those shared meanings. XME, however, had not put in place alternative strategies for facilitating the sharing of understanding. Although visits to distant sites and staff transfers took place, this was not sufficient to overcome some degree of misunderstanding generated by national and site cultural differences. Clearly some degree of education and the initiation of formal processes and protocols would be necessary to help achieve mutual understandings. Despite this, the different sites acted as repositories of knowledge to the benefit of the organization, although the value of these repositories was limited due to the lack of feedback mechanisms between the sites.

Collective knowledge retention occurs because of individual action. As one person needs information from another, they make enquiries and the knowledge is communicated from one person to another. As this communication proceeds from person to person, often with others listening in to conversations, it becomes embedded in the group knowledge retention structures. Thus collective knowledge retention is promoted by bottom-up means as well as top-down means.

The case of the XME group, with the three very different sites shows the variability in knowledge retention strategies, issues and failings. By examining how these three sites remember, we can draw conclusions and construct theories that start to answer the complex question: "How do organizations retain knowledge?" The next chapter sets out the theory and implications that have emerged from this study.

Chapter 7
Theory and Implications

"T.G.I.F.—Thank God, it's Friday" chants Sanjay as he hurries past. Well, the new recruit has survived the week. She still has to make sense of it all; the politics, tea room etiquette, the networks and even just where things are. All she has learnt at the previous job has stood her in good stead. And the people still seem nice, although the manager has a short fuse. The stocky man whose seat she accidentally pinched was even pleasant this morning. Everything's a trade-off, but all in all, she thinks her new job is working out pretty well.

Introduction

People within organizations need to recall knowledge of events, of how to perform actions, of past behavior, and of the behavior and relationships pertaining to individuals associated with the organizations. Organizations, through the actions of individuals, build structures and processes to remember and recall this knowledge. Individuals need to be able to retain knowledge so that they can cope and prosper in various environments.

So, how do organizations remember? And even more importantly, how **can** organizations remember in terms of optimally retaining and recalling knowledge? This chapter sets out the theory that has been generated during the course of this research study and covers the emergence of dominant knowledge retention systems in organizations and the influences upon them; the communication of knowledge across organizations; and the management of knowledge retention.

The Development of Knowledge Retention Structures in Organizations

Proposition 1

This study shows that the way that knowledge structures become dominant is subject to influences that derive from humans and human action. Repeated use of the

P. O'Toole, *How Organizations Remember: Retaining Knowledge through Organizational Action*, Organizational Change and Innovation 2, DOI 10.1007/978-1-4419-7524-9_7,

knowledge retention structure by humans reinforces the structure's degree of dominance within the organization. This study shows that the direct influences on the dominance of knowledge retention structures are:

- The individual, who is influenced by current and previous experience
- The subculture/functional group in which the individual works and to which the individual contributes
- The requirements of the organizational leaders which are influenced by social structures, current and future experience and
- External factors, such as the requirements of regulating and investment entities

The literature, on the other hand, emphasizes the influence of group social structures on the individual and the effects of leaders on the organization as a whole. The role of the individual, and their individual knowledge retention structures, within the organization is generally understated with a few exceptions (Nord & Fox, 1996; Ackerman & Halverson, 2000), such as the capacity of high level individuals to be knowledge resources; the intractability of knowledge "silos" (people who will not share knowledge) (Senge et al., 1999); and mediators of social learning processes such as boundary spanners (Tushman & Scanlan, 1981). Where these authors have concentrated on individuals with specific characteristics, this study shows that individuals at all levels will affect knowledge retention structures through the way that individuals bring their own knowledge to bear on the way that work is done, and the way individuals work in concert with each other. Although the power held by the individual can be a factor in how they influence knowledge retention structures, influence can also be exerted through the informal formation of lobby groups, or the collective recognition of a good idea.

Implication

The individual needs to be acknowledged as an integral part of the knowledge retention process, rather than just individuals who are deemed to have knowledge especially valuable to the organization. The actions of individuals will affect the dominance of other knowledge retention structures with whom the individuals act in concert, and organizational leaders need to take into account the human component when making decisions.

Proposition 1.1

The study shows that the individual knowledge retention structures can retain knowledge of considerable significance to the organization, for example, the XME Australia staff's personal logbooks. Although each logbook was used only by one staff member, and ordered in an idiosyncratic way, the logbooks were used as an important reference with regard to the development of products, records of meetings and agreed actions and so forth.

Implication

Organizational leaders need to recognize that local knowledge retention structures used by individuals may retain considerable value to the organization in the knowledge they hold, and individuals should be encouraged to:

- Make this knowledge available at a group level if appropriate and
- Protect the knowledge retention structure with the organization providing the necessary infrastructure, e.g., fireproof filing cabinets in the case of personal logbooks or providing electronic means of data capture

Proposition 1.2

The study also shows that individuals arranged their work environments in a way that called on previous experience and their individual procedural knowledge retained in their own cognitive knowledge retention structures, facilitating smoother progress of work completion. Polanyi (1967) dealt with the tacit knowledge required to perform tasks, but his analysis stopped within the body of the participant, he did not explore the role of objects in eliciting procedural memory from people performing tasks. Theoretically, this links the cognitive memory work of Tulving (1985a, b) and Singley and Anderson (1989) in relation to procedural memory, with the constructivist notion of knowledge being situated in the environment.

Implication

Theoretically, this means that while the individual's knowledge is situated, the individuals can reproduce the situation when they move to new environments by importing the same or similar objects and ordering them in similar ways to the old environments.

At an organizational level, if individuals are prevented by organizational rules from arranging their work space and formulating their own knowledge retention structures according to their own preferences, this may impede the effectiveness of the individual until the individual becomes accustomed to the predetermined situation. The implication for organizational leaders is that, particularly where the organization embraces programs that call for standardization, the organization still empowers the individual with sufficient latitude to effectively use their own knowledge in producing results.

Proposition 1.3

Various individuals coming from different levels of the organization were found in this study to be significant knowledge retention structures within the organizations studied. The emergence of these individuals as significant knowledge retention structures did not depend solely on their level of knowledge or position within the organization, but also because of such factors as:

- The individual's willingness to help others, and ability to elicit epistemic and social trust and
- Their physical position in the organization/work environment which meant that others perceived they may have knowledge regarding particular equipment or the location of a senior member of the organization, which in turn caused these individuals to take such actions such as learning the required knowledge, instituting a repository of documents and so forth

Although Stein (1989) warns of inappropriate "knowledge reputations" within organizations, these non-structural factors in the development of individuals as knowledge retention structures are rarely covered in the literature, with some exceptions such as Adler (2002) who explore the issue of trust as a feature of the knowledge economy. For Adler, however, trust is a coordinating mechanism of the knowledge economy, and there is no recognition that trust can be based on factors that are not actually related to the knowledge retained (i.e., social trust) and therefore may lead to levels of trust disproportionate to the knowledge retained by the individual.

Implication

The implications here are twofold. Firstly, where individuals become significant knowledge retention structures in the organization, it becomes important for the organization to ensure that these individuals really do possess the knowledge that other people require. Secondly, where organizational leaders need to create a role relating to knowledge needed by others in the organization, the ability of the potential incumbents to incite both epistemic and social trust needs to be part of the selection process.

Proposition 1.4

This study illustrated the importance of the individual's personal autonomy in ensuring that knowledge retention structures are still viable. In XME Ireland, personal autonomy was diminished in the role of the production operators who had to comply with standardized procedures. The production operators, however, could and did work with engineers to identify problems. This acted to review and streamline procedures. Working through the engineers meant that changes made to improve the processes that were standardized across the organization, in other words, the knowledge retained was continually reviewed and evaluated while the product remained consistent.

Implication

The personal autonomy of an individual is a necessary part of ensuring that knowledge retention structures remain effective and viable. The implication for organizations is that to structure roles to diminish the autonomy of the individual is to diminish the individual's capacity to improve the knowledge retention structures and ultimately, improved ways of working. Where it is seen that personal autonomy needs to be diminished to ensure standardization of work outcomes, individuals should at least be given a way of communicating problems and possible solutions to a person centrally responsible for work improvements.

Proposition 2

This study showed that the dominance of specific knowledge retention structures emerges from both bottom-up (i.e., the organizational members) as well as top-down sources (the organizational leaders). The influence of top-down and bottom-up factors cause shifting dominance in knowledge retention structures over time. Although there is considerable literature with regard to how organizational leaders may introduce new technologies, for example, there is little investigation regarding the bottom-up influences or the interaction of top-down and bottom-up influences at a theoretical level.

Implication

Knowledge retention structures are numerous, dynamic, and complex. The multidirectional influences on knowledge retention structures mean that management can be at best partial and subject to a series of trade-offs.

Proposition 2.1

Organizational leaders are subject to influences from outside entities that cause knowledge retention structures to be formed that must be explicit and centralized so that required information can be communicated to these external entities.

Implication

In terms of knowledge management, organizational leaders must ensure that certain knowledge retention structures exist in predetermined formats so that the organization can comply with the demands of external regulators and stakeholders.

Proposition 2.2

This study found that lack of support by organizational leaders did not preclude the retention of knowledge within organizations. Two examples observed in this study were:

- When organizational leaders refused to recognize past errors, knowledge of past errors was captured by stories told by organizational members and
- When members of the organization who did not trust DO_IT, the centralized ICT knowledge structure, created their own recording systems

Although Gabriel (1995) acknowledged the alternative viewpoint captured by organizational stories, there has been little in the literature concerning the unmanaged knowledge retention structures that are not ratified by management.

Implication

Unmanaged knowledge retention structures may have benefits for the organization. Stories offer a perspective on past leadership performance that organizational leaders could learn from (if they listened); stories also enable leaders to offer a more positive version of events if the story contains distorted information. The individual recording systems, for example, acted as a backup and confirmation to DO_IT. These unmanaged knowledge retention structures can offer value to the organization even though the organizational leadership may not support them. In addition, where unmanaged knowledge retention structures capture memories of the past that are unpopular, a tactic of silence on behalf of the organization's leaders is unlikely to prove effective. A more useful tactic would be to counter the richness of stories, for example, with other stories that resonate with members of the organization.

Proposition 2.3

An individual knowledge retention structure becomes more widely used when others become aware of its usefulness. In some cases, a particular knowledge structure became dominant when members of the organization lobbied for its widespread acceptance by the organization, e.g., the engineering action report. Individuals may create and amend both specific knowledge retention structures such as a form or a procedure, or use an existing physical feature, such as the managers' car park being used to monitor managers' movements in XME Australia. Over the long term, the individuals may change the dominance of the class of knowledge retention structures. See also Proposition 1.4.

Implication

Organizational leaders may improve organizational effectiveness by taking notice of knowledge retention structures and endorsing those that contribute to organizational effectiveness.

Proposition 3

The activity of individuals and their interaction with their environment shapes the knowledge retention structures of the organization in a structurated way (Giddens, 1984). Thus as the knowledge retention structures of the organization are reviewed and altered, so are those knowledge retention structures of the individual.

Proposition 3.1

Specific knowledge retention structures, such as forms or a new process come into being continually in organizations. These knowledge retention structures, however, will conform to particular classes of retention structures, with particular dimensions, that are habitual to individuals and/or groups. Thus it was the norm for XME Australia Accounting to create a process and then document it, and retain the document on the organizational server. On the other hand, it was the norm for R&D people to use personal logbooks. Thus, the dominance of a particular class of knowledge retention structure will tend to conform to the group culture or the habit of the individual, which is itself a knowledge retention structure. This confirms a constant theme of the literature concerning the influence of structure and culture on organizational operations in general (for example, Berg (1985), Brown and Starkey (1994), and Hall (1996)).

Continually utilizing a class of knowledge retention structure may also affect the culture of the organization, e.g., if a department has to maintain extensive explicit records, the department may be influenced to gradually change its culture in line with the need to keep the records in an orderly fashion. Thus XME Australia Accounting developed high standards of order to cope with the need to keep records orderly.

Implication

Organizational leaders who wish to introduce new methods of retaining information need to ensure that the existing social structures will allow or enable the implementation of the desired innovation. Where the existing social structures do not allow or enable the implementation, either cultural change may need to be planned and initiated or implementation of the new knowledge retention structure deferred or canceled.

Proposition 3.2

The physical environment holds significant messages for individuals within organizations and reinforces structural boundaries. This confirms the work of Gagliardi (1990) and other authors. In XME Australia, a payroll clerk had to cope with working on confidential information in an open plan office. This caused a degree of stress in her working life caused by her physical environment—determined by her status in the organization—being inconsistent with her level of access to knowledge. Clearly the physical environment, structural status, and level of access to knowledge need to be consistent to facilitate the performance of the work.

Implication

Where cultural and/or structural change is contemplated, organizational leaders need to examine the cultural and structural messages retained within the physical environment, as these messages can serve to reinforce the existing structure and culture. Where the physical environment is inconsistent with either the structure of the level of knowledge access, problems will occur in the performance of job roles.

Proposition 4

In this study the processes of the organizations were seen as extremely significant knowledge retention structures. Although individuals have an important part to play as knowledge retention structures, processes that individuals contributed to were often seen to be effective in retaining knowledge where individual action in retaining knowledge was ineffective. Successful processes were observed in XME USA where the physical environment in the form of in trays, signs and labeling, and documents were structured so that a series of actions by individuals was facilitated leading to desired results. In this study, a comparison of sites showed that processes that incorporated certain features had a higher chance of success. These features are:

- More than one person has to complete stages of the process
- The people involved in the process agree to follow the process
- One stage of the process relies on the completion of another stage of the process – this is a built in mechanism for prompting feedback when a stage is not completed
- Various feedback mechanisms are built into the process, such as the point shown above
- The physical environment is arranged so that sufficient physical affordance is constructed to facilitate the process's completion (Gibson, 1979)

Implication

Processes rely on each stage of the process being completed, which relies on each participant in the process completing their assigned tasks. Thus organizational leaders need to ensure that compliance occurs, and that appropriate feedback mechanisms are built in to the processes. If compliance does not occur then the process breaks down and people form their own individual ways of working. Hence, where people use a central bank of files, it becomes necessary that they will all replace the files according to the index system so that the next person who needs them may find the files. If the agreed ways of working are not followed on an ongoing basis, it is likely that people will start creating their own copies of the files so that they can do their work. This is a variation of Scribner's (1986; 1997; 1997) least-effort theory, but where Scribner applied this theory in terms of the mental structures and processes of individuals, this study shows that people will arrange their workplaces and ways of working to minimize frustration and facilitate the smooth completion of a work process, provided that this arrangement does not conflict with their own standards relating to how the work should be done.

Proposition 5

Organizations need to explicitly designate responsibility for explicit collective knowledge retention structures to be viable on an ongoing basis. Thus in XME Australia, part of the structure included job functions dealing with drawing and procedure maintenance, maintenance of the network. Where there was no designated function, e.g., to maintain the databases used internationally, there were complaints from other sites due to the slow implementation of changes and updated data. Although the literature deals with the importance of creating knowledge management roles, the necessity for designating responsibility for maintaining collective explicit knowledge structures has been omitted.

Implication

The implication of this is that organizational leaders need to evaluate the importance of knowledge retention structures, particularly explicit ones, to the organization and allocate appropriate resources to their maintenance.

Retaining Knowledge Through Communication

Proposition 6

This study shows that there is a significant relationship between the temporal, geographical, or structural distance between individuals attempting communication and the ease with which effective communications can be established.

Proposition 6.1

The study showed that ease of communication was achieved most readily where the people communicating were in close proximity to each other. Thus, the people in the XME Australia R&D area enjoyed continual communication until a number of them were sent to other premises. This supports the work of Pedler et al. (1991/1997) and Davenport and Prusak (1998). The proximity that facilitates communication, however, can have disadvantages. In XME Australia and XME USA, where the organizations were structured to have different levels of knowledge access, it was difficult to keep certain information confidential. The noise that verbal communication entailed also meant distraction and interruptions for people doing detailed tasks.

Implication

The implication of this finding for organizational leaders is that the management of physical workspaces needs to take into account the structure of the organization. The need for verbal, face to face communication between the members of the organization must be weighed against the need to maintain restrictions on the information to be communicated to different levels of the organization, and the potential for distraction of people from their primary tasks. Where a high level of communication is required, organizational leaders should query whether restricted information is necessary to the achievement of organizational objectives, or simply a structural and cultural artifact that could be reviewed to the benefit of the organization.

Proposition 6.2

In XME Australia, the largest site, the development of departments facilitated a cultural distance between different subcultures. This meant that, as groups worked to achieve different goals and different priorities emerged, their understanding of the goals and priorities of other subcultures diminished. The members of one subculture may develop a low opinion of another subculture because of these different priorities and because of the other subculture's lack of knowledge about what was important. This extends the work by Trice (1993) and Schein (1996) and Van Maanen and Barley (1985) who identified the significance of subcultures, particularly occupational subcultures, within organizations, that different subcultures have different goals, and that subcultures have consciousness of difference with other subcultures respectively. This study, however, illustrates that as well as recognition of difference between subcultures, friction is not only caused by different priorities, but by a degree of disdain caused by a recognition of another subculture's lack of knowledge of one's own priorities.

Implication

Organizational leaders need to be aware that the structural distance occasioned by functional department can cause some friction as people work to different objectives and priorities. People of one subculture may have low opinions of another subculture where the other subculture fails to understand the central priorities of the first subculture. This situation needs to be managed by promoting communication mechanisms and common language among the different subcultures. See Proposition 7.2.

Proposition 7

Much of the literature depicts the tacit and explicit dimensions of knowledge as two separate elements, with only a few exceptions, such as Tsoukas (1996). This study showed that knowledge will have both tacit and explicit dimensions and that knowledge will have more or less tacitness/explicitness depending on its nature. Proposition 2.1 outlined how external influences cause certain knowledge retention structures to be explicit and centralized. Although this form of knowledge (for example, items needed to complete a company tax return) is in the form of recorded transactions, the format and details of the knowledge is predetermined by the Australian Taxation Office. Usually, people completing these returns have training and experience in completing these tax returns, and thus although the forms are explicit, there are tacit assumptions relating to that knowledge that are understood due to common training and experience. On the other hand, many communications will have a discernible tacit element that may either facilitate or impede communications. It was seen in all the research sites that the good-natured banter that took place facilitated communication, where misunderstandings over tacit messages caused by different cultures impeded communication.

Proposition 7.1

This study showed that a certain affability and banter in communications within the same site facilitated communications within those sites. Goffee and Jones (2001) argued that too much sociability could be detrimental, although Trice (1993) saw banter as a means of managing emotions in an acceptable way. It was seen in this study that a laughing encounter meant that two or more people shared a small piece of their personal past in a positive way, which facilitated future communication. Although the literature (e.g., Doz et al., 2001; Szulanski, 1996; Adler, 2002) discussed the importance of communication, there is very little concerning banter, humorous interactions, and the benefits that these types of communications bring to the organization.

Implication

Banter and humor are elements of organizational communications that cannot be directly managed by organizational leaders. The value of these type of interactions is generally tacit and difficult to specifically allocate to given organizational goals. These elements should be acknowledged and valued within organizations for the importance in facilitating communication. It is also suggested that these types of communication would be a fruitful area for future research.

Proposition 7.2

This study shows that communication difficulties caused by distance can be compounded by distant national cultures. People in different cultures regarded, formulated, and used email messages in different ways, which caused individuals to misinterpret the tacit messages contained in the text. This extends the work of Shulman (1996) who pointed out that email simply causes communication to be faster, rather than better.

Implication

Although email messages are generally considered an explicit means of communication, the tacit messages embedded in emails can be misinterpreted by the receiver in ways that cause friction. Organizations can at least partially manage this situation by promulgating knowledge about the way different sites communicate and by introducing email protocols that are company-wide.

Proposition 7.3

Visits by members of one site to other sites has been common in the literature as means of overcoming the effects of distance and cross-cultural friction between sites (e.g., Davenport and Prusak (1998), Adler & Cole (1993)) but in the research sites in this study, this was not always the case. Although visits sometimes alleviated communication problems, which was also noted by Doz et al. (2001), at times the visit itself changed the behaviors of the host organization, so that the visitor took away mistaken impressions.

Implication

Organizational leaders cannot depend on one-off visits between members of organizations to alleviate communication problems. Where staff visits are an organizational strategy to promote communication, a continuous program of visits is needed. It may also be helpful to debrief members of staff after returning from visits by another staff member who is familiar with the visited site.

Proposition 8

This study showed that with regard to unmanaged communication, the communication or message needed to resonate with the emotions or a view, belief, or perspective of the person receiving a message. Although this view, belief, or perspective may relate to the person's life in general, there was typically a comment on some facet of the organization embedded within the communication. Evidence of this resonance was particularly observed in the stories told within the organization. Where an organizational leader attempts to suppress knowledge of an event or a fact, the event or fact may be captured by a story.

Implication

Unmanaged communications, where accessible by organizational leaders, may be a rich source of information concerning the climate of the organization and beliefs of the people about the organization. These unmanaged communications, however, may be a means of retaining knowledge that organizational leaders may prefer suppressed.

Proposition 8.1

A story is likely to be remembered and repeated where the listeners' emotions are engaged by the story.

Implication

Significant stories will continue in organizations without repeated narratives by the listeners, as the engagement of listeners' emotions makes them empathize with the story. Organizational leaders who wish to use stories as a cultural device (as promoted by Snowden (2000b)) need to concentrate on the emotional aspects of the story, and choose stories that are likely to resonate with the experience and pre-existing knowledge of the audience.

Proposition 8.2

Individuals within organizations may assume the informal role of "storyteller." This role presupposes that the individual has skills in framing stories to engage the emotions of listeners. A story told may not have any particular power, but the framing of the story, and the telling of accompanying stories, can contribute to the cultural beliefs within the organization, with no regard to the hierarchical level enjoyed by the storyteller. Boje (1991) noted that managers can effectively use storytelling as a means to transmit cultural messages, which was observed in XME Australia, as the new CEO told stories to explain new ways of working, but there is little literature on the storyteller at lower levels of the organization.

Proposition 9

This study showed that where distance is acknowledged, mechanisms can be introduced to facilitate more effective communication.

Implication

Where organizations implement strategies that involve creating distance between individuals and groups that need to interact, some effort and investment should be made to overcome the issues created by the distance.

Proposition 9.1

Within all four sites, communication was facilitated by the cordial relationships, trust and respect for colleague's competence. As distance increased, however, the ease of communication diminished. One person with XME Australia successfully fostered the communication by entering into social relationships with distant colleagues by including in his messages personal (non-threatening) enquiries and social chat.

Implication

Differences created by distance and cross-cultural friction can be overcome where people actively attempt to foster cordial relations with distant counterparts.

Proposition 9.2

This study showed that communications improved where formal processes were implemented, e.g., the protocols followed in the Military division meant that all four members knew the progress of work in both XME Australia and XME Ireland. On the other hand, although XME Ireland may have benefited from the Quality Management System providing a voice to its members, communication across national boundaries suffered because the System was not designed to transcend national boundaries.

Implication

Proposition 4 noted that processes achieve what individuals cannot achieve alone. It is seen here that formal processes can also improve communications by providing an avenue or channel for individuals. Organizational leaders need to ensure that these formal channels exist for the use of these members so that communications, both horizontal and vertical, can occur effectively.

Proposition 9.3

The experience in the XME Group showed that a shared central artifact such as an integrated ICT system for significant operations can provide a common language, as well as technical benefits. Davenport and Prusak (1998, p. 98) pointed out that a "common language is essential to productive knowledge transfer"; this study shows that the language can have a shared system as the basis for that language. The integrated ICT system, however, did have severe drawbacks in terms of limited functionality and technical support.

However, the Quality Management System did not facilitate communications to the same extent, probably because the QMS had widely different levels of applicability in different departments, and because the language fostered by the QMS related to administration surrounding the work, rather than to the work itself. Thus communication is fostered where the common language is widely spread and central to the organization's operations.

Implication

This finding means that organizational leaders can promote improved communications by providing a common means of achieving work objectives throughout an organization so that a common language is present in the organization. This benefit of providing this common means or artifact, however, must be weighed against the availability of training, support, and prior industry knowledge relating to such to a central artifact.

Proposition 10

This study showed that although different cultures and operations within different sites of an organization can lead to communication problems, these differences can also add value to an organizational group as the site takes on the role of knowledge resource or retention structure for the rest of the organizational group. This confirms the work of Moorman and Miner (1997), who argued that high memory dispersion can work against the creation of new knowledge in different organizational units. As each site in this study developed a different focus and competency set, they could build on each other's knowledge. The challenge for XME in this case is to effectively harness the knowledge created in each site and diffuse it across the organization, with feedback mechanisms in place to assist organizational learning on an international level. Although there are organizations that have effectively created strategies and processes to communicate and utilize knowledge from different organizational sites, equally there are companies that facilitate one-way knowledge communication only, where the knowledge created in one site is imposed on others (Kulkki, 2002). This latter model of communication more closely resembles the situation in the XME group.

Implication

Attempts to standardize sites within one organizational group can not only cause cross-cultural problems in the marketplace (Doz et al., 2001) but can deprive the organizational group of the knowledge that can be created in each site.

Managing Knowledge Retention Structures

Proposition 11

The actions and choices of organizational leaders have a direct impact on the promotion or impediment of knowledge retention. Organizational leaders shape the organization's knowledge retention structures in terms of infrastructure, human resources, culture, structure, and processes.

Implication

When making decisions, organizational leaders need to be aware of and acknowledge the ramifications of those decisions on the knowledge retention structures of the organization. A decision, for example, not to fund an organizational intranet as in XME Australia, meant that the organization was deprived of a knowledge retention structure with the ability to decrease duplication of records, delays in receiving important information and to improve the communication between sites.

Proposition 12

Organizational leaders are also directly responsible for the strategies to protect the knowledge retention structures of the organization. The importance of these strategies to the organization can be determined by the level of resources and the level of accountability in terms of such things as disaster prevention and recovery plans and so on. The protection of knowledge is severely underrated in the knowledge management literature.

Implication

Generally, knowledge management is understood from the perspective of creating knowledge management (usually ICT) tools, but the ongoing maintenance of these tools and their protection from viruses is rarely addressed. The input of the organizational leader is well illustrated in XME Australia, where the former Managing Director oversaw backup procedures for the organization's server DAT tapes, but not much else. The new CEO, however, elevated the priority of proper disaster prevention and recovery planning.

Organizational leaders need to address the protection of knowledge within the organization at a strategic level. The increased reliance on electronic explicit knowledge structures makes protection of these resources highly significant to the organization.

Proposition 13

This study also showed how the structure and culture of the organization are significant in relation to the effectiveness of knowledge retention. Structural boundaries can dramatically affect perceptions of how widely knowledge should be disseminated. The culture of the organization also has an impact on effective knowledge retention in terms of preventing knowledge rigidities through people having the autonomy to evaluate knowledge effectiveness. In XME Australia, there was a culture of trying things out and trying to improve, which seemed to be a normal part of the way people worked. This constant testing of viability, particularly at the mid- and lower levels of the organization meant that obsolete knowledge was recognized as such. This further confirms the work of Senge (1992) and Nonaka (1994) and further links knowledge retention structures to the activity of humans. Adler (2002) predicted that trust would be necessary in a knowledge-intensive society and that this trust would be built on values of epistemic trust. This study showed that trust was also built partially on a social element related to individual's demeanor and appearance. The degree of commonality and exchanged banter also promoted effective knowledge retention as outlined in Proposition 7.

Implication

Organizations need to promote a culture and structure that promotes openness, trust, and autonomy if communication of knowledge is an organizational value. Structure and culture are themselves knowledge retention structures that will cause knowledge to be retained in more or less people at more or less levels of the organization. Clearly the more people to retain the knowledge at more levels of the organization, the less likely is its loss. Similarly, openness and trust is necessary for people to ensure that organizational leaders are quickly appraised of problems and issues that arise.

Proposition 14

This study showed that an organization cannot succeed in completely embedding knowledge in retention structures outside of the individual. Although the Fordism movement has advocated the embedding of knowledge in procedures, processes, and machines rather than in individuals who can leave the company, this cannot occur because procedures, processes, and machines cannot review and update the knowledge embedded within them. Epple et al. (1996) also noted that knowledge could not be embedded solely in these non-human structures.

In XME Australia, the production operators needed only soldering skills to start their jobs, and worked from procedures and drawings. They still used their problem solving skills, however, to decrease the amount of reworking of defective products. In addition, although not a lot of knowledge was embedded within the production operators in comparison to the XME Australia production operators, the Irish engineers were extremely knowledgeable, and continually reviewed drawings and processes. Because the engineers were part of a professional group, they worked according to the accepted norms of the professional group. This meant that if an engineer left XME Ireland, another engineer could use the documentation to understand and work with the local knowledge. If the production operators left, the organization could replace them with another person with soldering skills and train them using the documentation and the knowledge of the other operators. Thus, the documentation could be seen to retain local knowledge and any new engineers could use their professional knowledge to interpret and use the documentation. The majority of knowledge was therefore not simply embedded in the documentation, but also in the professional body of knowledge common to engineers.

Implication

This finding again confirms the place of the individual in retaining knowledge within the organization but also shows how knowledge can be embedded in structures outside the organization, i.e., the body of knowledge of the engineers. The engineers created drawings and procedures to capture the local knowledge of the product. They assumed the role of ensuring that the knowledge retained was viable. Although the knowledge was embedded in the drawings and procedures, the significant role of the engineers needs to be taken into account.

This has implications with regard to organizational structure. Organizations should not rely on embedding knowledge in explicit or non-human forms. People have to be part of the knowledge retention process, but the vulnerability of knowledge loss can be diminished by using group structures either internal or external to the organization as knowledge retention structures. Where jobs are structured so that a significant portion of the local knowledge is explicit, and other knowledge is embedded within a profession, the knowledge is less vulnerable to being lost when an incumbent leaves the organization. This is an alteration to Fordism; instead of people being de-skilled as such, the skills are transferred to other, professional people of the organization who use their professional knowledge in concert with explicit knowledge retention structures.

Proposition 15

Knowledge audits are often cited as significant tools in knowledge management. This study extends the notion of knowledge audits to embrace the semantic/episodic/procedural dimensions in addition to the individual/collective dimensions and tacit/explicit dimensions cited in the literature. In XME Australia's R&D area, for example, the collective episodic knowledge retention structures were sparse, however the individual episodic knowledge retention structures, in the form of the personal log books were a significant part of the organization. These log books, however, were vulnerable to vagaries of fortune. The organization did not even provide a fireproof cabinet in which to store completed logbooks.

Implication

Knowledge retention structures within organizations are found in large numbers at all levels in the organization. If an organization is to manage these knowledge retention structures, a useful classification system is needed to highlight vulnerabilities and deficiencies. The protection of knowledge differs according to its dimension. The knowledge retention model synthesizing individual/collective, semantic/episodic/procedural, and tacit/explicit dimensions enables organizations to ascertain whether different useful classes of knowledge are being retained and properly protected. For example, in the XME Australia R&D department, there was little collective/episodic/explicit knowledge, which meant that the lived experience of projects would walk out the door if specific individuals left the company. Examining the knowledge retention structures in the light of this model highlights vulnerabilities in knowledge retention structures.

Proposition 16

The study showed that knowledge retention structures can change dimensions over time. Tacit knowledge may be explicated or an individual knowledge retention structure may be shared with others to become collective. For example in XME USA, the knowledge of an unusual product structure changed from collective/tacit to individual/tacit as people left the organization. The knowledge was then documented on the DO_IT system, which meant that the knowledge was changed to collective/explicit. Although Nonaka (1991) promoted deliberate knowledge conversion, there is little that theorizes on how knowledge retention structures change over time with turnover, obsolescence of technology, or adoption of new technology and so on.

Implication

Continuous knowledge audits are necessary because knowledge dimensions change over time. This process may be deliberately managed as described by Nonaka (1991) or it may occur through one individual generating an effective knowledge retention structure, and others adopting it. It may also occur due to departures of staff from the organization, and knowledge retention structures being forgotten.

Proposition 17

As organizations grow and become more complex, the jobs within the organization become more specialized. This means that the issue of backing up roles becomes a significant issue within the organization. In XME USA, for example, the adoption of function departments, and the hiring of professional staff meant that it became more difficult for the General Manager to back up the managers, although, working in concert, the managers could back up the General Manager.

Implications

Organizational leaders need to plan for the eventuality that individuals who fill various roles throughout the organization may not be indefinitely employed by the organization. Small organizations are not exempt from this necessity, because it may be the owner or Managing Director who is the key knowledge retention structure, and who may be vulnerable to accident if not to other opportunities.

Conclusion

These propositions and their implications illustrate the need in organizations to formulate focused, cohesive strategies pertaining to knowledge management. Organizations also need to acknowledge vulnerabilities in organizational infrastructure and recognize the role played by local and unmanaged knowledge retention structures. The building of effective knowledge retention structures closely reflects the building of an effective organization that can utilize the knowledge resources that exist both within and outside of its boundaries.

References

Ackerman, M. S., & Halverson, C. A. (2000). Reexamining Organizational Memory. *Communications of the ACH, 43*(1), 59-64.

Adler, P. S. (2002). Market, Hierarchy, and Trust: The Knowledge Economy and the Future of Capitalism. In W. C. Chun & N. Bontis (Eds.), *The Strategic Management of Intellectual Capital and Organizational Knowledge* (pp. 23-43). Oxford: Oxford University Press.

Adler, P.S., & Cole, R.E. (1993). Designed for Learning: A Tale of Two Auto Plants: *Sloan Management Review, Spring,* 85-93.

Allee, V. (1997). *The Knowledge Evolution: Expanding Organizational Intelligence*. Boston, MA: Butterworth-Heinemann

Alvesson, M. (1993). Organizations in rhetoric: knowledge intensive firms and the struggle with ambiguity. *Journal of Managment Studies, 30*(6), 997-1015.

Amburgey, T. L., & Miner, A. S. (1992). Strategic Momentum: The Effects of Repetitive, Positional and Contextual Momentum on Merger Activity. *Strategic Management Journal, 13*, 335-348.

Anand, V., Manz, C. C., & Glick, W. H. (1998). An Organizational Memory Approach to Information Management. *Academy of Management Review, 23*(4), 796-809.

Anderson, J. R. (1995). *Cognitive psychology and its implications* (4th ed.). New York: W.H. Freeman.

Anderson, J. R. (2000). *Cognitive Psychology and Its Implications*. New York: Worth.

Anderson, J. R., Reder, L. M., & Simon, H. A. (1996). Situated Learning and Education. *Educational Researcher, 25*(4), 5-11.

Anderson, J. R., Reder, L. M., & Simon, H. A. (1997). Situative Versus Cognitive Perspectives: Form Versus Substance. *Educational Researcher, 26*(1), 18-21.

Anderson, M. C., & Neely, J. H. (1996). Inference and Inhibition in Memory Retrieval. In E. L. Bjork & R. A. Bjork (Eds.), *Memory* (pp. 237-313). San Diego: Academic Press.

Andriansson, L., & Hjelmquist, E. (1991). Group processes in face-to-face computer-mediated communication. *Behaviour & Information Technology, 10*(4), 281-296.

Anolli, L., Ciceri, R., & Infantino, M. G. (2002). From "blame by praise" to "praise by blame". Analysis of vocal patterns in ironic communication. *International Journal of Psychology, 37*(5), 266-276.

Anonymous (2001). Business people fail to see importance of business continuity planning until it's too late; IT managers poorly supported in disaster recovery planning. *M2 Presswire*.

Anonymous (2003). Zycko: UK companies unprepared for terrorist attack; One third of UK companies fail to back-up data daily; Over 80 per cent do not use mirrored storage on separate sites; 91 per cent fail to back up data weekly. *M2 Presswire,* pp. 1+. , 24/3/03.

Argyris, C. (1992/1999). *On Organizational Learning* (2nd ed.). Oxford: Blackwell Business.

Argyris, C. (1993). *Knowledge for action*. San Francisco: Jossey-Bass.

Argyris, C., & Schön, D. A. (1978). *Organizational Learning*. San Francisco: Jossey-Bass.

Ashforth, B. E., & Fried, Y. (1988). The Mindlessness of Organizational Behaviors. *Human Relations, 41*(2), 305-329.

Assmann, J. (1995). Collective Memory and Cultural Identity. *New German Critique, 65*, 125-133.

Atkins, P., Simmons, I., & Roberts, B. (1998). *People, Land and Time: An Historical Introduction to the Relations between Landscape, Culture and Environment*. London: Arnold.

Baets, W. R. (1998). *Organizational Learning and Knowledge Technologies in a Dynamic Environment*. Boston: Kluwer Academic Publishers.

Banaji, M. R. (2001). Implicit Attitudes Can Be Measured. In H. L. Roedinger, J. S. Nairne, I. Neath, & A. M. Surprenant (Eds.), *The nature of remembering* (pp. 117-150). Washington: American Psychological Association.

Barrozzo, M.C.D., & Penna, T.J.P. (1994). Unlearning in Neural Networks with Many Neuron Interactions. *International Journal of Modern Physics*, 5(3), 503-512.

Berg, P.-O. (1985). Organization Change as a Symbolic Transformation Process. In P. J. Frost, L. F. Moore, M. R. Louis, C. C. Lundberg, & J. Martin (Eds.), *Organizational Culture* (pp. 281-299). Beverley Hills: Sage.

Berman, S. L., Down, J., & Hill, C. W. L. (2002). Tacit Knowedge as a Source of Competitive Advantage in the National Basketball Association. *Academy of Management Journal, 45*(1), 13-31.

Birch, H. G., & Rabinowitz, H. S. (1951). The negative effect of previous experience on productive thinking. *Journal of Experimental Psychology, 41*, 121-125.

Blackler, F. (2002). Knowledge, Knowledge Work and Organizations: An Overview and Interpretation. In W. C. Chun & N. Bontis (Eds.), *The Strategic Management of Intellectual Capital and Organizational Knowledge* (pp. 47-65). Oxford: Oxford University Press.

Bogner, W. C., Thomas, H., & McGee, J. (1999). Competence and Competitive Advantage: Towards a Dynamic Model. *British Journal of Management, 10*(4), 275-290.

Boisot, M. (1998). *Knowledge Assets: Securing Competitive Advantage in the Information Economy*. New York: Oxford University Press.

Boisot, M. (2002). The Creation and Sharing of Knowledge. In W. C. Chun & N. Bontis (Eds.), *The Strategic Management of Intellectual Capital and Organizational Knowledge* (pp. 65-78). Oxford: Oxford University Press.

Boje, D. (1991). The Storytelling Organization: A Study of Story Performance in an Office Supply Firm. *Administrative Science Quarterly, 36*, 106-126.

Bonner, D. (2000). The Knowledge Management Challenge: New Roles and Responsibilities for Chief Knowledge Officers and Chief Learning Officers. In J. J. Phillips & D. Bonner (Eds.) (pp. 3-19). Leading Knowledge Management and Learning: ASTD.

Boyce, M. E. (1996). Organizational story and storytelling: a critical review. *Journal of Organizational Change, 9*(5), 5-26.

Brand, S. (1994). *How Buildings Learn: What happens after they're built*. New York: Viking.

Braverman, H. (1974) Labor and Monopoly Capital: The Degradation of Work in the Twentieth Century. New York: Monthly Review Press.

Brown, A. D., & Starkey, K. (1994). The Effect of Organizational Culture on Communication and Information. *Journal of Management Studies, 31*(6), 807-828.

Brown, J. (2003). Survey warns IT managers to make disaster recovery top priority. *Computing Canada, 29*(4), 6.

Burgess, J. (2001). Workforce Developments and the Knowledge Economy in Australia. *Business/ Higher Education Round Table, July 2001*(11).

Burrell, G. (1997). *Pandemonium-Towards a Retro-Organization Theory*. London: Sage.

Burton-Jones, A. (1999). *Knowledge Capitalism: Business, Work, and Learning in the New Economy*. Oxford: Oxford University Press.

Cameron, K.S. & Whetten, D.A. (1981) Perceptions of Organizational Effectiveness over Organizational Life Cycles. *Administrative Science Quarterly*, 26, 525–544.

Casamayou, M. H. (1993). *Bureaucracy in Crisis: Three Mile Island, the Shuttle Challenger, and Risk Assessment*. Boulder: Westview Press.

Choo, C. W. (2002). Sensemaking, Knowledge Creation and Decision Making: Organizational Knowing as Emergent Strategy. In W. C. Chun & N. Bontis (Eds.), *The Strategic Management of Intellectual Capital and Organizational Knowledge* (pp. 79-88). Oxford: Oxford University Press.

Cohen, G. (1996). *Memory in the real world* (2nd ed.). Hove: Psychology Press.

Cohen, M. D. (1991). Individual Learning and Organizational Routines: Emerging Connections. *Organization Science, 2*(1), 135-139.

Cohen, M. D., & Bacdayan, P. (1994). Organizational Routines are Stored as Procecedural Memory: Evidence from a Laboratory Study. *Organization Science, 5*(4), 554-568.

Collinson, D. (1994). Strategies of Resistance: Power, Knowledge and Subjectivity in the Workplace. In J. M. Jermier, D. Knights, & W. R. Nord (Eds.), *Resistance & Power in organizations* (pp. 25-68). London: Routledge.

Cook, S. D., & Brown, J. S. (1999). Bridging Epistemologies: The Generative Dance Between Organizational Knowledge and Organizational Knowing. *Organizational Science, 10*(4, July-August), 381-400.

Cook, S. D., & Yanow, D. (1996). Culture and Organizational Learning. In M. D. Cohen & L. S. Sproull (Eds.), *Organizational Learning* (pp. 430-459). Thousand Oaks, CA: Sage.

Coopey, J. (1995). The Learning Organization, Power, Politics and Ideology. *Management Learning, 26*(2), 193-213.

Coopey, J. (1996). Crucial gaps in the Learning Organization: Power, politics and ideology. In K. Starkey (Ed.), *How Organizations Learn* (pp. 348-367). London: International Thomson Business Press.

Cross, R., & Baird, L. (2000). Technology Is Not Enough: Improving Performance by Building Organizational Memory. *Sloan Management Review, 41*(3), 67-78.

Crowley, H., & Himmelweit, S. (Eds.). (1992). *Knowing Women: Feminism And Knowledge.* Cambridge, UK: Polity Press.

Cyert, & March. (1963). *The Behavior of the Firm.* Englewood Cliffs, NJ: Prentice Hall.

Cyert, R. M., & Goodman, P. S. (1997). Creating Effective University-Industry Alliances: An Organizational Learning Perspective. *Organizational Dynamics, 25*(4), 45-57.

Czarniawska, B. (1997). *Narrating the Organization Dramas of Institutional identity.* Chicago: University of Chicago Press.

Davenport, T. H., & Prusak, L. (1998). *Working Knowledge: How Organizations Manage What They Know.* Boston, Ma: Harvard Business School Press.

Delbridge, A., Bernard, J., Blair, D., Butler, S., Peters, P., & Yallop, C. E. (1997). *Macquarie Dictionary* (3rd ed.). North Ryde: Macquarie Library.

Denning, S. (2007). *The secret language of leadership : How leaders action through narrative* San Francisco, : Jossey-Bass.

Dhar, V. (2001). The Role of Machine Learning in Organizational Learning. In T. K. Lant & Z. Shapira (Eds.) *Organizational Cognition: Computation and Interpretation* (pp. 15-37). Mahwah, NJ: Lawrence Erlbaum Associates.

Domingues, J. M. (1997). Social memory, social creativity and collective subjectivity. *Social Science Information, 36*(3), 469-492.

Dougiamas, M. (1998). *A journey into Constructivism,* [Internet]. Available: http://www.dougiamas.com/writing.constructivism.html [2002, 15/11/2002].

Doxtater, D. (1990). Meaning of the Workplace: Using Ideas of Ritual Space in Design. In P. Gagliardi (Ed.), *Symbols and Artifacts: Views of the Corporate Landscape* (pp. 107-128). Berlin: Walter de Gruyter.

Doz, Y., Santos, J., & Williamson, P. (2001). *From Global to Metanational: How Companies Win in the Knowledge Economy.* Boson, Ma: Harvard Business School Press.

Drucker, P. F. (1995). *Managing in a Time of Great Change.* New York: Truman Talley Books.

El Sawy, O. A., Gomes, G. M., & Gonzalez, M. V. (1986). *Preserving Institutional Memory: The Management of History as an Organizational Resource.* Paper presented at the Academy of Management.

Epple, D., Argote, L., & Devadas, R. (1996). Organizational Learning Curves: A Method for Investigating Intra-Plant Transfer of Knowledge Acquired Through Learning by Doing. In M. D. Cohen & L. S. Sproull (Eds.), *Organizational Learning* (pp. 83-100). Thousand Oaks: Sage.

Fahey, L., & Prusak, L. (1998). The Eleven Deadliest Sins of Knowledge Management. *California Management Review, 40*(3), 265-276.

Field, L. (2000). *The emotional underbelly of organizational learning.* Paper presented at the Emotions in Organizations: The Contributions of Psychoanalytic Approaches, London.

Fischer, G.-N. (1997). *Individuals and Environment: A Psychosocial Approach to Workspace* (Atkin-Etienne, Ruth, Trans.). Berlin: Walter de Gruyter.

Foucault, M. (1972/1980). *Power/Knowledge: Selected Interviews and Other Writings* (C. Gordon, L. Marshall, J. Mepham, John & K. Soper, Trans.). New York: Pantheon Books.

Foucault, M. (1977). *Discipline and Punish: The Birth of the Prison*. London: Penguin Books.

Gabriel, Y. (1993). Organizational nostalgia-Reflections of 'The Golden Age'. In S. Fineman (Ed.), *Emotion in Organizations* (pp. 118-141). London: Sage.

Gabriel, Y. (1995). The Unmanaged Organization: Stories, Fantasies and Subjectivity. *Organization Studies, 16*(3), 477-501.

Gabriel, Y. (1997). *An Introduction to the social psychology of insults in Organizations*, London.

Gabriel, Y. (1998). The Use of Stories. In G. Symon & C. Cassell (Eds.), *Qualitative Methods and Analysis in Organizational Research* (pp. 135-160). London: Sage.

Gagliardi, P. (1990). Artifacts as Pathways and Remains of Organizational Life. In P. Gagliardi (Ed.), *Symbols and Artifacts: Views of the Corporate Landscape* (pp. 3-38). Berlin: Walter de Gruyter.

Gargiulo, T. L. (2005). *The strategic use of stories in organizational communication and learning*. Armonk, NY: M.E. Sharpe.

Garrison, J. (1998). Toward a pragmatic social constructivism. In M. Larochelle, N. Bednarz, & J. Garrison (Eds.), *Constructivism and education* (pp. 43-60). Cambridge: Cambridge University Press.

Garud, R., Jain, S., & Kumaraswamy, A. (1999). An Integrative Perspective for Managing Knowledge. In J. F. Porac & R. Garud (Eds.), *Cognition, Knowledge and Organizations* (Vol. 6, pp. 195-214). Stamford: JAI Press Inc.

Gasparino, C., & Smith, R. (2001, 25/09/2001). Rebuilding Wall Street: Merril, Lehman Faced Hurdles in Relocating to Backup Offices. *Wall Street Journal*, pp. C 1.

Gaver, W. W. (1996). Situating Action II: Affordances for Interaction: The Social is Material for Design. *Ecological Psychology, 8*(2), 111-129.

Geertz, C. (1983). *Local Knowledge: Further Essays in Interpretive Anthropology*. New York: Basic Books, Inc.

Gherardi, S. (2006). *Organizational knowledge: The texture of workplace learning*. Malden, MA: Blackwell Publishing.

Gibson, J. J. (1979). *The Ecological Approach to Visual Perception*. Boston: Houghton Mifflin.

Giddens, A. (1984). *The Constitution of Society*. Cambridge: Polity Press.

Gieryn, T. F. (2000). A space for place in sociology. *Annual Review of Sociology, 26*, 463-496.

Goffee, R., & Jones, G. (2001). Organizational Culture: a Sociological Perspective. In C. L. Cooper, S. Cartwright, & P. C. Earley (Eds.), *The International Handbook of Organizational Culture and Climate* (pp. 3-20). Chichester: John Wiley & Sons Ltd.

Gopalakrishnan, S. (1997). Organizational Innovation and Strategic Choices: A Knowledge-Based View. *Academy of Management, Proceedings '97*, 422-426.

Gottfied, H. (1994). Learning the score: The duality of control and everyday resistance in the temporary-help service industry. In J. M. Jermier, D. Knights, & W. Nord (Eds.), *Resistance & Power in organizations* (pp. 102-117). London: Routledge.

Grant, R. M. (1996). Prospering in Dynamically-competitive Environments: Organizational Capability as Knowledge Integration. *Organization Science, 7*(4), 375-387.

Grant, R. M. (2000). Shifts in the World Economy: The Drivers of Knowledge Management. In C. Despres & D. Chauvel (Eds.), *Knowledge Horizons: The Present and the Promise of Knowledge Management* (pp. 27-53). Boston: Butterworth Heinemann.

Greeno, J. G. (1997). On Claims That Answer the Wrong Question. *Educational Researcher, 26*(1), 5-17.

Hall, R. H. (1996). *Organizations: Structures, Processes and Outcomes*. New Jersey: Prentice Hall.

Hansen, C. D., & Kahnweiler, W. M. (1993). Storytelling: An Instrument for Understanding the Dynamics of Corporate Relationships. *Human Relations, 46*(12), 1391-1409.

Harwood, V. (2001). Foucault, Narrative and the Subjugated Subject: Doing Research With a Grid of Sensibility. *The Australian Educational Researcher, 28*(3), 141-166.

Hedberg, B. (1981). How organizations learn and unlearn. In P.C. Nystrom & W.H. Starbuck (Eds.). *Handbook of Organizational Design* (pp. 3-27). London: Oxford

Hellström, T., & Raman, S. (2001). The commodification of knowledge about knowledge: knowledge management and the reification of epistemology. *Social Epistemology, 15*(3), 139-154.

Henderson, R. M. (1996). Technological Change and the Management of Architectural Knowledge. In M. D. Cohen & L. S. Sproull (Eds.), *Organizational Learning* (pp. 359-375). Thousand Oaks: Sage.

Hitt. M.A., Ireland, R.D., & Hoskisson, R.E. (2003). *Strategic management: Competitiveness and globalization* (5th ed.). Cincinnati, Ohio: Thomson-South Western.

Huber, G. P. (1996). Organizational Learning: The Contributing Processes and the Literature. In M. D. Cohen & L. S. Sproull (Eds.), *Organizational Learning* (pp. 124-162). Thousand Oaks, CA: Sage.

James, W. (1987/1995). The Will to Believe. In P. K. Moser & A. vander Nat (Eds.), *Human Knowledge: Classical and Contemporary Approaches* (pp. 203-214). New York: Oxford University Press.

Jarvis, P. (2009). Learning to be an expert: Competence development and expertise. In K. Illeris (Ed.), *International perspectives on competence development* (pp. 99-109). London: Routledge.

Kaplan, R.S. & Norton, D.P. (1996). *The Balanced Scorecard.* Boston, Ma: Harvard Business School Press.

Keller, C. M., & Keller, J. D. (1996). *Cognition and tool use: The blacksmith at work.* Cambridge: Cambridge University Press.

Kelley, C. M., & Lindsay, D. S. (1996). Conscious and Unconscious Forms of Memory. In E. L. Bjork & R. A. Bjork (Eds.), *Memory* (pp. 33-63). San Diego: Academic Press.

Kerfoot, K. (1999). Creating the Forgetting Organization. *Dermatology Nursing, 11*(1), *75-76.*

Kessler, E. H. (2001). The Idols of Organizational Theory: From Francis Bacon to the Dilbert Principle. *Journal of Management Inquiry, 10*(4), 285-297.

Kim, D. H. (1993). The Link between Individual and Organizational Learning. *Sloan Management Review, Fall*, 37-49.

Kingery, W. D. (1993). Technological Systems and Some Implications with Regard to Continuity and Change. In S. Lubar & W. D. Kingery (Eds.), *History from Things: Essays on Material Culture* (pp. 215-230). Washington: Smithsonian Institute Press.

Kogut, B., & Zander, U. (1992). Knowledge of the Firm, Combinative Capabilities and the Replication of Technology. *Organizational Science, 3*(3), 383-397.

Kransdorff, A. (1998). *Corporate Amnesia: Keeping know-how in the family.* Oxford: Butterworth Heinemann.

Kulkki, S. (2002). Knowledge Creation of Global Companies. In W. C. Chun & N. Bontis (Eds.), *The Strategic Management of Intellectual Capital and Organizational Knowledge* (pp. 501-522). Oxford: Oxford University Press.

Lakatos, I. (1978). *The methodology of scientific research programmes.* Cambridge: Cambridge University Press.

Lant, T. K. (1999). A Situated Learning Perspective on the Emergence of Knowledge and Identity in Cognitive Communities. In J. F. Porac & R. Garud (Eds.), *Cognition, Knowledge and Organizations* (Vol. 6, pp. 171-194). Stamford, Co.: JAI Press Inc.

Lantz, A. (2001). Meetings in a distributed group of experts: Comparing face-to-face, chat and collaborative virtual environments: *Behaviour & Information Technology, 2001(20), 2+*

LaNuez, D., & Jermier, J. M. (1994). Sabotage by Managers and Technocrats: Neglected patterns of resistance at work. In J. M. Jermier, D. Knights, & W. R. Nord (Eds.), *Resistance and Power in Organizations* (pp. 219-251). London: Routledge.

Larochelle, M., & Bednarz, N. (1998). Constructivism and education: beyond epistemological correctness. In M. Larochelle, N. Bednarz, & J. Garrison (Eds.), *Constructivism and education* (pp. 3-20). Cambridge: Cambridge University Press.

Lei, D., Hitt, M., & Bettis, R. (1996). Dynamic Core Competencies through Meta-Learning and Strategic Context. *Journal of Management, 22*(4), 549-569.

Lebie, L., Rhoades, J., & MacGoth, J. (1995). Interaction process in computer mediated and face-to-face groups, *Internation Journal of Computer Supported Cooperative work, 4*(2-3), 127-152.

Leithwood, K., Leonard, L., & Sharrat, L. (2000). Conditions Fostering Organizational Learning in Schools. In K. Leithwood (Ed.), *Understanding Schools as Intelligence Systems* (Vol. 4, pp. 99-124). Stamford,: JAI Press Inc.

Leonard, D., & Sensiper, S. (1998). The Role of Tacit Knowledge in Group Innovation. *California Management Review, 40*(3), 112-132.

Leonard-Barton, D. (1992). Core Capabilities and Core Rigidities: A Paradox in Managing New Product Development. *Strategic Management Journal, 13*, 111-125.

Leonard-Barton, D. (1995). *Wellsprings of Knowledge: Building and Sustaining the Sources of Innovation*. Boston, Ma: Harvard Business School Press.

Levitt, B., & March, J. G. (1996). Organizational Learning. In M. D. Cohen & L. S. Sproull (Eds.), *Organizational Learning* . Thousand Oaks, CA: Sage.

Lincoln, Y. S. (2000). Paradigmatic Controversies, Contradictions, and Emerging Confluences. In N. K. Denzin & Y. S. Lincoln (Eds.), *Handbook of Qualitative Research* (2nd ed., pp. 163-188). London: Sage.

Livio, N., & Rietz, S.A. (1986). *Storytelling: Process and Practice*. Littledon, Co.: Libraries Unlimited Inc.

Locke, J. (1987/1995). An Essay Concerning Human Understanding. In P. K. Moser & A. vander Nat (Eds.), *Human Knowledge: Classical and Contemporary Approaches* (pp. 126-145). New York: Oxford University Press.

March, J. G. (1996). Exploration and Exploitation in Organizational Learning. In M. D. Cohen & L. S. Sproull (Eds.), *Organizational Learning* (pp. 101-123). London: Sage.

Marks, I., & Tobeña, A. (1990). Learning and Unlearning Fear: A Clinical and Evoluntary Perspective. *Neuroscience & Biobehavioral Reviews, 14*, 365-384.

Marquandt, M., & Reynolds, A. (1994). *The Global Learning Organization: Gaining Competitive Advantage Through Continuous Learning*. New York: Irwin.

Martin, J., Feldman, M. S., Hatch, M. J., & Sitkin, S. B. (1983). The Uniqueness Paradox in Organizational Stories. *Administration Science Quarterly, 28*(September), 438-453.

Matthews, J. H., & Candy, P. C. (1999). New dimensions in the dynamics of learning and knowledge. In D. Boud & J. Garrick (Eds.), *Understanding Learning at Work* (pp. 47-64). New York: Routledge.

McDowell, A. (2002). Trust and information: the role of trust in the social epistemology of information science. *Social Epistemology, 16*(1), 51-63.

Mentzas, G., Apostolou, D., & Young, R. (2001). Knowledge networking; a holistic solution for leveraging corporate knowledge. *Journal of Knowledge Management, 5*(1), 94-106.

Moorman, C., & Miner, A. S. (1997). The Impact of Organizational Memory on New Product Performance and Creativity. *Journal of Marketing Research, 34*(February), 91-106.

Moorman, C., & Miner, A. S. (1998). Organizational Improvisation and Organizational Memory. *Academy of Management Review, 23*(4), 698-724.

Morris, C. G. (1988). *Psychology: An Introduction*. Englewood Cliffs, NJ: Prentice Hall.

Nelson, R. R., & Winter, S. G. (1982). *An evolutionary theory of economic change*. Cambridge, Mass.: Belknap Press of Harvard University Press.

Newman, M. (2001). Routines in Chaos, Employees Cope With Makeshift Offices. *New York Times*, pp. B 9. 3/10/01.

Nonaka, I. (1991). The Knowledge-Creating Company. *Harvard Business Review, November-December*, 96-104.

Nonaka, I. (1994). A Dynamic Theory of Organizational Knowledge Creation. *Organizational Science, 5*(1), 14-37.

Nonaka, I. (2002). A dynamic theory of organizational knowledge creation. In C. W. Choo & N. Bontis (Eds.), *The strategic management of intellectual capital and organizational knowledge* (pp. 437-462). New York: Oxford University Press.

Nonaka, I., & Konno, N. (1998). The concept of "Ba": Building a foundation for knowledge creation. *California Management Review, 40*(3), 154-174.

Nonaka, I., & Reinmoeller, P. (2000). Dynamic Business Systems for Knowledge Creation. In C. Despres & D. Chauvel (Eds.), *Knowledge Horizons: The Present and the Promise of Knowledge Management* (pp. 89-113). Boston: Butterworth Heinemann.

Nonaka, I., Toyama, R., & Konno, N. (2000). Seci, ba and leadership: A unified model of dynamic knowledge creation. *Long Range Planning, 33*, 5-34.

Nonaka, I., von Krogh, G., & Voelpel, S. (2006). Organizational knowledge creation theory: Evolutionary paths and future advances. *Organization Studies, 27*(8), 1179-1208.

Nord, W. R., & Fox, S. (1996). The Individual in Organizational Studies: the Great Disappearing Act? In S. R. Clegg, C. Hardy, & W. R. Nord (Eds.), *Handbook of Organizational Studies* (pp. 148-174). London: Sage.

Nystrom, P. C., & Starbuck, W. H. (2004). To avoid organizational crises, unlearn. In K. Starkey, S. Tempest & A. McKinlay (Eds.), *How organizations learn: Managing the search for knowledge* (pp. 100-111). London: Thompson Learning.

O'Toole, K. M. (1999). *Organizational Memory: The Structures and Processes of Collective Remembering*. Unpublished MA, Flinders University, Adelaide, SA.

O'Toole, K. M. (2001). Learning through the physical environment in the workplace. *International Education Journal, 2*(1), 10-19.

O'Toole, K. M. (2003). *Building knowledge retention structures and systems in organisations*. Unpublished PhD, Flinders University, Adelaide, South Australia.

O'Toole, P. (2010). Locating space in qualitative research: Questioning culture through the corporeal. In M. Savin-Baden & C. H. Major (Eds.), *New approaches to qualitative research: Wisdom and uncertainty* (pp. 121-130). London: Routledge.

O'Toole, P., & Talbot, S. (in press). Fighting for knowledge: Developing learning systems in the Australian Army. *Armed Forces and Society*.

O'Toole, P., & Were, P. (2008). Observing places: Using space and material culture in qualitative research. *Qualitative Research, 8*(5), 621-639.

Organization of Economic and Cultural Development (OECD). (1996). *The Knowledge-Based Economy* .

Oldham, G. R., & Rotchford, N. L. (1983). Relationships between Office Characteristics and Employee Reactions: A Study of the Physical Environment. *Administrative Science Quarterly, 28*, 542-556.

Orr, J. E. (1990). Sharing Knowledge, Celebrating Identity: Community Memory in a Service Culture. In D. Middleton & D. Edwards (Eds.), *Collective Remembering* (pp. 169-189). London: Sage.

Papert, S. .(2003) *Jean Piaget*, [Internet]. Time.com. Available: http://www.time.com/time/time100/scientist/profile/piaget03.html [Accessed: 2003, 15/01/03].

Pedler, M., Burgoyne, J., & Boydell, T. (1991/1997). *The Learning Company: A Strategy for Sustainable Development* (2nd ed.). London: McGraw-Hill.

Penrose, E. T. (1980). *The Theory of The Growth of the Firm* (2nd ed.). Oxford: Basil Blackwell.

Phillips, D. C. (1995). The Good, the Bad, and the Ugly: The Many Faces of Constructivism. *Educational Researcher, 24*(7), 5-12.

Pojman, L. P. (2001). *What Can We Know? An Introduction to the Theory of Knowledge* (2nd ed.): Wadsworth Thomson Learning.

Polanyi, M. (1962). *Personal knowledge : towards a post-critical philosophy*. London: Routledge & K. Paul.

Polanyi, M. (1967). *The tacit dimension*. London,: Routledge & K. Paul.

Popper, K. R. (1959). *The Logic of Scientific Discovery*. New York: Basic Books.

Porac, J. F., & Garud, R. (Eds.). (1999). *Cognition, Knowledge and Organizations* (Vol. 6). Stamford, Connecticut: JAI Press.

Prahalad, C. K., & Hamel, G. (1990). The Core Competence of the Corporation. *Harvard Business Review, May-June*, 79-91.

Proshansky, H. M., Fabian, A. K., & Kaminoff, R. (1995). Place-identity: physical world socialization of the self. In L. Groat (Ed.), *Giving Places Meaning* (pp. 87-114). London: Harcourt Brace & Company.

Reber, A. S. (1993). *Implicit learning and Tacit Knowledge: An Essay on the Cognitive Unconscious*. New York: Oxford University Press.
Reber, A. S. (1995). *Dictionary of Psychology* (2nd edn ed.). London: Penguin Books.
Renshaw, P. (1998). Sociocultural Pedagogy for New Time:Reframing Key Concepts. *The Australian Educational Researcher, 25*(3), 83-100.
Roberts, K., & Grabowski, M. (1996). Organizations, Technology and Structuring. In S. R. Clegg, C. Hardy, & W. R. Nord (Eds.), *Handbook of Organizational Studies* (pp. 409-423). London: Sage.
Robins, A., & McCallum, S. (1999). The consolidation of learning during sleep: comparing the pseudorehearsal and unlearning accounts. *Neural Networks, 12*, 1191-1206.
Rosen, M., Orlikowski, W. J., & Schmahmann, K. S. (1990). Building Buildings and Living Lives: A Critique of Bureaucracy, Ideology and Concrete Artifacts. In P. Gagliardi (Ed.), *Symbols and Artifacts: Views of the Corporate Landscape* (pp. 69-84). Berlin: Walter de Gruyter.
Roth, G., & Kleiner, A. (1998). Developing Organizational Memory Through Learning Histories. *Organizational Dynamics, Autumn*, 43-60.
Rousseau, D. M., & Parks, J. M. (1993). The Contracts of Individuals and Organizations. *Research in Organizational Behavior, 15*, 1-43.
Ryle, G. (1949). *The Concept of Mind*. London: Hutchinson.
Saint-Onge, H. (1996). Tacit Knowledge: The Key to the Strategic Alignment of Intellectual Capital. *Strategy & Leadership, March/April.*
Saint-Onge, H. (2000). Shaping Human Resource Management Within the Knowledge-Driven Enterprise. In J. J. Phillips & D. Bonner (Eds.) (pp. 275-299). Leading Knowledge Management and Learning: ASTD.
Sandelands, L. E., & Stablein, R. E. (1987). The Concept of Organizational Mind. *Research in the Sociology of Organizations, 5*, 135-161.
Schacter, D. L. (1996). *Searching for memory : the brain, the mind, and the past* (1st ed.). New York, NY: BasicBooks.
Schein, E. (1996). Three Cultures of Management: The Key to the Learning Organization. *Sloan Management Review*(Fall), 9-19.
Schön, D. A. (1987). *Educating the Reflective Practitioner: Toward a New Design for Teaching and Learning in the Professions*. San Francisco: Jossey-Bass.
Schwartzman, H.B. (1989). *The meeting: Gatherings in organizations and communities*. New York: Plenum Press.
Scribner, S. (1986). Thinking in action: some characteristics of practical thought. In R. J. Sternberg & R. K. Wagner (Eds.), *Practical intelligence: Nature and origins of competence in the everyday world* (pp. 13-30). Cambridge: Cambridge University Press.
Scribner, S. (1997a). Knowledge at work. In E. Tobach, R. J. Falmagne, M. B. Parlee, L. M. W. Martin, & A. S. Kapelman (Eds.), *Mind and social practice: Selected writings of Sylvia Scribner* (pp. 308-318). Cambridge: Cambridge University Press.
Scribner, S. (1997b). Mind in action: A function approach to thinking. In E. Tobach, R. J. Falmagne, M. B. Parlee, L. M. W. Martin, & A. S. Kapelman (Eds.), *Mind and social practice: Selected writings of Sylvia Scribner* (pp. 296-307). Cambridge: Cambridge University Press.
Seekings, D. (1981) *How to organize effective conferences and meetings*. London; Kogan Page.
Seely Brown, J., & Duguid, P. (1996). Organizational Learning and Communities-of-Practice: Toward a Unified View of Working, Learning, and Innovation. In M. D. Cohen & L. S. Sproull (Eds.), *Organizational Learning* (pp. 58-82). Thousand Oaks, CA: Sage.
Senge, P. M. (1992). *The Fifth Discipline: The Art & Practice of The Learning Organization*. Sydney: Random House.
Senge, P., Kleiner, A., Roberts, C., Ross, R., Roth, G., & Smith, B. (1999). *The Dance of Change: The Challenges of Sustaining Momentum in Learning Organizations*. London: Nicholas Brealey.
Shields, C., & Newton, E. (1994). Empowered Leadership: Realizing the Good News. *Journal of School Leadership, 4*(March), 171-196.

Shotter, J. (1990). The Social Construction of Remembering and Forgetting. In D. Middleton & D. Edwards (Eds.), *Collective Remembering* (pp. 120-138). London: Sage.

Shulman, A. D. (1996). Putting Group Information Technology in its Place: Communication and Good Work Group Performance. In S. R. Clegg, C. Hardy, & W. R. Nord (Eds.), *Handbook of Organization Studies* . London: Sage.

Silins, H. & Mulford B. (2002). Leadership and School Results. In K. Leithwood & P. Hallinger (Eds.), *Second International Handbook of Educational Leadership and Administration* (pp. 561-612). Dordrecht: Kluwer Academic Publishers.

Simon, H. A. (1996). Bounded Rationality and Organizational Learning. In M. D. Cohen & L. S. Sproull (Eds.), *Organizational Learning* (pp. 175-187). Thousand Oaks, CA: Sage.

Singley, M. K., & Anderson, J. R. (1989). *The Transfer of Cognitive Skill.* Cambridge MA: Harvard University Press.

Smelser, N. J., & Baltes, P. B. (Eds.). (2001). *International Encyclopedia of the Social and Behavioral Sciences* (Vol. 4). Amsterdam: Elsevier.

Snowden, D. (2000a). The Social Ecology of Knowledge Management. In C. Despres & D. Chauvel (Eds.), *Knowledge Horizons: The Present and the Promise of Knowledge Management* (pp. 237-265). Boston: Butterworth Heinemann.

Snowden, D. (2000b). Storytelling and Other Organic Tools for Chief Knowledge Officers and Chief Learning Officers. In J. J. Phillips & D. Bonner (Eds.) (pp. 237-252). Leading Knowledge Management and Learning: ASTD.

Sole, D., & Edmondson, A. (2002). Bridging Knowledge Gaps: Learning in Geographical Dispersed Cross-Functional Development Teams. In W. C. Chun & N. Bontis (Eds.), *The Strategic Management of Intellectual Capital and Organizational Knowledge* (pp. 587-604). Oxford: Oxford University Press.

Solovy, A. (1999). The Unlearning Curve. *Hospital & Health Networks, 73*(1), 30.

Spender, J.-C. (1996a). Making Knowledge the Basis of a Dynamic Theory of the Firm. *Strategic Management Journal, 17*(Winter Special Issue), 45-62.

Spender, J.-C. (1996b). Organizational knowledge, learning and memory: three concepts in search of a theory. *Journal of Organizational Change, 9*(1), 63-78.

Spender, J.-C. (1998). The Dynamics of Individual and Organizational Knowledge. In C. Eden & J.-C. Spender (Eds.), *Managerial and Organizational Cognition* (pp. 13-39). London: Sage Publications.

Spender, J.-C. (2000). Managing Knowledge Systems. In C. Despres & D. Chauvel (Eds.), *Knowledge Horizons: The Present and the Promise of Knowledge Management* (pp. 149-168). Boston: Butterworth Heinemann.

Spender, J.-C. (2001). Management's Options in the Knowledge Economy. *Business/Higher Education Round Table, July 2001*(11).

Stafford, S. P. (2001). Epistemology for Sale. *Social Epistemology, 15*(3), 215-230.

Stanford University, M. R. L. (2001). *Stanford Encyclopedia of Philosophy*, [Internet]. Stanford University. Available: http://setis.ibrary.usyd.edu.au/stanford/archives/sum2002/entries/epistemology-social [Accessed 2002, 11/11/02].

Starbuck, W. H. (1996). Unlearning ineffective or obsolete technologies. *International Journal of Technology Management, 11*(7-8), 725-737.

Stein, E. W. (1989). *Organizational Memory: A Socio-Technological Framework and Empirical Research.* Unpublished PhD, University of Pennsylvania.

Stein, E. W. (1995). Organizational Memory: Review of Concepts and Recommendations for Management. *International Journal of Information Management, 15*(2), 17-32.

Sternberg, R. J. (1999). *Cognitive psychology* (2nd ed.). Fort Worth: Harcourt Brace College Publishers.

Stinchcombe, A. L. (1990). *Information and Organizations.* Oxford: University of California Press.

Strati, A. (1990). Aesthetics and Organizational Skills. In B. A. Turner (Ed.), *Organizational Symbolism* . New York: Walter de Gruyter.

Styhre, A. (2003). *Understanding knowledge management*. Malmö, Sweden: Copenhagen Business School Press.
Szulanski, G. (1996). Exploring Internal Stickiness: Impediments to the Transfer of Best Practice Within the Firms. *Strategic Management Journal, 17*(Winter Special Issue), 27-43.
Trembly, A. C. (2002). Tech is both an enemy and an ally in the struggle to maintain security. *National Underwriter, 106*(35), 37-38.
Trice, H. M. (1993). *Occupational Subcultures in the Workplace*. Ithaca, New York: ILR Press.
Tsoukas, H. (1996). The Firm as a Distributed Knowledge System: A Constructionist Approach. *Strategic Management Journal, 17*(Winter Special Issue), 11-25.
Tulving, E. (1972). Episodic and semantic memory. In E. Tulving & W. Donaldson (Eds.), *Organization of Memory* . New York: Academic Press.
Tulving, E. (1985a). *Elements of episodic memory*. Oxford: Oxford University Press.
Tulving, E. (1985b). How Many Memory Systems Are There? *American Psychologist, 40*(4), 385-398.
Tulving, E. (2001). Origin of Autonoesis in Episodic Memory. In H. L. Roedinger, J. S. Nairne, I. Neath, & A. M. Surprenant (Eds.), *The Nature of Remembering: Essays in Honor of Robert G. Crowder* (pp. 35-54). Washington, DC: American Psychological Association.
Tulving, E., & Donaldson, W. (1972). *Organization of Memory*. New York: Academic Press.
Turner, J. H. (1986). *The Structure of Sociological Theory* (4th ed.). Chicago, Il.: The Dorsey Press.
Tushman, M. L., & Scanlan, T. J. (1981). Characteristics and External Orientations of Boundary Spanning Individuals. *Academy of Management Journal, 24*(1), 83-98.
Van Maanen, J. (1979/1983). Reclaiming qualitative methods of organizational research: A preface. In J. Van Maanan (Ed.), *Qualitative methodology* (pp. 9-18). Newbury Park, Ca: Sage.
Van Maanen, J., & Barley, S. R. (1985). Cultural Organization: Fragments of a Theory. In P. J. Frost, L. F. Moore, M. R. Louis, C. C. Lundberg, & J. Martin (Eds.), *Organizational Culture* (pp. 31-53). Beverley Hills: Sage.
Vann, K., & Bowker, G. C. (2001). Instrumentalizing the truth of practice. *Social Epistemology, 15*(3), 247-262.
Vaughan, D. (1990). Autonomy, Interdependence and Social Control: NASA and the Space Shuttle Challenger. *Administrative Science Quarterly, 35*(2), 225-257.
Vaughan, D. (1997). The Trickle-Down Effect: Policy Decisions, Risky Work, and the *Challenger* Tragedy. *California Management Review, 39*(2), 80-103.
Volkema, R.J. & Niederman, F. (1995) Organizational meetings: Formats and information requirements. *Small group research, 26(1), 3-24.*
von Glasersfeld, E. (1984). An Introduction to Radical Constructivism. In P. Watzlawick (Ed.), *The Invented Reality: How Do We Know What We Believe We Know? Contributions to Constructivism* (pp. 17-40). New York: W.W. Norton & Company.
von Hippel, E. (1994). "Sticky Information" and the Locus of Problem Solving: Implications for Innovation. *Management Science, 40*(4), 429-439.
von Krogh, G. (1998). Care in knowledge creation. [Electronic Version]. *California Management Review*, 40, 133-153. Retrieved June 3, 2010.
von Krogh, G., Ichijo, K., & Nonaka, I. (2000). *Enabling Knowledge Creation: How to Unlock the Mystery of Tacit Knowledge and Release the Power of Innovation*. Oxford: Oxford University Press.
von Krogh, G., Lyles, M., Mahnke, V., & Rogulic, B. (1999). Preparing the Organization for New Competencies: A Process Perspective of Integrating Knowledge and Competence. In J. F. Porac & R. Garud (Eds.), *Cognition, Knowledge and Organizations* (Vol. 6, pp. 57-78). Stamford, Co.: JAI Press Inc.
von Krogh, G., & Roos, J. (1995). *Organizational Epistemology*. New York: St Martin's Press.
Wagner, R. K., & Sternberg, R. J. (1986). Tacit knowledge and intelligence in the everyday world. In R. J. Sternberg & R. K. Wagner (Eds.), *Practical intelligence: Nature and origins of competence in the everyday world* (pp. 51-83). Cambridge: Cambridge University Press.

Walsh, J. P., & Ungson, G. R. (1991). Organizational Memory. *Academy of Management, 16*(1), 57-81.

Weick, K. E. (1979a). Cognitive Processes in Organizations. *Research in Organizational Behavior, 1*, 41-74.

Weick, K. E. (1979b). *The Social Psychology of Organizing*. Reading, MA: Addison Wesley.

Weick, K. E. (1993). The Collapse of Sensemaking in Organizations: The Mann Gulch Disaster. *Administrative Science Quarterly, 38*(*Missing), 628-652.

Weick, K. E. (1995). *Sensemaking in Organizations*. Thousand Oaks, Ca: Sage.

Weick, K. E., & Roberts, K. (1996). Collective Mind in Organizations: Heedful Interrelating on Flight Decks. In M. D. Cohen & L. S. Sproull (Eds.), *Organizational Learning* (pp. 330-358). Thousand Oaks, CA: Sage.

Wenger, E. (1999). *Communities of practice : learning, meaning, and identity*. Cambridge: Cambridge University Press.

Wenger, E. (2000). Communities of Practice: The Structure of Knowledge Stewarding. In C. Despres & D. Chauvel (Eds.), *Knowledge Horizons: The Present and the Promise of Knowledge Management* (pp. 205-225). Boston: Butterworth Heinemann.

Wiig, K. M. (2000). Knowledge Management: An Emerging Discipline Rooted in a Long History. In C. Despres & D. Chauvel (Eds.), *Knowledge Horizons: The Present and the Promise of Knowledge Management* (pp. 3-26). Boston: Butterworth Heinemann.

Wimbauer, S. Klemmer, N., & van Hemmen, J. L. (1994). Universality of Unlearning. *Neural Networks, 7(2)*, 261-270.

Winter, S. G. (1998). Knowledge and Competence as Strategic Assets. In D. A. Klein (Ed.), *The Strategic Management of Intellectual Capital* (pp. 165-). Boston: Butterworth-Heinemann.

Yates, J. (1988). *Creating Organizational Memory: Systematic Management and Internal Communication in Manufacturing Firms, 1880-1920.* : MIT Sloan School of Management.

Yi, J. Q. (2002). Facilitating Learning and Knowledge Creation in Community of Practice: A Case Study in a Corporate Learning Environment. In E. Coakes, D. Willis, & S. Clarke (Eds.), *Knowledge Management in the Socio-Technical World: The Graffittti Continues.*

Zarraga, C., & Bonache, J. (2005). The impact of team atmosphere on knowledge outcomes in self-managed teams. *Organization Studies, 26*(5), 661-681.

Index

Kolibri 360 GmbH
Ferdinand-Jühlke-Straße 7
99095 Erfurt, Deutschland
produktsicherheit@kolibri360.de